# FINANCIAL ANALYSIS OF M&A INTEGRATION

# FINANCIAL ANALYSIS OF M&A INTEGRATION

Stuart Ferguson, Ph.D.

**McGraw-Hill**

New York   Chicago   San Francisco
Lisbon   London   Madrid   Mexico City
Milan   New Delhi   San Juan   Seoul
Singapore   Sydney   Toronto

*The McGraw·Hill Companies*

1 2 3 4 5 6 7 8 9 0   DOC/DOC   0 9 8 7 6 5 4 3

ISBN 0-07-140211-X

McGraw-Hill books are available at special quantity discounts to use as premiums and sales promotions, or for use in corporate training programs. For more information, please write to the Director of Special Sales, Professional Publishing, McGraw-Hill, Two Penn Plaza, New York, NY 10121-2298. Or contact your local bookstore.

 This book was printed on recycled, acid-free paper containing a minimum of 50% recycled, de-inked fiber.

**Library of Congress Cataloging-in-Publication Data**

Ferguson, Stuart, Ph. D.
  Financial analysis of M&A integration  /  by Stuart Ferguson.
     p. cm.
  ISBN 0-07-140211-X (hardcover : alk. paper)
  1. Consolidation and merger of corporations—Finance—Mathematical models.
2. Consolidation and merger of corporations—Management.   I. Title: Financial analysis of M and A integration.   II. Title: Financial analysis of M & A integration.
III. Title.
    HG4028.M4F47  2003
    658.1'6—dc21

                                                          2002156078

# CONTENTS

# ACKNOWLEDGMENTS

PEOPLE DON'T WRITE BUSINESS BOOKS because they have a vision of getting rich. There are very few writers who enjoy the success of Tom Peters, Stephen Covey, and Jim Collins. The rest of us have something to say and pray for the opportunity to see our words in print as evidence that we once had a profound thought or a great idea. The kindnesses of many people have created an opportunity for me to share my thoughts with you.

Susan, my wonderful wife of nearly 20 years, is the dearest, most understanding, and most forgiving person in the world. She has had to have all of these fine traits to tolerate with good cheer my many quirks and fancies, misdeeds and misdirections, set-tos and setbacks. Through it all she has given me courage and patience enough to pursue my vision of a full life.

Our daughter, Maddie, has not seen as much of me as either of us would have liked over the past 2 years when I was writing my Ph.D. dissertation and then putting this book together. I owe her camping trips, time on trout streams and tennis courts, and my undivided attention so that we can reconnect our lives like they used to be.

My son, Stuart Webster, has been a great supporter of my work. He and his wife, Shellie, and our granddaughters, Stephanie and Sophie, have given me many joyful moments of relaxation between my writing sessions. And my father, Stuart Woodrow Ferguson, who passed away before this book was published, always gave me warm encouragement in spite of his daunting health issues.

My second family, Marjorie and John Claghorn and their children, provided a lot of comic relief and recreation that helped me bring a recharged body, mind, and spirit to this project.

Many thanks to my editors, Kelli Christiansen and Janice Race, and the great people at McGraw-Hill for their support of my ideas and their hard work in translating them into readable text. Thanks, also, to Alexandra Reed Lajoux, who suggested that my work might be of interest to McGraw-Hill and facilitated my connection with Kelli.

I stood on the shoulders of a giant when I wrote this book. Daniel Denison deserves a tremendous amount of respect and gratitude from the business community for his work in correlating organization cultures with business performance. People like Edgar Schein, John Kotter, James Heskett, and Rossabeth Kanter have invested their lives in understanding what makes organizations tick (or not tick), and they have also had a great influence on my thinking.

To all of you who have been so helpful in your own known and unknown ways, thank you.

# INTRODUCTION

Companies that have cultivated their individual identities by shaping values, making heroes, spelling out rites and rituals, and acknowledging their cultural network have an edge. These corporations have values and beliefs to pass along—not just products. They have stories to tell—not just profits to make. They have heroes whom managers and workers can emulate—not just faceless bureaucrats. In short, they are human institutions that provide practical meaning for people, both on and off the job.[1]

THIS BOOK IS INTENDED TO ADDRESS the unique phenomena that occur when two vastly different subjects, financial performance and organizational cultures, intersect because of business combinations such as mergers and acquisitions. As a writer, I have the challenge of serving the interests of a very broad spectrum of people who are interested, and perhaps expert, in one of the two subjects and curious or perhaps ignorant about the other. Someone once said about the horrible multipurpose ballparks that were erected in the 1970s, "Anything built to serve more than one purpose will probably do all of them poorly." To avoid creating something that is universally dysfunctional, I've written three separate parts, which, taken as a whole, present a complete package discussing business combinations and organization cultures. The style is designed for reader functionality. People familiar with one discipline or the other will probably want to look over the chapters dedicated to their field or subject of expertise either for review or to understand my particular bent on the subject. Each chapter provides background information, a discussion of the chapter topic, usually an example of a business situation (either good or bad), and a summary. The chapters are written in such a way that a reader can determine his or her own command of the topic and approach it as either an expert seeking a refresher or a novice starting from scratch.

The first part, "M&A from A to Z," discusses the history and purpose of business combinations, the various types of business combinations, and the process involved in these combinations. It draws on my 30-plus years of professional experience in business planning, operations, and management. The second part, "Understanding and Analyzing Organization Cultures," discusses the concept of organizational cultures, their nature and characteristics, and methods of cultural assessment. Part 3, "QUOCA—Quantitative Organization Culture Analyses," describes a unique, quantitative tool for evaluating the implications for financial performance of the respective cultures involved in business combinations. The book in its entirety provides (1) an in-depth explanation of the business combination process, including its success rate and a leading cause for M&A underperformance; (2) an understanding of the most underrated asset and misunderstood barrier to the success of business combinations—the combining businesses' unique cultures; and (3) an innovative approach to improving the success of mergers and acquisitions by determining the financial and competitive impacts of their individual and combined cultures.

One of the most daunting elements of gaining wisdom is decoding the meaning of the terms used by the particular expert. Terms such as *vision, mission,* and *purpose* may either be used interchangeably or have such narrow meanings to meet the expert's objectives (another word with a myriad of meanings) that the reader's newfound knowledge may not fit very well into his or her own jargon or add much to his or her existing knowledge. One of my goals in assessing and understanding organization cultures is to consistently use a set of terms that are both descriptive and functional. While these terms may be specific to my perspective and writings, perhaps they will create a groundswell of universal acceptance from our modest group of interested people and eventually stamp out global confusion and communication barriers through the use of simple, consistent, functional terms. My purpose is not to refute the wisdom of experts but to impart as much knowledge as possible to my readers. Figure I-1 illustrates and briefly explains the hierarchy of the descriptive and functional terms as used within this book.

## THE VISION STATEMENT

For the purpose of getting the most out of this book, I will define terms that are critical to an understanding of business organization financial and cultural performance. First, humans create organizations with a vision for changing their current circumstances into something more advantageous. The vision, when articulated in business, is a statement of

**Figure I-1** *Hierarchy of Business Functional Terms*

the desired future purpose of the organization. It is time bound at the discretion of the visionaries, usually the board of directors, the CEO, and the president of the enterprise. For technology companies, the envisioned future state may be a few months away; more traditional businesses may set their envisioned future state 5 or more years away. For example, the vision statement for my business, Organization Change Resources, LLC, is:

> By the end of calendar year 200_, OCR will be the leading provider of Quantitative Organization Culture Analyses (QUOCA) for North American middle-market businesses involved in mergers and acquisitions.

It is important that the vision statement be descriptive of where the organization wants to be rather than prescriptive of how the vision is going to be created. Vision statements often require input from organization outsiders, such as experts on the external business environment, including technology, regulatory changes, the cost and availability of critical resources, ripple effects from other industries, and so on. Experts on the internal environment, such as senior line and staff people, should be included in the visioning process, not only for their contribution to the statement, but to get early buy-in for the change initiatives needed to realize the desired future of the organization.

## THE PURPOSE STATEMENT

The purpose statement describes (in greater detail than the vision statement) what the organization does, for whom, where, why, when, and how. It is the responsibility of the board of directors, the CEO, and the president to create, monitor, and amend the purpose statement as needed. The purpose statement is also put together with input from internal and external experts in order to assure its adequacy and accuracy.

The functions of a clearly defined purpose statement are to (1) articulate and promulgate the theme of the business; (2) provide a sense of the organization's direction to employees, customers, suppliers, and other stakeholders; (3) rouse interest, support, and action on the part of the employees and the other vested stakeholders, such as suppliers; (4) stimulate creativity; and (5) determine and collect the requisite resources. If properly stated, communicated, and implemented, the purpose statement results in consistency and unity of effort throughout the organization, from the boardroom to the cubicles and shop floors. At the time of this writing, my business's purpose statement is:

> The purpose of Organization Change Resources LLC is to create and provide organization culture assessment and development products and services for small to midsize (>$5 Million to <$500 Million annual gross revenue) businesses in the 48 contiguous United States. Our products and services will be innovative, cost-effective, and of the highest quality and will result in the increased success of all our stakeholders.

The purpose statement is our elevator speech. When we are asked by anyone, anywhere, at any time what OCR does, we can succinctly, accurately, and consistently answer questions about what we do and for whom, where, why, and how we do what we do. Our resources are specifically aligned to achieve this unique purpose.

Purpose statements have finite lives that are dependent on the organization's internal and external environments. If the organization's purpose changes, either intentionally or unintentionally, or if elements of the external or internal environment change, the organization will fail unless the leadership formally acknowledges, accepts, and communicates the new purpose and realigns resources to it. Each enterprise can have only one purpose that describes the unique niche the organization fills within the business environment. When (not if) the environment changes, the purpose must be reviewed to see if the changes affect the appropriateness of the purpose statement and or/the resources required to achieve the stated purpose. Survival requires reconciliation of the purpose/environment conflict by adaptation or changing location (think, *market*). Inaction or inappropriate action will only result in the business's perishing.

## THE CREDO

Many organizations complement their purpose statement with a formal expression of their core values. Such a credo or value statement overtly expresses the specific desired assumptions, beliefs, and behaviors that the organization's constituents are to express and employ on behalf of the organization and its stakeholders. Credos often include statements about fair pricing, equal opportunity, community involvement, and so on and function as a guiding light for the conduct and decision making of the enterprise's people.

The Johnson & Johnson credo (see Figure I-2) is frequently held up as a living example of the positive influence a value statement can make during both normal and challenging circumstances. During the two Tylenol poisoning incidents, the 40-year-old credo served as a foundation for J&J's chairman, Jim Burke, to conduct what is often regarded as the gold standard for crisis management. For Jim, a long-time family friend, the response to the situation was merely another expression of the beliefs he had embraced throughout his climb to the top of the J&J organization: "The credo is a unifying force for our corporation. It guides us in everything we do. It represents an attempt to codify what we can all agree upon since we have highly independent managers."[2]

The credo for my own business is a little simpler but fulfills the same function of expressing our philosophical and operational "true north":

OCR believes:

- That our greatest challenge and responsibility is to make a positive contribution to each person we have the opportunity to work with.
- That our success is tied directly to the success of our clients.
- We should treat all information as confidential concerning

the business and affairs of our clients, prospects, affiliates, and colleagues.

- We should continually strive to improve our knowledge, skills, abilities, and techniques in order to provide the most effective services for our clients.
- In our clients' ability to succeed and our ability to help you achieve success.

---

**Figure I-2** *The Johnson & Johnson Credo*

We believe our first responsibility is to the doctors, nurses, and patients, to mothers and all others who use our products and services. In meeting their needs everything we do must be of high quality. We must constantly strive to reduce our costs in order to maintain reasonable prices. Customer's orders must be serviced promptly and accurately. Our suppliers and distributors must have an opportunity to make a fair profit.

We are responsible to our employees: the men and women who work with us throughout the world. Everyone must be considered an individual. We must respect their dignity and recognize their merit. They must have a sense of security in their jobs. Compensation must be fair and adequate, and working conditions clean, orderly and safe. Employees must feel free to make suggestions and complaints. There must be equal opportunity for employment, development, and advancement for those qualified. We must provide competent management, and their actions must be just and ethical.

We are responsible to the communities in which we live and work and to the world community as well.

We must be good citizens—support good works and charities and bear our fair share of taxes. We must encourage civic improvements and better health and education.

We must maintain in good order the property we are privileged to use, protecting the environment and natural resources.

Our final responsibility is to our stockholders. Business must make a sound profit. We must experiment with new ideas. Research must be carried on, innovative programs developed, and mistakes paid for. New equipment must be purchased, new facilities provided, and new products launched. Reserves must be created to provide for adverse times.

When we operate according to these principles, the stockholders should realize a fair return.

---

*Source:* Johnson & Johnson web site, www.jnj.com.

## THE MISSION STATEMENT

Business is well known for borrowing terms and recasting them to suit a particular need or to metaphorically describe a certain thing. Such is the case with the term *mission*, which had first religious and later diplomatic definitions. Well down the list of definitions in my trusty dictionary[3] is the following use: "a specific task with which a person or group is charged." Clearly, the term has been broadened for business use to include more than just a "specific task." In fact, some use the term *mission statement* to explain the reason for the organization's existence. I prefer a more specific, perhaps military-based, definition that serves to focus on what is, at this point in time and for a stated period of time, the focus of the organization. The mission, to me and in this book, refers to the things the organization must do in order to accomplish its purpose and eventually fulfill its vision. As such, the mission is the time-based link between what the organization wants to do (purpose) and how the overall group, the hierarchy, and each of the individuals is going to do it via the succession of *goals and objectives, strategies, tactics, jobs, duties, tasks,* and *assignments.*

Here is how we state the mission for Organization Change Resources:

> The OCR Mission is to create and capitalize on opportunities to establish the organization as the leading authority on and preferred provider of Qualitative Organization Culture Analyses (QUOCA) for mid-market mergers and acquisitions.

My business is extremely focused, and so the mission statement is brief and to the point. The larger the organization, of course, the broader the mission and the mission statement. However, the statement should be focused on the three or four (or, at the most, five) things that the organization *absolutely, positively must do if it is to survive and prosper.* The mission statement, then, is the transition between the long-term purpose and vision of the business and the specific activities that must be accomplished.

## GOALS AND OBJECTIVES

Goals and objectives are prescriptive outcomes accomplished in an appropriate sequence and with an appropriate sense of priority in order to accomplish the organization's mission and fulfill its purpose. Ideally, goals and objectives are SMART—that is:

Simple, in terms that allow for universal understanding

Measurable, so that achievement and progress toward achievement can be objectively monitored and operational adjustments can be made

Achievable, to build confidence, provide closure, and avoid frustration

Responsibility for achievement is clearly stated and understood

Time-based for accountability, sequencing, and prioritization

Setting goals and objectives, communicating them, and measuring their accomplishment are the responsibilities of senior organization leaders such as division and department heads, with input and coordination from line and staff peers and approval by executive management. My current OCR goals and objectives are:

1. Complete writing the *Financial Analysis of MBA Integration* first draft by August 1, 2002.
2. Arrange two speaking engagements per month for the next twelve months with M&A trade groups and service firms to promote the book and OCR services.
3. Get one new culture assessment client and complete one QUOCA per month through the end of 200_.
4. Perform post-QUOCA services for a minimum of 50% of culture assessment clients.

## STRATEGIES

As outcomes, goals and objectives state what and how much is to be done, when, where, and by whom, but they do not say *how*. Strategies are the overarching, broadly descriptive plans and methods for meeting goals and objectives. Strategies are the domain of division and department heads, with considerable input from direct subordinates such as line managers and those responsible for organization resources such as manpower, systems, supplies, and budget. An example of my strategy to meet the second OCR objective is:

Network with and demonstrate QUOCA to enterprises engaged or interested in mergers and acquisitions such as XYZ Pharmaceuticals, consulting firms, investment banks, business brokers, local university MBA and business undergrad departments, law and accounting firms within a 75 mile radius from Princeton.

## TACTICS

Strategies are supported and accomplished through tactics, which are usually developed and implemented by managers, supervisors, foremen, and group leaders. Like goals and objectives, tactics must be SMART, and they serve as the marching orders for the organization's teams and individual contributors. My tactics for accomplishing the strategy stated previously are:

1. By December 31, develop a prioritized contact list with names, titles, addresses, phone and fax numbers and email addresses of decision makers in target enterprises. Use contact data base, organization member lists and network to develop contact list.
2. Develop a phone script and prototype email and letters; initiate contact with identified people between January 6 and 31. Describe QUOCA; create a presentation style and parameters; offer descriptive white paper; specify follow up.
3. By January 6, develop a five to eight page white paper that describes the QUOCA process, value and strategic advantage.
4. Follow up as promised; sell the presentation based on innovation and value.

## JOBS, DUTIES, TASKS, AND ASSIGNMENTS

Teams, work groups, task forces, and individuals contribute to the organization's desired outcomes by performing assigned or self-determined jobs, duties, tasks, and assignments. These are the day-to-day activities and efforts by people that, in sum, implement the tactics and strategies, achieve the goals and objectives, and fulfill the purpose of the organization. Just as innumerable grains of sand make a beach, the loftiest outcomes of organizations are the composite of routine individual efforts. And that is the fundamental point of this book. Without a sense of mission, a degree of consistency balanced with adaptability, and the personal involvement of the entire organization, the individual efforts may not add up to fulfillment of the organization's purpose.

Four cultural traits, Mission, Consistency, Adaptability, and Involvement, make up the overall culture of the enterprise. Cultural shortcomings have direct impacts on the completion of tasks and duties, the implementation of tactics and strategies, the achievement of goals and objectives, and the wherewithal to meet today's purpose and achieve tomorrow's vision. Our ability to measure and modify the organization's culture traits is as important to success as the measurement and management of cash flow, inventory, and supplies.

## MEASURING ORGANIZATIONAL EFFECTIVENESS IN ACCOMPLISHING DESIRED OUTCOMES

Human survival has always been dependent upon our ability to survey our environment and respond appropriately. What stimuli to respond to, the nature of the response, and the results of those responses are the bases for virtually all aspects of our well-being. In situations in which we are alone, our personal repertoire of sensory perception, experience, knowledge, skills, and abilities determines the situational stimulus that creates a specific response that leads to an outcome. When we function as part of a group, our behavior is influenced by such organization cultural elements as the attitudes, values, opinions, assumptions, and norms of the group. And to the extent that the contributions of the group members accumulate to produce the outcomes of the group, the nature of these cultural elements directly influences the success of the group members and the people and enterprises that depend, in part or in whole, upon their success.

In the past, the measurement of cultural characteristics has been predominantly subjective and qualitative, such as:

- The organization is "strong" or "weak."
- People's attitudes are "positive" or "negative."
- Teamwork is "good" or "bad."
- The organization has a sense of its mission or it doesn't.
- People care about their work or they don't.
- Things "fall between the cracks" or they don't.

Because of the subjective and qualitative nature of such cultural observations, it is very difficult to measure the culture and to state its impact on the organization's ability to meet its goals and objectives and to fulfill its purpose. Most enterprises define their success through measures and ratios referenced to "dollars" that are familiar, quantitative, and universally understood by most business stakeholders. Qualitative information, such as "They run a tight ship," may momentarily capture the interest of businesspeople, but it has no utility when measuring and forecasting performance parameters. And that is the irony of these "soft" but critically important characteristics of business. Cultures direct the behaviors of people on the job in ways that determine their:

- Productivity
- Creativity
- Efficiency
- Effectiveness
- Ability and desire to solve problems
- Ability and desire to make quality products and perform quality services

Organization cultures have been shown to have a direct impact on the performance and competitiveness of businesses. Yet cultural characteristics are seldom factored into business decisions. This phenomenon is doubly true in business combinations. If the variables that make up the culture of a single organization are not regularly factored into the decisions and expectations of that business, imagine how difficult it will be to figure out the impact of combining two cultures into a single one through a merger or an acquisition. Professionals who are involved and experienced in mergers and acquisitions acknowledge that cultural differences are difficult to factor into the price and performance calculations for the deal.

My research shows that five out of six business combinations do not fulfill the financial expectations on which the deal was predicated. In fact, while two out of every six deals added no synergy to the financial performance of the combined business, three out of six deals actually produced lower financial results than when the businesses had operated independently.[4]

It is no surprise that stakeholders eventually tire of the poor results and often try to restore the predeal financial performance of the acquisition initiator by selling the acquired company, usually at a loss. When the costs of researching, cogitating, planning, offering, negotiating, closing, integrating, and operating poor combinations are added up and compared to the rewards of the deal, the impact on stakeholders, including management, board members, employees, suppliers, customers, and communities, is staggering. And from the preceding discussion, you won't be surprised to learn that the leading causes of poor M&A performance are the qualitative "people" matters such as synergy, communication, and cultural issues. In fact, you might say, "Somebody oughta do somethin' about these crummy deals!" And that is what this book is for.

# FINANCIAL ANALYSIS OF M&A INTEGRATION

PART

# M&A FROM A TO Z

# THE HISTORY, PURPOSE, AND EXPECTATIONS OF BUSINESS COMBINATIONS

> While the business man has endured long nights of abasement, and engineered many hours of harmonious agreement, he has known very few and brief periods of genuine triumph.[1]

THE OBJECTIVES OF THIS CHAPTER are to help the reader to understand the historical reasons why mergers and acquisitions are done the way they are today, to develop a working knowledge of the reasons buyers want to buy and sellers want to sell, and to understand how changes in management philosophy have paralleled changes in mergers and acquisitions and, consequently, why organization cultures have a significant impact on the success or failure of business combinations.

Mergers and acquisitions are routine news. From neighborhood combinations like Jones Deli buying Smith Take-Out to megadeals such as AOL buying Time Warner, businesses see nothing but opportunity and symbiosis in their desire to add something to their existing assets and capabilities. The reasons for such deals are diverse, and the rationale for the expectations that they will be successful is based almost entirely on the projected financial aspects of these deals.

While each combination has its own idiosyncrasies, the typical M&A process today has been somewhat standardized through trial and error. This chapter provides an extensive overview of the merger and acquisition process, from its most general aspects such as its history, purpose, and expectations to increasingly specific observations regarding the impacts of combinations on the cultures of the organizations involved.

## HISTORY, PURPOSE, AND EXPECTATIONS

Combinations have been a part of the human condition since Adam met Eve, and basically for the same reason: Two can often create things that it would be impossible for either of them to create alone. Combinations in pre-Industrial Revolution America consisted mostly of the formation of partnerships between firms, usually sole proprietorships, that were in either the same or complementary businesses. The compelling reason for such combinations—which is also the reason behind today's small, medium, large, and monstrous deals—was to make more money. That having been said, however, the nature of combinations has evolved considerably, especially in the last one hundred years or so.

Since the decade before the beginning of the twentieth century, there have been five distinct waves of business combination activity. Each wave has occurred in a unique business environment created by innovation, including vision and technologies, the courage to change the nature of business, and specific opportunities within the marketplace. And each wave has had a tremendous impact on the shape of industries, the nature of business, the dynamics of the economy, and the quality of life in the United States and the world.

Beginning in the 1890s, there were thousands of horizontal mergers combining small and medium-sized companies within the same (horizontal) industry to form such giants as United States Steel, Standard Oil, DuPont, and General Electric, although these combinations were somewhat slowed by the Sherman Anti-Trust Act of 1890 and significantly impacted by the Clayton Act and the creation of the Federal Trade Commission of 1914. However, the courts gradually eroded support for and enforcement of these laws, and another round of combinations began in 1925 and ran through 1931. The deals in this era were primarily vertical, with companies buying other players (suppliers or customers) in their vertical market. Major companies formed by these combinations included American Cyanamid, RCA, and General Foods.

The Great Depression, the Second World War, and very tough government laws ended this era of combinations and forced businesses that proposed mergers or acquisitions to meet difficult standards in order to demonstrate that they were not creating monopolies.

The boom of the 1950s created conglomerate mergers, in which the initiating company increased its profits by acquiring firms with different products, services, and markets. Between 1961 and 1968, Litton Industries made 79 acquisitions, Gulf & Western made 67, and Teledyne, which had no assets in 1960, took over 125 firms.

In 1976, a series of megadeals began with Mobil's purchase of Montgomery Ward for $1.6 billion. What followed, thanks in part to the pro-business administrations of Presidents Reagan and George H. W. Bush, was such a flurry of vertical, horizontal, and conglomerate combinations that some 250 of the 1980 *Fortune* 500 did not survive intact to the 1990 list.

The period from the 1990s through the present has seen some of the largest deals ever. These have included virtually all of the historical combination types, such as the:

• Media conglomeration between Time Warner and AOL
• Transnational deal between Daimler and Chrysler
• Recent $80 billion Pfizer-Pharmacia deal
• Huge number of vertical and horizontal mergers and acquisitions in the financial services industry among broker/dealers, banks, and insurers

## THE EVOLUTION OF BUSINESS MANAGEMENT

Coincident with the changes in mergers and acquisitions in the time period from roughly 1890 through the present, significant changes (see Table 1-1) took place in the design, management, and operations of businesses. American enterprise evolved from traditional organizational designs like command-and-control management systems and bureaucratic, centralized business structures to empowerment of employees, decentralized operations, and self-management. Business management was forced to accept the social dynamics of a nomadic workforce, the technical power of instantaneous worldwide communication, and employee demands for greater power, control, and autonomy in their work.

These critical dynamics—vertical and horizontal expansion of businesses; changes in the capitalist environment, such as regulations, better communications and transportation, and more informed buyers; and the adaptation of business management to both internal and external organizational environmental factors—had a significant impact on the success of mergers and acquisitions. No longer could accountants and

**Table 1-1**   *Organizational Dynamics of the Twentieth Century*

| Traditional Organizational Design Factors | Modern Organizational Design Factors |
| --- | --- |
| Unskilled workforce | Educated, sophisticated employees |
| Temporary workers | Career-oriented employees |
| Simple, physical work | Complex, intellectual work |
| Centralized organization | Decentralized organization |
| Slow, unreliable communications | Communications accelerating to nearly instantaneous |
| Knowledge available to only a few | Knowledge widely available |
| Mechanical technology | Fast evolution and availability of electronic, chemical, and biological technologies |
| Mechanical views—simple causes and simple effects | Organic views—complex causes and broad effects |
| Stable markets and supplies—limited suppliers | Fluid markets, supplies, and suppliers |
| Rigid bureaucracy, sharp lines between hierarchy levels | Greater team orientation, blurred organization lines |

market analysts simply combine balance sheets and market share to calculate aggregate revenues and determine the return on investment for the combined businesses. Differences in how the businesses were organized, how they booked and reported income and expenses, their histories and leadership styles, their respective visions of the future, how they viewed and used technology, and the amount of power and knowledge that was shared caused huge difficulties in making the deals work. The compatibility of the cultures being combined became a significant factor in the success of the deal.

Like all business activities, the number of mergers and acquisitions in any given year is subject to many forces and factors, and so it varies on a continuum from merger madness such as that during the mid-1990s to the relative few that have come about since the turn of the millennium. In the early and mid-1990s, the United States enjoyed a boom economy, the lifting of barriers to global markets, and the proliferation of e-business, creating a "no holds barred" environment for combinations. In some deals, figuring out the potential symbiosis that motivated the players stretched the imagination. And some of the deals were between strange bedfellows. For example, AOL, which had been merely a gleam in an entrepreneur's eye a decade earlier, merged (and received top billing) with Time Warner, which had absorbed Turner Communications only a year or so earlier.

Since the downturn in the U.S. economy in 2000, high-profile mergers and acquisitions such as the Pfizer-Pharmacia deal have been relatively rare. But the small and middle-market deals that make up the vast majority of combinations continue to take place because the motivation for these deals is not affected as much by the large-scale economic concerns that seem to drive or deter the larger deals. The prime motivators for small and middle-market deals include:

- Incremental technological advances that threaten or create opportunity for the business
- The need to cash out nonpublic equity
- The need for succession of ownership or management
- Economic drivers for horizontal or vertical integration
- Loss of competitive advantage

Thus, low profile middle-market business combination activity remains very high. In 2000, there were more than 10,000 mergers and acquisitions. And one expert[2] stated that the value of Internet-related merger and acquisition deals alone topped $116 billion in 2000, 73 percent more than in 1999 and seven times more than in 1998.

In spite of the drop-off in the overall number of business combinations over the past few years, the cycle will eventually turn and stranger, larger mergers and acquisitions will again capture the headlines. No one can guess when the deal flow will see an upswing or what the nature of those deals will be. But one thing is certain: Unless the root causes of M&A underperformance are identified and resolved, there is no reason to believe that the abysmal track record of losses, failures, and divestitures will change. To that end, perhaps the best use for this lull in deal flow is to get smarter on such dynamics as the cultures of organizations and their impact on the performance of business combinations.

## SUMMARY

The history of business management theory and practice has paralleled the history of business combinations. Today's wide variety of vertical, horizontal, and conglomerate-forming deals represents an agglomeration of the deals characteristic of very specific eras that reflected the business demands of the time. General Electric consolidated literally scores of inventors and small manufacturers. General Foods brought together farmers, grain storage and distribution, food processing, finished food production, and marketing and distribution, enabling millions of people to have access to inexpensive, high-quality, nonperishable foods. The conglomerates of the 1950s provided investors with ownership in and dividends from businesses whose markets were so broad that they were virtually immune to economic dips and dynamics.

Meanwhile, advances in the availability of personal communications, social and economic changes, and better understanding of psychology influenced the evolution of management philosophy from typical command and control in the period when the M&A phenomenon began to today's era of empowerment, autonomy, and self-management. Business combinations are no longer simply a matter of combining balance sheets. More and more, they must recognize the unique nature of the businesses being combined in order to realize the rewards and benefits that are expected from the deal.

# DANCING WITH STRANGERS: THE MERGER AND ACQUISITION PROCESS

*The sweet murmurs of admiration for a thousand successes are painfully drowned out by the wails of a single failure.*

THE OBJECTIVES OF THIS CHAPTER are to help the reader to know the sequence and content of the steps in the typical M&A process, to begin to understand how the cultures of the combining businesses affect the success of the deal, and to stimulate thought concerning how the M&A process can better anticipate and accommodate the cultural differences of the combining businesses.

To understand the nature of cultural differences and the financial implications of these differences when organizations combine, we must first develop an awareness of where and how the cultural characteristics come into play during the M&A process. For example, the strategic directions and visions of the two businesses will always be different because the business strategy of the seller is to sell and the business strategy of the buyer is to buy.

Further, there are several specific points in the M&A process where cultural differences will reveal themselves. If these differences are not recognized as threats to the deal and dealt with, they can have a significant, long-term unfavorable impact on the financial performance of the deal. Therefore, the purpose of this chapter is to discuss the typical merger and acquisition processes (they are slightly different, as will be discussed later) and the mindset and motivation of the combining parties to build a foundation for understanding when, where, how, and why differences in the cultures of combining companies can affect the financial performance of the deal.

Given the number of business combinations involving businesses of many different types and sizes and the number of different people involved in them, it is easy to understand that each deal is a unique transaction. However, there are many commonalities as well, including the parties' basic motivations, the general process, and the usual steps. This chapter is written to be as inclusive of the many variations as possible.

## MOTIVATIONS FOR MERGERS AND ACQUISITIONS

There are many ways to view, understand, and classify business combinations, and we will very probably look at deals from nearly all of these perspectives at one place or another in this book. One way is to look behind the deal—that is, to define the strategic objectives of the deal participants.

The buyer is usually the initiator and driver of an M&A transaction. There are as many reasons for buyers to buy as there are buyers. However, one way to look at deals is to classify them by the buyer's strategic motivation. Table 2-1 describes five distinct types of M&A and corresponding buyer objectives.

**Table 2-1** *M&A Types and Their Objectives*

| M&A Type | Strategic Objectives |
|---|---|
| Overcapacity | The acquirer reduces overall industry capacity, gains market share, and improves efficiency through acquisition of a competitor; e.g., Daimler-Benz buys Chrysler |
| Geographic roll-up | Acquisitions expand the acquirer's physical presence; e.g., Banc One buys many local banks |
| Product/market extension | The acquired products complement or extend the market of the acquirers' products; e.g., Quaker Oats buys Snapple |
| Research and development | The acquirer buys technological advances rather than building them in-house; e.g., Microsoft's acquisition/licensing of complementary software |
| Industry convergence | The acquirer establishes a new industry by assembling resources from existing businesses; e.g., Will Durant puts General Motors together |

Another way to look at acquisitions is from the perspective of the value that the acquired business will add to the assets of the acquirer, such as the following factors:

- Revenue enhancement
- Cost reduction
- Vertical and/or horizontal operational and financial synergies or economies of scale
- Growth to satisfy pressures from investors
- Underutilized resources
- Entrepreneurs with large appetites
- A desire to reduce the number of competitors (increase market share)
- A need to gain a foothold in a new geographic market (especially if the current market is saturated)
- A desire to diversify into new products and services

Mergers, because of the implied relationship of key people within the enterprises going forward, have a different set of objectives for both parties, such as:

- To improve process engineering and technology
- To increase the scale of production in existing product lines
- To vertically integrate the production process
- To redeploy excess capital in more profitable or complementary uses
- To obtain tax benefits

In some rather rare cases, the buyer may purchase the proprietary assets of a competitor, supplier, or customer and shut the acquired business down, retaining only those people who are directly associated with operating, maintaining, or advancing the technology. This type of business combination is noteworthy because it is the only type of deal in which the cultures of the two organizations are not significant to the long-term success of the transaction.

## THE SELLER'S AGENDA

As the old saying goes, "It takes two to tango." We have looked at types of deals and motives for deals from the buyer's perspective, but what motivates the seller to sell? Reasons include:

- The desire to retire
- Lack of successors
- Business adversities
- Inability to compete

Unlike the buyer, who seldom has a sense of urgency about a combination, sellers often are under the gun to do a deal. With reference to the preceding list, the owner may have sudden health problems, find out that his child wants to surf in Bali instead of running the family business, or discover that his industry's equivalent of Wal-Mart is about to move into town. These factors play an important role in the attractiveness of the deal to prospective suitors and the ultimate price paid. Buyers often drag out the combination process in order to put price pressure on the seller or to force concessions in the negotiations. Being in the driver's seat, the buyer has a great deal more control over the final outcome of the deal. The beginnings of ill will, the exodus of key employees, and difficult integration creep into the deal if the seller and its people regard the acquirer as a shark (or worse).

## MERGER OR ACQUISITION?

Whether a particular combination is a merger or an acquisition is best determined by the structure of the financial arrangements involved in the deal rather than the jargon of the business community and the press. There are many cases in which, in order to assuage the fears of employees, customers, and suppliers, an acquisition is announced as a merger. Some experts in business combinations contend that there is no such thing as a merger, and it is certainly true that very few combinations, if any, are actually mergers of equals. Perhaps the most recent example in which the folly of believing that a combination is a union of equals has been revealed is the heavy hand that Daimler has recently wielded over Chrysler, although the combination had been announced as a "union of equals." Even in true acquisitions, the term *merger* is used as a synonym for "takeover." Some of this is due to the language of accounting conventions. For various technical reasons, the term *merger* can be preferable to *acquisition* for financial accounting purposes. However, the lion's share of combination deals are in fact acquisitions in terms of the type of funding mechanism and the allegiance of the management team.

If there is a bias in discussing the combination process and the impact of cultures on the success of deals, it is clearly toward acquisitions because they are the most common type of business combination.

## A BUSINESS OPERATOR BECOMES A BUSINESS BUYER

The buyer usually begins the business combination process. In some cases a business broker may initiate a search on behalf of a prospective seller, but once a buyer decides that it is interested, the overall process and the steps that are followed are fairly consistent. The merger and acquisition process often begins with introspection to determine what success looks like and why that form of success is attractive to the organization. As the phrase goes, "The journey of a thousand miles begins with a single step." This first step sets the direction and begins the buildup of momentum toward the goal, which is ultimately the increased profitability, improved operations, and greater probability of prosperity and long-term survival of the acquiring business.

Figure 2-1 illustrates the steps in the typical merger or acquisition. Each step will be discussed in order to provide insight into and understanding of the nature of the step itself as well as to gain insight into how cultural differences come into play. As a result, the steps in the merger and acquisition process and the related discussion should be looked at from two perspectives. The first is to understand the purpose and process of the step itself. The second is to understand the implications of the step for the people in the organization, their ongoing activities, and their assumptions about the organization that dictate their attitudes, values, opinions, behaviors, and actions for the purpose of providing their safety and security in the workplace.

## DEFINING THE GOALS AND DEVELOPING THE STRATEGY OF THE DEAL

The merger and acquisition process is usually initiated by something amorphous on the buyer's part—an idea, a revelation, a dream, a nightmare. Once the concept is formed, it often leads to consideration of the pluses and minuses of doing the deal; if the net sum is positive, the plan for moving ahead begins to be formed. The initial step is to articulate the rationale behind the idea for a merger or acquisition. These are the goals and strategies of the deal. The following list describes the typical activities involved in this phase of the combination process:

- Develop specific financial and market objectives for the combination, such as sales volume growth, internal rate of return, increase in market share, deeper/higher vertical integration, and greater geographic reach.

**Figure 2-1** *Steps in the Typical Merger and Acquisition Process*

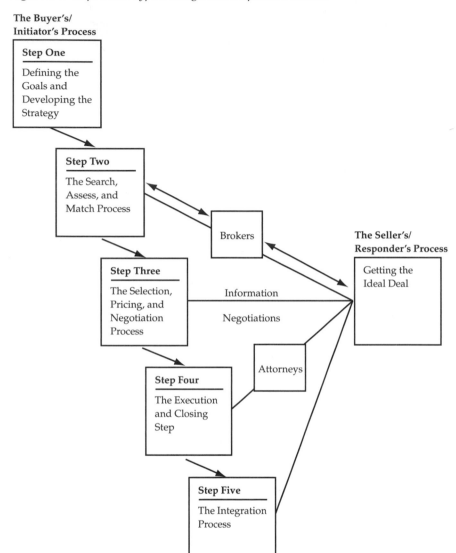

- Determine the nature of the combination—merger, acquisition, or joint venture.
- Develop a profile for the ideal combination candidate, including such factors as geographic location, products or services offered, current market share, gross sales, and so on. If possible, specify deal killers such as debt level or potential liabilities.

- Prepare the due diligence package, including materials desired from the acquisition/merger candidate.

The official beginning of the typical deal generally takes place in a board or marketing meeting in which the desire to increase earnings is stated in one form or another and the possible strategies for doing so are discussed. In part, the motivation for such thinking is based, somewhat understandably, on the fear that if the company is not aggressively directing its own growth, it will become the target of a firm that is. The choice, in the most succinct terms, is "build or buy." The firm can build new capacity, design new products, and launch new advertising campaigns despite the high cost and the uncertainty that the return on the investment (ROI) of money, time, and opportunity costs will meet the expanded profit expectations of the business. Or the company can quietly begin a search for an organization with proven performance that can add the desired capabilities. External factors such as the cost and availability of capital, market pressures, the degree of merger and acquisition activity in the firm's market sector, and myriad other issues will influence the build or buy decision.

Since profit equals revenue less expenses, the desire to increase profits means that the company must either increase revenue or decrease costs. The target of a merger or acquisition must add value to the initiator of the combination in some manner that drives the profit equation in a more profitable direction. Value capture can be derived from several key sources, and depending upon the circumstances of the merger, some will be more valuable than others, according to experts.[1] For example, it is generally useful to consider the following areas when identifying sources of value:

*Growth-oriented (revenue drivers)*

- New products, service offerings, markets, customer segments, distribution channels
- Enhanced market presence, market capture
- Enhanced product development efficiency (leveraged R&D, internal best practices)
- Combined technologies or capabilities
- Leveraged sales force
- Increased capture of the value chain

*Efficiency-oriented (cost drivers)*

- Integrated supply chain
- Leveraged procurement volume

- Production footprint optimization
- Facility optimization
- Vertical integration or deintegration
- Distribution channel optimization
- Sales force optimization
- Headquarters consolidation
- Support function consolidation (human resources, finance, IT)

*Other (intangible drivers)*

- Financial value (balance sheet items, taxes, etc.)
- Optimized programs and policies (e.g., benefits programs)
- Rationalization and/or elimination of special projects, etc.
- Additional alliances or relationships

True mergers differ from acquisitions in many respects and may be initiated by either party. In a classic merger, there is no buyer or seller, although one party may take the lead by initiating the proposal or contact. Data gathering, due diligence, and key decisions are bilateral. Postmerger integration and other dynamics of transition are more collaborative than with acquisitions. But as relatively friendly as mergers appear, they are not without their own challenges. According to merger veterans:[2]

> Even in the most scrupulously planned and executed merger unexpected issues arise that can make those involved question whether the upside potential is really worth the pain.

## DEFINING THE IDEAL DEAL

We have been focusing on the buyer or merger initiator's process; however, to be fair and complete, it is important to consider the other side of the coin—the seller's process. The selling process may be self-initiated, or it may be prompted by an unsolicited inquiry regarding the owner's interest in selling all or some of the business's assets or activities. The seller's steps typically involve this sequence of activities:

1. Deciding to sell, setting sale objectives, and determining the timing
2. Establishing the logistics by putting together an advisory team, optimizing the value of the business, and preparing an initial valuation
3. Developing a marketing strategy (if self-initiated), including identifying potential buyers or selecting an intermediary

4. Selecting the ideal buyer through executing nondisclosure agreements and participating in the due diligence and preliminary negotiations
5. Participating in the final negotiations and structuring of the deal
6. Preparing for closing and integration
7. Closing
8. Engaging in postclosing activities, including compensation confirmation and implementation of the integration/turnover plan

## THE SEARCH, ASSESS, AND MATCH PROCESS

Once the initiator has decided upon the motivation, structure, and financing of the deal and the characteristics of the ideal target company, it begins looking for its new asset. Again, each deal is different, but for the most part, this phase of the combination process includes the following activities:

- Based on the type of combination, determine and assemble a combination team (managers, attorneys, accountants, and investment bankers) and begin the search for combination candidates.
- Initiate a search for prospective combination candidates based on the identified criteria. This step is often performed by or with a business broker.
- Prepare and perform due diligence analyses of the prime candidates.
- Screen the candidate list and due diligence information for deal killers.
- Select primary and secondary merger/acquisition candidates.

At some point in the M&A process, the initiator, either directly or indirectly through a broker, initiates the compilation of a list of prospective target companies. Publicly available information such as Department of Commerce data, tax and other government filings, marketing materials, web sites, and so on is used to add or eliminate prospects in light of the initiator's needs. For vertical integrations, lists of existing customers and/or suppliers provide a pool of known candidates with whom the firm has successful, mutually beneficial working relationships from which a promising combination can be launched. For horizontal combinations, lists of competitors can be obtained from sources ranging from simple local resources such as the Yellow Pages to trade associations and trade show participants. Firms with complementary products, services, and geographic and demographic markets should be included in the prospect list.

Target company lists for conglomerate-forming or expanding combinations are more difficult to develop quickly. Generally speaking, this is due to the desire to supplement profit by acquiring businesses with external environment variables and cycles different from those of the initiating company. Consequently, virtually any business in a different market from the conglomerating firm is a candidate. As a result, the vision of the strategic fit must precede the identification of prospective target companies.

Subsequently, a team is assembled from either internal human assets or outside experts and consultants, or, typically, a combination of insiders and outsiders. The critical competencies of the team are:

- The ability to envision and articulate the optimum combined entity and its outcomes
- In-depth knowledge of the combining businesses' markets, their dynamics, their variables, and their histories
- In-depth knowledge of the production process for the product or service, from R&D through distribution
- The ability to identify and quantify the features of the prospective combining businesses into accurate *pro forma* statements so that the most financially advantageous opportunity is determined and executed
- In-depth familiarity with tax and regulatory issues related to the operations of the individual and combined businesses, including environmental, federal security, labor, and employment laws and the implications of the Hart-Scott-Rodino Act regarding premerger notification requirements
- The ability to structure the most advantageous legal relationship between the combining companies
- The ability to source and assemble the most advantageous financial structure for the combination
- Knowledge and sincere appreciation of organization culture fundamentals and the potential impact of cultural mismatches on the success of the deal

Eventually, the prospect list is whittled down to one to three companies, upon which in-depth scrutiny is performed via the due diligence process. This analytical process is intended to confirm the promise of postcombination success through an in-depth and systematic scrutiny of the seller's business by a team of professionals whose skills match the nature of the issues. The overall due diligence process has two very diverse elements: legal and operational. In the former, the buyer or merger team reviews documents and data regarding the following:[3]

1. Corporate matters such as letters of incorporation, operating licenses, bylaws, shareholder lists, and minutes of directors' and shareholders' meetings
2. Financial matters, including audited financial statements, tax returns, contracts, equity agreements, and budgets
3. Management and employment matters, such as employment agreements, union contracts, EEOC and other regulatory compliance files, employee benefit plans, personnel policies and procedures, and consultant/contract employee agreements
4. Tangible and intangible assets of the seller, including lists of real property; patents and other proprietary assets; lease contracts for buildings and equipment; verification of liquid assets like stock certificates, deposits, and bonds; and so on
5. Material contracts and obligations of the seller, describing any and all obligations to third parties
6. Miscellaneous materials such as press releases, management résumés, community activities, donations, directorships of employees, and so on

The second, or operational, due diligence includes scrutiny of the critical operational elements of the target company. While many of the areas appear similar to those reviewed during the financial due diligence, the operational analysis is concerned with the functionality and compatibility of the combining firms' production processes. Aspects of the operations that are typically reviewed are:[4]

1. History and background of the business's:
   - Strategy
   - Products
   - Acquisitions and other external ventures
   - Technology
   - International trade
2. Products and/or services, including:
   - Product/service literature
   - Market strengths and advantages

- Sales and earnings to date
- Sales and earnings projections
- New products being developed

3. Market dynamics, such as:
   - Market environment
   - Growth, breadth, and depth of products in the market
   - Competitive advantages and proprietary strengths
   - Pricing position
   - Importance of service
   - Quality requirements
   - Cyclical market trends
   - Industry profitability
   - Barriers to entry of competitors
   - Constraints on foreign competitors
   - Resources required to compete

4. Distribution characteristics, such as:
   - Types of distribution systems
   - Distribution channels
   - Competitors' distribution systems and channels
   - Projection of distribution changes

5. Technology, including:
   - Compatibility of business systems
   - Patent situation
   - Complexity and maturity of each business's technology
   - Volatility of technology in chosen markets
   - Proliferation of technology to other products or services
   - Identification of technical leaders in the domestic and global markets
   - R&D status and commercial applications of innovations

6. Manufacturing capabilities from the perspective of integrating the companies: systems, cost to upgrade to required quality standards, and ability to expand to meet future needs. Specific criteria include:
   - The condition and capabilities of physical facilities
   - Plans for new facilities
   - Production capacity
   - Availability of raw materials and other supplies

- Quality standards
7. Organization, including:
   - Identification of key personnel
   - Identification of the true organization leaders
   - Whether a sound, well-thought-out integration plan can be developed before the acquisition
8. Financial projections, including the acquired company's:
   - Approach to taxes
   - Approach to inventory accounting
   - Current financial projections
   - Sources and uses of revenues
   - Deal-relevant calculations, such as breakeven point, sensitivity analyses, and major risks/opportunities
9. Competitor analyses, such as:
   - The names and locations of competitors and their products or services
   - Their product literature, including price lists
   - Customer input
   - A comparative grid that candidly compares the combined firm's products or services with those of a ranked list of competitors
10. Strategic considerations, including gaps in the combined entities' products, markets, technology, and management relative to those of its competitors

The rather nebulous line between "finding matches" and "making a selection" depends on how many viable candidates there are that come close to the buyer's requirements. For our purpose, we will suppose that there is more than one prospect and that the final selection depends upon the financial opportunities and pricing implications of each prospect.

## POSTSCRIPT

The search, assess, and match step of the merger and acquisition process is ripe for improvement via a greater understanding of the cultural differences between the prospectively combining organizations. The problems leading to the failure or underperformance of many business combinations can and should be identified and recognized during this phase of the M&A process. There are effective techniques available that can identify the strengths and weakness of the cultures in objective financial terms, such as:

- The impact of the cultures on the payback period for the deal
- Information that may refute assumptions about the combined market share of the new entity
- Citations of organization differences that may extend the integration phase

For now, the reader should know that there are resources available to those involved in mergers and acquisitions that can be used to objectively identify, prevent, or modify potentially disastrous business combinations. It is the fundamental premise of this book that the use of objective culture analyses such as Quantitative Organization Culture Analyses (QUOCA) can significantly improve the outcome of many mergers and acquisitions.

## THE SELECTION, PRICING, AND NEGOTIATION PROCESS

### Selecting a Partner
The accumulated due diligence information is typically analyzed and summarized by the team of financial professionals and becomes the basis for the "go/no-go" decision on prospects for the combination and the eventual determination of the amount of compensation and the form of the compensation scheme. In the precombination steps, the emphasis is on the financial implications of the deal. Buyers typically concentrate on the numbers they have gathered in the due diligence process, such as what the target business is worth, what price premium, if any, to pay, what the tax implications of the deal may be, and how to structure the transaction.

The decision to do a deal with a selected enterprise is usually based on the combined balance sheet of the companies, projected cash flows, and hoped-for return on investment. In most instances, members of the buyer's team come entirely from financial positions or backgrounds; they therefore bring a strong financial mindset to their work, and their judgments are based on financial models and ratios. There is a tendency for "hard" criteria to drive out "soft" matters in these deals, with the result that organizational or cultural issues tend to be scoffed at and disregarded.

While the due diligence process has traditionally been a financial analysis, many experts assert that it is never too early to determine, acknowledge, and confront issues that will make integration of the businesses difficult and the achievement of financial goals impossible. These faults may not be deal killers or showstoppers by themselves, but if there are several of them and, in their aggregate, they are serious enough, the candidate should be rejected or the price structure of the deal should be recalculated. According to experts, showstoppers include:[5]

- *Distrust and incompatibility between management representatives.* Issues of trust and compatibility that arise as a result of the precombination planning and negotiation process may signal difficulty in working together after the deal.
- *Difficulties in working out governance arrangements.* Problems in working out the management team for the combined entity and the roles of key individuals can be a hint of problems to come after the deal is done.
- *Lack of sufficient talent to manage both ongoing operations and the transition.* Not having enough managerial talent to deal with both core business tasks and the combination puts huge demands on the combined management team.
- *Need for significant coordination costs to obtain synergies.* Achieving the envisioned synergies and advantages is often much more costly, difficult, and time-consuming than initially anticipated. Time, money, technology, and other investments required to obtain synergies may divert resources from other important operational areas.
- *Disruptions associated with the combination.* Going through the process of combining the companies can disrupt business operations and create significant costs, problems with customers, or opportunities for competitors.
- *Threats to customer relationships as a result of the combination.* Customers may feel differently about the combined entity because of its new ownership, its size and position, or other factors that lead them to view the new organization negatively.
- *Postcombination talent drains.* Key managerial, technical, or professional talent may not want to remain because of their feelings about the new owners or partners, the nature of the new company, or real or perceived threats to their careers. Often the best and the brightest are the most mobile.
- *Negative impact on the workforce and communities.* When the gains anticipated from the combination require significant layoffs, there may be harm to the workforce and the communities in which the company operates.

- *Postdeal hangover.* If the process of making the deal has been con-
  tentious enough, it can create significant bad blood that will be difficult to overcome during the combination phase.
- *Incompatible values and cultures.* Core values and cultures that are
  significantly different are very difficult to combine. Different
  heroes, myths, and artifacts create different attitudes, values, and
  opinions. *How* and *why* people do things is just as important as *what*
  they do. Barriers to collaboration can affect anything from order
  processing to invoicing and everything in between.

Notice how many of these showstoppers are people issues, subjective in nature and very difficult to quantitatively factor into the economic
models that are used for due diligence go/no-go decisions. These issues,
if they are truly showstoppers, somehow have to be incorporated into
the decision-making process if bad deals are to be avoided.

Quite often the process for selecting the combination partner boils
down to identifying the enterprise that has the fewest flaws and the greatest potential for return on investment. The calculation of return on investment usually ignores the warts and wrinkles that were discovered in the
course of looking for showstoppers because these issues are considered
qualitative rather than quantitative. QUOCA was developed specifically to
convert these soft issues into financial and competitive performance information that can be factored into the matching process so that the enterprise
that has the greatest "hard" and "soft" potential for success is selected.

### Determining the Price of the Combination

Determining the offering price can be quite involved and is often performed by a team of finance, accounting, and business brokerage experts.
The offer price is influenced by the following factors and their elements:

*Revenue factors*

- Combined gross revenues
- Combined market share
- Revenue enhancement by vertical and horizontal market synergies
- Revenue enhancement from bundling products and services
- Product/service leverage, such as follow-on sales

*Expense factors*

- Production and distribution efficiencies
- Marketing and sales efficiencies

- Customer service efficiencies
- Greater purchasing power for supplies, raw materials, utilities, etc.
- Reduction of overhead costs from:
  - Increased leverage in buying and overseeing insurance and benefit programs
  - Combining staff functions such as payroll, accounting, legal services, human resources, organization development, IT, communications, investor relations, facility management and maintenance, and so on
  - Reduction of facility requirements and costs, such as property taxes, energy, insurance, security, and so on, as a result of the combination
- Transaction costs, including:
  - Attorneys', consultants', accounting, and brokerage fees
  - Licenses, registrations, filings, and so on
  - Shutdown, decommissioning, cleanup, maintenance, caretaking, and so on, of redundant facilities
  - Compensation packages and related expenses for redundant personnel
  - Liquidation of equity options in the acquired business
  - Fees and penalties for restructuring existing legal agreements such as contracts and leases
- The cost of capital and the ongoing debt service as a business expense
- The dilution of equity for existing stockholders
- The impact of the deal on company valuation
- The future cost and availability of operating capital

Generally, the go/no-go decision is based upon the financial upside of the deal compared to the acquiring business's "hurdle rate," or desired internal rate of return. This somewhat subjective number is unique to every business because it is based on a combination of the company's cost of capital, its cash flow, and its time horizon for calculating the net present value of the deal. Needless to say, the go/no-go decision and the purchase price of the deal are dependent upon accurate calculation of the variables that affect the amount and timing of the net income from the deal. If aspects of the deal that affect the assumptions that go into the decision and the pricing are ignored, disappointment is inevitable. As we shall see in subsequent sections, the factors that go into calculating the

IRR (cost of capital, cash flow, and the time horizon) can all be influenced by weaknesses in cultural characteristics.

The differences in the cultures must be recognized and factored into the *pro forma* calculations of future revenues and expenses as well as into the internal rate of return and the offer made by the buyer to the seller or, in the case of a merger, into the valuation of the deal. Mismatched cultures can have a negative impact on the following financial measures and operational factors:

- Return on investment (ROI)
- Return on sales (ROS)
- Return on equity (ROE)
- Return on assets (ROA)
- Payback period for the combination
- Market share
- Sales growth
- Product or service quality
- Time to market for new products and services
- Product or service innovation
- Employee satisfaction, turnover, effectiveness, and efficiency

Each of these financial implications of cultural differences should be factored into the *pro forma* calculations for the deal in order to fully reflect the likely financial performance of the deal.

### Financing the Combination

Once the due diligence information has been amassed and a target has been selected, a great deal of work remains to be done to secure the financing. Most of the issues that must be resolved in the financing package are based upon *pro forma* calculations of profitability, estimates of cash flows, and the use of funds for the deal.

There are several financing options,[6] each with its optimum application. The options fall into two distinct categories: purchase (acquisition) or pooling of interest (merger). It is worth noting that both the purchase and the type of financing for the deal are arranged by finance professionals, who rely almost entirely on financial information. While "soft" issues regarding the organizations' cultures are a concern, in few deals does anyone take the time to calculate the financial implications of the "people stuff" for the price or likely outcomes of the deal. The features of the financing options are:

1. In the purchase scenario:
   - One company buys another. The purchased company ceases to exist.
   - The assets and liabilities of the acquired company are assumed at fair market value.
   - The difference between fair market value and the purchase price is accounted for as goodwill.
2. In the pooling-of-interest approach:
   - The two companies combine to form a new entity.
   - The assets and liabilities of the combined entity are based on the recorded value of the assets.
   - Goodwill cannot be recognized.

Financing is generally not an obstacle to closing a merger or acquisition. For example, of the deals reported canceled in a recent year, only 7 percent of the cancellations were due to financing problems.[7] Of the combinations that did go through, the breakdown of financing was as follows:

| | |
|---|---|
| All cash | 58.7% |
| All stock | 6.0% |
| Combination | 17.4% |
| Undisclosed | 17.9% |

An important driving force for investors is the liquidity of the invested assets. For example, sources of cash for a purchase combination include commercial banks, investment banks, venture capitalists, and private investors. For the most part, commercial banks are driven by interest income; if they are the source of cash, the deal is financed through debt over its life, and the deal is built around the combination's ability to repay.

Investment banks, venture capitalists, and private investors are motivated by the desire to multiply the value of their investment, with a fairly specific window for when that return is to be achieved. Therefore, the synergy or value added from combining the two companies is strategically more important to these financial partners than to commercial banks with their debt financing. For these investors, the issue of liquidity, or when they will get their money back with growth, is paramount. One way of achieving liquidity is through an initial public offering, in which the public becomes the owner of the company through the purchase of its tradable stock. Another option for liquidity is for the combined company to be acquired by or merged with another firm, thereby paying the investors back for their risk and the growth that happened because of their investment and their management tenure. Both exit strategies count on increases in income, market share, or other value-added aspects of the business to enable the investors to realize profit from the initial merger or acquisition. Ignoring cultural issues in determining the price for the initial deal can have a huge impact on the return on investment from the exit deal.

## Negotiating the Deal

Discussions of the terms and conditions of the deal usually have their warts and wrinkles, but fewer than a quarter of the deals that are proposed fall apart because of irresolvable issues. The amount, nature, and timing of compensation are the common sticking points. The way these issues are resolved is usually in keeping with the companies' gut desire to do the deal. If there is a strong desire to execute the transaction, a way will be found to overcome problems. In some cases, however, the fear of life after the deal or other gut emotional issues can cause an endless list of little problems that complicate negotiations unreasonably. This hidden or unaddressed agenda is an organization cultural issue—the seller's vision is different from what the seller has professed or acknowledged. Like a groom being left at the altar by an uncertain bride, the buyer may find that the seller hasn't honestly confronted life after the marriage. More money is seldom enough of an incentive to get the nervous seller to reconsider the deal, and the transaction becomes unsalvageable.

The style and spirit of the negotiation process can be a bellwether for the ease or difficulty of the integration process. Some fundamental cultural characteristics become evident during these discussions, such as:

- How the representatives work to achieve agreement on conflicting points of view
- The commitment to the parties' specific goals and objectives and the reasons behind them
- The willingness of each party to empathize with the other party's perspective and to factor that information into its negotiation stance
- Core values such as honesty and integrity in the parties' approach to negotiating the deal in good faith

Significant problems with negotiations should alert the acquiring team to potential integration issues should the negotiations eventually lead to closing the deal. The initiating company may want to use a quantitative organization culture analysis to reveal the basis for the difficulties in the negotiations, and to factor the results into another go/no-go decision, the valuation, and, if appropriate, the integration process.

## THE EXECUTION AND CLOSING

Little has been written about the actual closing. Generally, it is somewhat anticlimactic in that papers merely need to be signed by the parties to execute the terms and conditions negotiated as part of the due diligence, valuation, and financing steps. However, although very few deals fall apart structurally at closing, many lasting impressions that significantly influence working relationships and other elements critical to the long-term success of the operational integration are formed at closing.

In most small and middle-market deals, setting and executing the closing is largely a matter of logistics. In the case of large deals and megadeals, logistics gives way to scrutiny and approval by regulators such as the Securities and Exchange Commission as the major factor in the consummation of the combination.

## THE INTEGRATION PROCESS

After the deal is closed, the philosophical and physical combination, or integration, of the businesses begins. Even though the process has had its share of challenges up to this point, it is not until the organizations begin the formal and informal processes of working together that the assumptions on which the deal was predicated are replaced by reality. Ideally, integration planning should occur prior to the actual closing and should address the most likely and most significant barriers to success. However, in most cases, transition teams made up of senior management from both sides of the deal are convened after the closing. The integration kickoff meeting generally identifies specific issues and the appropriate tactics to resolve them, along with responsibilities, budgets, and time frames.

Some merger and acquisition experts[8] advocate two integration programs, one for management and operational issues and another for cultural issues. The management and operational issues should include but not be limited to the following areas for both the acquiring and the target company, and a plan should be developed for integrating these areas:

- Quality control
- Promotion policies and career opportunities

- Performance evaluations
- Whether decision making is centralized or decentralized
- Job security
- Innovation

It's hard for experienced people not to add their personal thoughts to lists like this one. I am sure that everyone who has been through either a merger or an acquisition would have his or her own contributions. From my own experience, I would add:

- Policies and procedures
- Purchasing and spending guidelines and authorizations
- Regulatory compliance accountabilities

The cultural integration process is often regarded as the more difficult. Marks and Mirvis[9] state it very nicely:

> The optimism that energizes the decision to purchase a target or align with another firm carries into the combination phase in the form of high hopes and confident expectations. They are soon forgotten, however, as the grueling work of combination planning, the critical mass of personal stress and uncertainty, and the pervasive clash of cultures overwhelm people during the combination phase. Common problems besiege organizations and their people during this period, when the highs of doing a deal are replaced by the lows of making the deal work.

This is such an important issue for both the fate of combinations and the theme of this book that it deserves another expert commentary. Senn[10] avows:

> While it is clear that successful mergers and acquisitions must be based on strategic, financial and other vital objective criteria, ignoring a potential clash of cultures can lead to financial failure or at least a substantial diminution of expected results. Far too often, personnel and organizational issues are assigned a low priority during the pre-acquisition process. Other times they are an afterthought. Increasing evidence suggests cultural incompatibility is the single largest cause of failure to achieve projected performance, departure of key executives, and time consuming conflicts in the consolidation of businesses. When companies combine, a clash of cultures can turn potentially good business alliances into financial disasters.

Cultural integration requires recognizing that there is a very high probability that the cultures differ in the strength of their beliefs and assumptions concerning several key issues that dictate the behaviors of the cultures' people. Experts[11] have determined that the critical variables and elements of an organizational culture can be captured in the following characteristics:

- *Vision.* The organization has a shared view of its desired future state.
- *Strategic direction and intent.* This involves the organization's plan to "make its mark" on its industry.
- *Goals and objectives.* There is a clear sense of what needs to be done in order for the organization and its people to survive and prosper.
- *Core values.* Members of the organization share a set of values that creates a sense of identity and a clear set of expectations.
- *Agreement.* The organization is able to reach agreement on its critical issues as well as resolve differences when they occur.
- *Coordination and integration.* Different functions and units of the organization are able to work together productively to achieve desired outcomes.
- *Empowerment.* Individuals have the authority, initiative, and ability to manage their own work such that they have a sense of ownership and responsibility toward the organization.
- *Team orientation.* Value is placed on working cooperatively toward common goals for which all employees feel mutually accountable.
- *Capability development.* The organization continually invests in the development of employees' skills in order to remain competitive and meet ongoing operational needs.
- *Creating change.* The organization is able to create adaptive ways to prosper in its ever-changing business environment.
- *Organizational learning.* The organization receives, translates, and interprets signals from the environment into opportunities to encourage innovation, gain knowledge, and develop its capabilities.
- *Customer focus.* The organization understands and reacts to its customers, anticipates their future needs, and is driven to satisfy those needs.

The degree of cultural strength for these characteristics should determine the priorities, nature, and direction of the cultural integration activities. The four possibilities for the relative degree of characteristic strengths are:

1. Strong acquirer, strong acquired
2. Strong acquirer, weak acquired
3. Weak acquirer, strong acquired
4. Weak acquirer, weak acquired

The optimum situation, of course, is to have both organizations be strong in all of their cultural characteristics, but even in this case, since the companies' histories have not been shared, differences in how the cultures work will be apparent. For example, both companies can have great strengths in their core values, but the values can be as different as night and day.

As we will see in later chapters, the quantitative organization culture analysis process looks at the cultural characteristics and the strengths and weaknesses of the combining organizations on each characteristic to determine where, when, and how interventions should be used to smooth and shorten the cultural integration process.

There are several other factors that affect the difficulty of achieving organizational integration,[12] including the:

1. Degree of differentiation of organizational functions (low to high)
2. Number of units requiring integration (low to high)
3. Nature of integration relationships (pooled, sequential, or reciprocal)
4. Frequency of integration contact (rare to frequent)
5. Importance of integration to overall strategy (low to high)
6. Complexity and uncertainty of organizational information (simple and certain to complex and uncertain)

Some experts[13] believe that if the cultural differences are not adequately addressed in the integration process, the shock experienced by the members of the acquired company is similar to mourning. They state that:

> There is considerable evidence in the literature that the process of dealing with the loss of a loved one is the model after which all other forms of loss are patterned. And loss necessitates mourning. A disturbance in the organizational status quo precipitates a comparable process. It causes a loss of old and familiar patterns of functioning and administrative relationships as they are replaced by new ones. Working-through, mourning, and change thus appear to be intimately connected.

Clearly, the impact of a change in ownership comes from many sources of uncertainty and loss. The potential replacement of well-liked and respected leaders and the uncertainty of professional and personal prosperity and survival are two very obvious causes for angst. The process of mourning involves the following four phases:

*Phase One: shock.* A period of numbing that usually lasts from a few hours to a week and may be interrupted by outbursts of extremely intense distress and/or anger.

*Phase Two: disbelief or denial.* A period of yearning and searching for the lost figure and for a source of feelings of comfort and security that lasts several months and sometimes years.

*Phase Three: discarding or work-through.* A period of reorganization, forgiveness, acceptance, and recovery. This phase may last almost indefinitely.

*Phase Four: realization and acceptance.* A gradual mellowing and acceptance of the situation.

The first reaction to a disturbance, which often involves a withdrawal of or change in status, is *shock*. The person is reluctant to assimilate new information, especially if it is damaging to self-esteem. A short period of numbness often occurs, which may be punctuated by attacks of panic, outbursts of anger, and a sense of bewilderment that can spread unabated throughout the organization and create a state of chaos and panic. Critical organizational functions and processes may fail, or people may simply go through the motions in a ritualistic, mechanical way.

In the second phase, *disbelief* or *denial*, the individual or group will yearn and search for what has been lost. Employees feel a huge sense of anger and irritation, often directed toward the acquiring organization and its people. These deep-seated feelings manifest themselves as bursts of anger, sadness, personal recrimination, and guilt. People often blame themselves for mistakes or problems that impeded their employer's success and rendered their employer vulnerable to the acquisition. The emergence of the fight/flight and dependency reactions often comes during the disbelief phase. Fight behavior manifests itself in confrontations, arguments, and altercations. Flight behavior often takes the form of withdrawal reactions such as malingering, absenteeism, and extended vacation requests. During this phase, energy is often redirected from productive activities to what seems to be wasteful internal politics or is directed toward external agencies that are held responsible for the change.

The most prominent feature of the third phase, the *working-through* process, is the *discarding* of the old patterns of thinking, feeling, and acting and the accepting of the inevitability of the new situation. During this phase, people begin to accept the idea that they must acknowledge and embrace the situation. People then begin recognizing and replicating the new attitudes, values, opinions, behaviors, and actions of the reformed culture. The feelings of despair and frustration may occasionally re-emerge, but their frequency and duration will continue to decrease until they are extinguished, often along with a great deal of the memories of and feelings for the old culture.

The final phase is one of *realization and acceptance*. The irreversibility of the situation is accepted, and the new attitudes, values, opinions, behaviors, and actions are fully embraced by the employees. The redefined environment is now fully owned and accepted.

Because the phases of shock and disbelief are internally focused, they are most effectively addressed by influential and well-respected members of the acquired business's management team. On the other hand, the phases of discarding and realization are externally focused, and so the people and their organizations are ready for and receptive to external forces that can shape their transition to their new equilibrium. It is at this stage of the integration process that people from the acquiring business can have valuable, positive long-term impacts on the integration process and the financial success of the combination.

## FINANCIAL PERFORMANCE MEASURES

Business books are full of terms that describe one aspect or another of financial performance. The challenge here is to define, present, and discuss the terms that provide insight into combinations and the relationship of their performance due to their disparate cultures. In researching literature on the subjects of culture performance and business combination financial performance, the following terms were found to be of concern to both camps. Terms in italics are defined in the glossary of terms at the end of the book.

*Net income* is the ultimate measure of a company's financial performance because it is the measure of how much money the business makes. Net income is of interest to stakeholders because it translates into salaries, bonuses, dividend income from stock, perquisites, promotions, and so on. Net income increases when revenues go up or expenses go down, or, especially, when both occur simultaneously. Conversely, net income decreases or becomes net loss when revenues go down, expenses go up, or both occur simultaneously. In the world of enlightened self-interest, it is a good thing for a business's stakeholders when its net income increases and its competitors' net income decreases.

For companies whose *equity* is publicly traded, increased net income draws the attention of analysts, who rate investments in terms of earnings per share. When the company's earnings are good, more people want the stock and its price increases. When *stock prices* are high, bankers are more likely to offer the company favorable rates on loans, so its *cost of capital* is reduced, enabling it to achieve higher profits and/or cheaper growth. Good begets more good, and the upward spiral continues until something negative happens in the internal or external environment of the business.

Of course, when profits decrease or become losses, *earnings per share* decrease, fewer people want the stock, its price per share decreases, cheap capital disappears, and income is again reduced. Bad also begets more bad, and the downward spiral continues until something positive happens in the internal or external environment of the business.

The goal and prime motivation of every businessperson who envisions and executes a merger or acquisition is to enjoy increased net profits and the wonderful upward spiral and beneficial ripple effects. Unfortunately, most combinations don't produce the envisioned results. The next chapter will discuss the impact and the causes of merger and acquisition underperformance.

As we will discuss in the chapters that follow, the relative strengths of the cultural characteristics we mentioned earlier have a direct and profound impact on the financial performance of business combinations. For example, both Denison[14] and Fisher[15] cited evidence of a relationship between the strength of an organization's vision, strategic direction and intent, and goals and the organization's objective characteristics such as its:

- Profitability as measured by return on assets
- Sales and revenue growth
- Market share
- Sales/revenue growth
- Employee satisfaction

Quantitative organization cultural analyses are able to illustrate the cultural differences of the combining organizations in such a way that people on both sides of the deal understand the relative strengths and weaknesses of their respective businesses and the impact of the differences on the financial success of the deal. Such analyses provide input into these critically important elements of the business combination process:

- Envisioning the nature, purpose, and structure of the deal
- Understanding the nature of their own business culture
- Identifying the ideal candidate
- Making the go/no-go decision
- Determining the valuation of the deal
- Integrating the businesses

## SUMMARY

All business combinations are different, although they frequently follow a similar sequence of steps. Most of the decisions made during the process are financially oriented and are made by people with financial backgrounds. However, many of the identified causes of underperformance of mergers and acquisitions concern the "soft issues," such as the vision of the business, how decisions are made, the extent of empowerment that people have in performing their work, and the ability of the business to adapt to its ever-changing environment. There are important junctures in the deal-making process where cultural information could have an important influence on the decisions, and subsequently on the performance of the combination. What is needed is a mechanism that is accepted and used by M&A professionals to objectively factor cultural information into the combination process.

CHAPTER

# SO WHAT? THE IMPACTS AND CAUSES OF MERGER AND ACQUISITION UNDERPERFORMANCE

The issue of culture and sub-culture arises whenever two companies merge or one company acquires another. In the former case one attempts to blend two cultures into one without necessarily treating one or the other as dominant. In the latter case the problem of blending or assimilation is compounded by the fact that the total new unit will not have any shared history and one or the other subunit will feel inferior, threatened, angry and defensive.[1]

THE INTENT OF THIS CHAPTER is to allow the reader to develop an understanding of the impacts and ripple effects on the stakeholders that result from the failure or underperformance of mergers and acquisition; to know that ignoring or not assessing the cultural differences between the combining organizations can be a significant cause of M&A failure and underperformance; and to develop a need for knowledge regarding organization cultures, how to objectively measure them, and how to use this information to improve the performance and the likelihood for survival of combined businesses.

We are now armed with an understanding of the merger and acquisition processes and the financial measures and ratios used to gauge the success of mergers and acquisitions, and we are ready to confront the harsh realities of business combination underperformance. Specifically, this chapter is dedicated to investigating the most common causes of failure and underperformance and the impact of bad deals on the stakeholders of the combined organizations.

## THE EXTENT OF COMBINATION UNDERPERFORMANCE

It is often cited that most acquisitions fail to live up to the buyer's expectations. According to a recent Deloitte survey, only 32% of acquisitions could be deemed successful, i.e. transactions which had achieved their stated objectives within the planned time frame.[2]

Recent studies indicate that about 60% of transactions fail to deliver the value promised to shareholders of the acquiring company.[3]

Yet another heralded merger imploded last fall into a corporate wasteland. . . . Both chairmen, Chrysler's Eaton and Daimler's Schrempp, spouted effusively about future success—despite a 1998 joint study conducted by the two companies that showed 73% of all cross-border mergers fail to thrive.[4]

A.T. Kearney research shows that 56% of mergers do not succeed, failing to produce shareholder value.[5]

Experts disagree as to the exact percentage of mergers and acquisitions that underperform; however, no one is raving about the rate of combination successes or the monstrously high returns on investment from all of the deals that succeeded. In the case of the Daimler-Chrysler merger, even the companies' hired experts recognized the likelihood of failure and unsuccessfully counseled the parties against the deal.

Even if the odds of success are 50-50, it would seem that prudent businesspeople would consider any and all measures that would either improve the likelihood that the deal would succeed or, alternatively, clearly identify a deal that was bound to fail and should be avoided. The track record clearly illustrates that the old, financial models are inadequate at providing acquirers with all of the information they need in order to make decisions that lead to a high percentage of successful out-comes. Clearly, the abysmal performance record of mergers and acquisitions, regardless of the exact percentage of failures, needs to be improved for the sake of the stakeholders on all sides of these transactions.

## IMPACTS OF COMBINATION UNDERPERFORMANCE

The direct and indirect effects of failing or underperforming combinations are significant for owners, investors, lenders, employees, suppliers, customers, and communities. The employees of the combining companies are often the first to sense the causes of underperformance. Some attrition and turnover can be expected when organizations undergo any type of significant change, but early loss of the best and the brightest people can be an accurate bellwether of problems to come. These smart people are often quite astute in sensing whether change portends opportunity or peril, and if there is a hint of a combination misfit, their skills will open doors at welcoming competitors.

The demeanor of the individuals and the nature of the relationships developed during the due diligence, negotiation, and closing steps often influence the expectations and the reactions of employees in both of the combining organizations. Even combinations that are perceived to be favorable will create some uncertainties regarding the impending change. If the uncertainties are not addressed, they may generate anxiety and eventually have an impact on the productivity and profitability of both the acquiring and the acquired companies. Marks and Mirvis[6] have said:

> On average, employees [involved in a merger or acquisition] spent two hours per day obsessing on the potential impact of a combination rather than performing their work. Add this up across all employees, and it's easy to understand why combinations frequently yield such disappointing results.

The behavioral effects of living through a combination result in dramatically higher health costs for organizations. A survey of 177 combining companies found that one-third reported an increase in workers' compensation claims over a 15-month period. One in five companies said that their workers' compensation costs increased between 50 and 100 percent. This increase occurred in spite of the fact that 37 percent of the studied companies had reduced their employee head count by an average of 13 percent.

Unless something is done to mitigate these reactions, people will become immobilized by their concerns, and the actual integration of the businesses can become a marriage of the walking dead. Overman[7] reports that these "people problems" are particularly acute in the technology arena, where companies may engage in several mergers or acquisitions a year. Art Geis, Hay Consulting's leading expert on high-technology mergers and acquisitions, says:[8]

> In the rush to deal with the obvious issues and keep Wall Street happy, a detailed people plan spelling out strategies and tactics is omitted or glossed over. This can be catastrophic, because when people who have talents and skills crucial to the business plan are underutilized, the result is paralysis, delayed products, stalled sales and restless top talent looking at career options. These are costly, high-impact, long-term problems, not just temporary performance dips.

Problems such as these are by no means rare. Research strongly indicates that between two-thirds and three-quarters of the deals that are completed do not deliver on their financial projections, according to M&A experts. The outcomes and organizational synergies that were projected and promised to stakeholders, including investors, stockholders, and financial institutions, simply don't happen. Most combinations require much more time to fully integrate their operations than was projected.

The financial implications of poorly planned and integrated combinations include:

- Higher and unexpected business integration costs
- Higher operating costs
- Extended payback and return on investment time frames
- Loss of the best and the brightest people, with an accompanying loss of appeal as an employer
- A negative rather than a positive impact on market share
- Less rather than more innovation
- A longer time to market for new products and services
- Deterioration of customer service
- Loss of reputation and goodwill
- Litigation problems from disgruntled stakeholders
- Unanticipated write-offs for restructuring
- Potential losses and costs of divestiture of the acquired business

The conventional wisdom may be that people who are involved in mergers are not subject to such angst, since a merger is more of a consensual marriage than an arranged wedding. But experts[9] describe similar problems with mergers:

> There is no such thing as a merger of equals. One side always dominates, usually the side with the greater size or stronger, more aggressive management. Given this, it should not be surprising that more than half of all senior executives in acquired companies leave voluntarily within the first three years. Those executives who remain are often torn between angrily defending their pre-acquisition practices and succumbing to a kind of malicious obedience that takes pleasure in carrying out the new boss's obvious follies and refraining from saving him from himself. You need only observe a few of these emotional games to conclude that the only thing more corrupting than power is powerlessness.

The frustration and the human toll of poorly executed combinations manifest themselves in many ways, particularly in the acquired company. Experts[10] have noted that a common problem in merger and acquisitions is the psychological consequences of seller's remorse, where people in the acquired business interfere with or sabotage the buyer's steps to take over management of the combined organization. The people from the seller's business can be so accustomed to their own style of managing the organization that they are not open to changes in strategies or policies implemented by the buyer. As you can imagine, seller's remorse is most common when the principals of the acquired business remain involved as consultants or as minority owners. Problems like these can also be expected in mergers. However, they seem to be more profound in acquisitions, where the mantle of ownership and responsibility is more clearly passed from the seller to the buyer.

Marks and Mirvis[11] have identified another cultural phenomenon that affects the employees of the seller's company who remain. According to them, "survivor guilt" makes the remaining employees feel culpable for having been spared from the axe and depressed because of their inability to prevent additional layoffs. Survivor guilt is doubly unfortunate because it tends to be felt most intensely by those employees who were most loyal to the acquired business. When loyal employees feel that layoffs are unfair, their loyalty to the new organization drops more sharply, and their guilt intensifies more, than is the case with the less-committed survivors.

The early impacts of poorly executed combinations and underperformance can be the beginning of a downward spiral of lower income, lower valuation, extended payback period, higher cost of capital, and reduction of resources to attack the organization's problems. Unresolved problems can lead to layoffs, facility closings, divestitures, and eventually a write-off of the deal or the bankruptcy of the overall business. The impacts will be felt first by the primary stakeholders, such as employees, stockholders, bankers, customers, and suppliers, and then by the chain of secondary stakeholders, including the primary stakeholders' families, the businesses they patronize, their community, the tax base, the quality of the school system, and so on across their economic reach.

The history and statistics of mergers and acquisitions paint a pretty bleak picture for the stakeholders. Lynch[12] found that, based on their dismal financial performance, 80 percent of the deals should never have been done in the first place. Another study concluded that 95 percent of acquisitions displayed disappointing results. Apropos of this study, Lynch also stated, "most have died of corporate culture shock."

And all of these problems, reactions, negative impacts, and unintended consequences occur *after* extensive and expensive due diligence and with a partner that has been carefully selected because the experts have determined that the acquisition is a great strategic fit! As Davis[13] says:

> When one considers the millions of dollars that are spent on lawyers and accountants to prepare for the marriage, it seems ridiculously shortsighted not to spend a dime on checking out the compatibility of the two cultures.

## CAUSES OF COMBINATION UNDERPERFORMANCE

The causes for the failure of combinations are likely to be as diverse as the deals themselves. In a comprehensive effort to troubleshoot merger and acquisition underperformance, Marks and Mirvis[14] have divided the overall process into three phases: the *precombination phase*, which includes the period and activities prior to the closing; the *combination phase*, including the preparation for closing, the closing, and the activities immediately following closing; and the *postclosing phase*, which includes all of the long-term integration period and activities. Their research has identified unique root causes for combination failures in each phase, such as:

*The precombination phase*

- The buying or lead merger business has an unclear business strategy.

- The initiating company has a weak core business that is beyond salvation even with a strong partner.
- A poor combination strategy and/or incorrect combination assumptions.
- Pressure by stakeholders or advisers to do a deal.
- Hurried, incomplete due diligence.
- Unrealistic expectations of target company value.
- Overestimated synergies.
- Inflated expectations of return on investment.

*The combination phase*

- Integration of the businesses is perceived to be a distraction from "real work."
- Value-added and critical success factors are misunderstood.
- Psychological effects of the combination are denied or ignored.
- Culture clashes are denied or ignored.

*The postcombination phase*

- Unmitigated employee stress and organizational ineffectiveness.
- Rushed implementation of integration processes and programs.
- Insufficient resources deployed to facilitate successful integration.
- Unanticipated integration issues and obstacles.
- Poor coordination between and within suborganizations.
- Lack of or inattention to team building.
- Culture by default rather than by design.
- Missed or overlooked opportunities for organizational enhancement.
- Unintended impacts on employee attitudes and, hence, on business performance.

Direct your attention to the number of these factors that either directly or indirectly concern the cultures of the combining organizations, particularly the following:

- If the M&A strategy is uncertain, how can the initiator differentiate between a complementary and a detrimental target company?
- The due diligence process is incomplete and usually does not include a sufficient in-depth understanding of the initiator's culture to enable the initiator to know its own strengths and weaknesses and how they may affect the success of the combination.

- Unrealistic valuation of the target company usually includes igno-rance of the cultural traits that will either bar or delay the success of the deal.
- Organizational synergies are often overrated and overstated in order to push the deal ahead when, in fact, the sense of synergism is purely subjective.
- The overinflated expectations for return on investment from the deal often include rampant ignorance of cultural issues that can actually reduce market share and revenues while driving up operational costs.
- If the integration process is considered a barrier to getting "real work" done, how and when are working relationships going to be developed for the "real work" synergies that prompted the deal?
- The integration and postintegration phases virtually ignore the cultural differences and human performance issues that affect the morale, satisfaction, creativity, efficiency, and effectiveness of the people who create or add the value that becomes revenue and profits.

Note that each of these factors has the potential to have a significant impact on the success of the deal. Each factor relates directly to the "soft" business issues, such as creating synergy, picking the right people, resolving culture issues, integrating the organizations, improving com-munications, and performing better due diligence. The irony is that many of the initiators know that such issues are key to the success of combinations and yet ignore them in the decision-making and integra-tion process, because "people issues" are deemed to be qualitative rather than quantitative and therefore are discussed in jargon rather than rep-resented by numbers. This phenomenon has been created and perpetu-ated by the organizational separation and communication barriers between the traditional line functions of business planning, accounting, and market analysis and the human resources and organization devel-opment staff functions related to soft business issues.

In fact, the short- and long-term success of any combination of human organizations ultimately depends on the effective use of people. According to a human resource expert,[15] organizational and cultural problems are more likely to derail a merger than financial factors are. Only 28 percent of companies said that they did a good job of assessing the culture of their merging organizations before the deal, only 26 per-cent said that they had put the right people in the right roles during the merger, and a scant 15 percent said that they had successfully communi-cated the company's vision and goals after the union.

We have discussed the fact that merger and acquisition teams are usually made up of financial professionals, and this creates a bias toward their areas of expertise at the frequent and significant cost of ignoring the "people" issues. To that end, Schein[16] states:

> When the management of a company decides to merge with or acquire another company, it usually carefully checks the financial strength, market position, management strength, and various other concrete aspects pertaining to the other company. Rarely checked, however, are those aspects that might be considered cultural: The philosophy or style of the company; its technical origins, which might provide clues as to its basic assumptions; and its beliefs about its mission and its future. Yet a cultural mismatch in an acquisition is as great a risk as a financial, product, or market mismatch.

Experts Marks and Mirvis[17] agree that there is a financial bias from the outset of combinations:

> In the pre-combination phase, much of the emphasis is on financial implications. Buyers typically concentrate on the numbers: what the target is worth, what price premium to pay if any, what the tax implications may be, and how to structure the transaction. Executives entering an alliance, who scope out the size of the returns but neglect how they will be achieved also fit the typical scheme. The decision to do the deal is thus framed in terms of the combined balance sheet of the companies, projected cash flows and hoped-for return on investment.

This financial bias comes about as a result of two interrelated human factors. First, the predominantly financial positions or backgrounds of the members of the buyer's team leads them to base their judgments about how well the proposed combination will do on their familiar financial models and ratios. These "experts" seldom know very much about the actual technical aspects of their own industry, such as engineering, manufacturing, or marketing, and the associated dynamics. Nor do they have a great deal of experience in assessing a partner's capabilities in these areas of operations. As a second factor, there is:[18]

> The tendency for "hard" criteria to drive out "soft" matters in these cases: if the numbers look good, any doubts about, say, organizational or cultural issues tend to be scoffed at and dismissed.

We may think that poor combinations take place only with the U.S. business approach, but international merger and acquisition experts[19] make it clear that the phenomenon occurs outside our borders as well. Commenting specifically on the poor success rate of international deals, they state:

> Much more can be done to identify the "people" issues. The current approach to due diligence is too narrow and looks primarily at areas of legal, financial and tax risk. While this approach to risk analysis is understandable from the professional perspective, it does not sufficiently address the more dynamic concepts of employment and organizational design issues that actually enable a business to function. Human capital due diligence can usefully analyze the people side of the business and inform the broader risks assessment. Information gathered can be used to assess the cultural and organizational fit between two entities.

It is this bias toward "hard data" that is at the heart of this book. It is unreasonable to expect educated, experienced professionals to abandon their knowledge, skills, and abilities when they continue to be employed by people who want them to use those abilities to do mergers and acquisitions. So the question boils down to this: *If the "soft, people issues" can be measured and converted into financial terms, will the financial professionals use the additional information to improve the results of their merger and acquisition work?*

To answer that question, we will turn our attention first to the development of a practical, in-depth understanding of organizational cultures and then to the introduction of QUOCA, a unique method of improving business combinations by incorporating the cultural differences between the combining businesses into the due diligence, decision-making, valuation, and integration processes.

P A R T

# UNDERSTANDING AND ANALYZING ORGANIZATION CULTURES

# WHAT IS CULTURE AND HOW DO I KNOW IT WHEN I SEE IT?

One of the main problems in resolving intercultural issues is that we take culture so much for granted and put so much value on our own assumptions that we find it awkward and inappropriate even to discuss our assumptions or to ask others about their assumptions.[1]

THE GOAL OF THIS CHAPTER is to help the reader understand and recognize the elements, traits, and characteristics of organization cultures and to be able to relate cultural strengths and weaknesses to the financial and competitive performance of the organization.

## ORGANIZATION CULTURES

People issues in business involve the beliefs, assumptions, and subsequent behaviors of the members of a group of employees that are used for the survival, prosperity, and well-being of the individuals and the group. Collectively, the shared beliefs, assumptions, attitudes, values, opinions, behaviors, and actions of the people in the group make up the group's culture. Culture has many definitions. The dictionary[2] defines it as "the totality of socially transmitted behavior patterns, arts, beliefs, institutions and all other products of human work and thought characteristics of a community or population." Colloquially, *culture* has been defined as "how we do things around here."

Within the context of business, *organization culture* refers to the underlying values, beliefs, and principles that serve as the foundation for an organization's management system, along with the set of management practices and behaviors that both exemplify and reinforce those basic principles.

Perhaps the most useful way to think about culture is to view it as *the accumulated shared learning of a given group*, covering behavioral, emotional, and cognitive elements of the group members' total psychological functioning. Schein[3] states, "A group has a culture when it has had enough shared history to have formed . . . a set of shared assumptions."

Many of a culture's shared assumptions can be observed as overt behaviors, signs, and symbols. Other shared assumptions are best revealed through interviews and surveys. As you can imagine, over time, a group develops cultural norms for virtually every kind of individual and group behavior and interaction, such as:

1. Accepted patterns of thought and speaking that both guide and convey the beliefs, perceptions, thoughts, and language used by the members of the group and are taught to new members early in their socialization process.
2. Specific behaviors that newcomers must embrace and emulate in order to be accepted into the group.
3. Specific mannerisms and expressions for constituents to use when interacting with one another and with superiors, subordinates, and outsiders.
4. Stated or implicit indicators of values and standards of performance, such as "Work hard, play hard."
5. Social norms, including the language people use and the customs, traditions, and rituals that they follow when interacting.
6. Operational credos and value statements that proclaim the broad policies and ideological principles that guide the group's actions toward its stakeholders, such as the Johnson & Johnson credo given in the Introduction.
7. Widely proclaimed statements or slogans that describe the group's acceptable values or behaviors, such as "Quality is Job One!" or "At Avis, we try harder!"
8. Informal, undocumented knowledge, skills, and abilities that are transferred from one generation to the next.

All cultures have elements such as these, whether the group is a country, a region, a town, a family, a social club, a church, a company, a division, a factory, or an office. Of course, a business culture will be different from a family culture in terms of the specific types of behaviors that are appropriate for the environment. In their important book *Corporate Cultures*, authors Terrence Deal and Allan Kennedy[4] identify and define the specific, unique, and important elements of corporate cultures. Some of the specific elements that make business cultures different from other cultures to which an individual belongs are:

1. The external environment of the industry or market sector in which the business functions, including customers, suppliers, competitors, and regulators

2. The type of technology used and the degree of dependence upon it

3. The attitudes, values, opinions, beliefs, assumptions, behaviors, and actions, both proclaimed and explicit and unproclaimed and implicit, that members adopt for their safety, security, prosperity, and well-being

4. The accepted definition of "success" for the organization

5. The heroes who personify the culture's values and serve as role models

6. Artifacts such as workspace layout; the presence or absence of awards, slogans, or photos of high performers; official or unofficial uniforms or dress codes; the presence or absence of personal items such as family photos; and overt examples of hierarchy, such as reserved parking spaces, separate dining rooms, or out-of-bounds areas

7. The accepted and emulated rites, routines, and rituals for day-to-day success in the organization

8. A "grapevine" for unofficial communications that conveys what are acceptable behaviors and the related rewards, and also what are unacceptable behaviors and the related punishments

Every business and each group within a given business has a different culture by virtue of its not having shared the same culture-forming histories, heroes, goals, and so on. This becomes quite evident when we become familiar with two businesses in the same market that may become involved in a merger or acquisition. Some of the more overt behaviors or artifacts may seem identical, such as both groups agreeing on the maxim "A fair day's work for a fair day's pay," but how the maxim became a norm for each of the two groups and what "fair" may mean to each of them can be quite different and belie the assumption that the cultures have shared values.

For example, Company A may somewhat defensively interpret a "fair day" as punching in at 8:00 A.M. sharp and checking out at 5:00 P.M. sharp, with precisely 1 hour for lunch. There is no nonsense on company time; everything is precise. Company B may expect people to come in early, skip lunch, and work late in order to put in their "fair day." People in Company B often spend time chatting with one another about problems and ideas. Company B thus has a pretty relaxed environment. Chances are that each definition works for that company's culture. But if the businesses are combined, the people in Company A may consider the people in Company B to be butt-kissers and slackers, and the people at Company B may look at their new colleagues at Company A as clock-watchers and slackers.

This one, relatively minor difference in the meaning of an identical descriptive phrase can be the source of animosity, disrespect, and incompatibility. If you extrapolate the impact of all cultural differences, you can clearly understand why so many combinations don't work because of cultural issues.

## ORGANIZATION CULTURE CHARACTERISTICS

We are now armed with an understanding of the idea that every group of people with an adequate shared history will develop a culture that has many specific characteristics that distinguish it from the cultures of other groups. Since our goal is to determine the criteria for an effective method to objectively measure the nature and strength of the characteristics of an organization's culture, the next challenge is to define and understand the characteristics that tend to make some cultures better able than others to achieve their desired outcomes while meeting the needs of their members.

### Strong and Weak Cultures

The strength of a culture refers to the degree of depth, tenacity, and sanctity with which the elements of that culture are held by its members. In strong cultures, the elements of the culture are nearly sacrosanct, and in weak cultures they are regarded with near ambivalence. As Kotter and Heskett[5] state,

> In a strong corporate culture, almost all managers share a set of consistent values, and methods of doing business. New employees adopt these values very quickly. In such a culture, a new executive is just as likely to be corrected by his subordinate as by

his bosses if he violates the organization's norms. . . . They often make some of their shared values known in a creed or mission statement and seriously encourage all their managers to follow that statement. Furthermore, the style and values of a strong culture tend not to change much when a new CEO takes charge—their roots go deep.

It stands to reason that an organization that is truly committed to living its values, conforming to its beliefs, and emulating its acceptable behaviors will have more consistent outcomes than an organization that is ambivalent about the factors that determine, define, and motivate the acceptance of "appropriate" values, beliefs, and behaviors. Thus, for an effective assessment of organization cultures, it is necessary to be able to measure the degree to which the organization's constituents are committed to its assumptions and beliefs.

## Positive and Negative Cultures

Another element of objective, comparative organization culture analyses is measuring the positive or negative nature of a group's beliefs. For example, if a desired outcome that stimulates the behaviors of the Hell's Angels is to scare the hell out of the average person on the street, then the Angels' heroes, myths, and artifacts are extremely good at stimulating their desired behaviors and outcome. Could a socially unacceptable desired outcome such as "scaring the hell out of the average person" work for a mainstream business? Of course not, but we still see some pretty negative behaviors, such as rudeness, from people in mainstream businesses. On the other hand, so-called mainstream businesses have to set standards for behavior that result in positive outcomes such as quality and quantity of production, cooperative relationships, innovation and adaptability, revenue and profitability, and so on.

So while the relative strength of a culture is an important element of how its people behave, the positive or negative nature of the cultural norms is equally critical to the success of a business organization. We have all endured poor service, unresponsive salespeople, and shabby treatment at stores. If it occurs once, we assume that we are dealing with an unhappy employee; if we return and receive the same treatment from a different salesperson, we may assume that this is a coincidence. But when such behavior is the rule, regardless of the person behind the counter, we are experiencing a strong, but negative culture. Our reaction is to stop shopping at the store. And it's not much of a surprise when the store closes or is purchased by a competitor.

What happens when a company with a negative culture combines with a company with a positive culture? How can the successful business, with its strong positive culture, not be tainted by the strong negative culture of its acquisition? What are the greatest cultural threats to the long-run success of the combination? Should the baby be thrown out with the bath water, or can it be cleaned up in a fresh, new tub? What is good, what is bad, and what is really bad about the negative culture? What is it about us that makes us successful? What is it about us that we want to protect? What is it about us that we can improve to make us even more successful? How do we find out about all of this stuff in an objective, helpful manner? To paraphrase Freud, who said something like, "Recognizing you are nuts is half the battle for becoming sane," recognizing the cultural differences is half the battle for resolving them.

## Flexibility and Stability

Mergers and acquisitions frequently involve the combination of companies that are at different points in their life cycle. Organizations' cultures are dynamic and evolve over their lifetime. Adizes,[6] in his unique and innovative work, states:

> Organizations have life cycles just as living organisms do; they go through the normal struggles and difficulties accompanying each stage of the organizational life cycle and are faced with the transitional problems of moving to the next phase of development. Organizations learn to deal with these problems by themselves or they develop abnormal "diseases," which stymie growth—problems that usually cannot be resolved without external, professional intervention.

The metaphor of the life cycle of a business being like that of a living organism works very well to illustrate two important characteristics of organizational cultures: flexibility and control. For example, children enjoy a great deal of physical flexibility, which enables them to rebound from all types of perils and misfortunes, but they are not yet able to control their emotions and behaviors. Conversely, old people are physically less limber and less adaptable to the physical and philosophical challenges of life, but they have the self-control and discipline to avoid many dangers. The flexibility of youth enables survival in spite of poor control. The control of the aged compensates for their loss of flexibility. Survival, growth, and maturity somehow work to trade flexibility for control. Somewhere in the prime of life, even if for only a moment, the optimal combination of flexibility and control enables peak performance.

Like all metaphors, the comparison between organization cultures and human life cycles has its limitations. For the purpose of understanding the variations between cultures, the metaphor works better when the term *stability* is substituted for *control*. The meanings are very similar, but stability is a more appropriate term to contrast with flexibility because it is broader than control and includes, in addition to the ability to exert self-control, such other cultural characteristics as the long-term sense of vision and mission, the organization's strategic direction, and proven, broadly embraced core values.

As organizations age, they tend to become more bureaucratic, risk-averse, and conservative in their decision making. This aging process does not necessarily relate directly to the number of years the organization has been in business. Adizes[7] cites several examples of relatively new companies that have, for one reason or another, quickly become bureaucratic, risk-averse, and conservative. Conversely, some companies that have been around for well over a hundred years have managed to remain flexible, dynamic, willing to take reasonable risks, and willing to empower people to have a great deal of autonomy in their work.

When we understand the contrast between flexibility and stability, we can understand why some industries are far more likely to fall at one end of the continuum or the other. State-of-the-art technology companies have to be flexible. We expect financial institutions to be pretty stable. In fact, the debacles involving Arthur Andersen are typical of what happens when companies that are expected to be stability-oriented start creating new rules for their game.

The stability-flexibility continuum also has relevance *within industries*. The influence of different founders, key leaders, and other heroes as well as the different crises, victories, and so on will create different cultures in competing businesses. In my career, for example, I have worked with a number of different insurance companies, some of which were very flexible in defining their mission, their market, and the value they added for their clients, and some that were quite stable in the way they approached the nature of their business.

This continuum can apply *within organizations* as well. I would hope that the emergency room of our local hospital doesn't have to consult the "standard procedures" before acting every time someone is carted in with a trauma. And within the same organization, I hope that the cardiologists don't try to come up with some tricky new shortcut for my triple bypass operation.

Businesses with cultures that lean toward the flexibility end of the scale look at several measures to monitor their performance, including time to market of new products, percent of new products in the mix, and market share. Enterprises that lean toward stability are more concerned with financial performance measures that can be compared to those of their competitors and that serve the interests of external stakeholders such as lenders and stockholders. These stability measures include return on sales and return on assets.

## Internal and External Focus

Another continuum illustrating the variability of organizational cultures concerns the direction of the organization's focus in envisioning, planning for, and achieving its desired outcomes. On one end is a total external focus, indicating that the organization relies entirely on factors outside its organization and its span of direct control to determine its operational strategies. A sampling of parameters that are typically of concern to externally focused businesses includes regulatory changes and legal decisions; new technologies being used by suppliers, competitors, and customers; the cost and availability of capital; the cost and availability of supplies; and the employment market. Businesses that are acutely aware of their external environment are concerned about their financial performance as measured by market share and sales growth.

At the opposite end of the continuum is a complete focus on the internal environment, indicating that the organization relies entirely on factors within its own organization and span of control for decision making. Internally focused businesses concentrate on:

- Their core values and culture
- Their ability to vertically and horizontally coordinate activities within the organization
- The effectiveness of their decision making
- The capabilities and bench strength of their people
- Their ability to achieve agreement on what should be done and how to motivate employees to carry out the plan

Businesses with an extreme degree of internal focus objectively measure their performance using quality indices, return on investment, and employee satisfaction surveys.

Very few companies can survive at either extreme of any continuum. And, since all businesses suffer from limited resources, some trade-offs must be made. But companies that prosper find an appropriate balance between their external and internal focus so that they know what's going on both inside and outside the gates with enough depth and breadth to make good decisions.

## THE KEY ORGANIZATION CULTURE TRAITS: MISSION, CONSISTENCY, INVOLVEMENT, AND ADAPTABILITY

The Holy Grail for people who are interested in organization cultures has been the codification of culture traits so that the important variables can be observed and compared. Many people have attempted to devise a list of characteristics that is just broad enough to be useful in capturing the essence of an organization's attitudes, values, opinions, beliefs, assumptions, behaviors, and actions without being unwieldy.

Denison[8] identified four traits—Mission, Consistency, Involvement, and Adaptability—that enable experts and journeymen alike to capture a very workable set of culture characteristics for measuring and analyzing businesses and related each trait to specific financial and competitive performance measures such as profitability, sales/revenue, market share, quality, product development/innovation, and employee satisfaction.

These traits, which are discussed next, provide valuable information regarding:

- The comparative strengths of the cultural traits and characteristics of the organization
- The positive and negative aspects of the culture
- The extent of the organization's flexibility and stability
- The organization's relative degree of internal versus external focus
- The financial and competitive implications of the culture

### The Mission Trait

The organization's beliefs and assumptions regarding both stability and its awareness of the external environment are assessed and illustrated by the Mission trait. These cultural characteristics play an important role in the enterprise's ability to focus on its long-term vision while at the same time maintaining the flexibility necessary to be relevant and viable in an ever-changing marketplace. A tight-loose relationship between their destination and the path of their journey enables sailors to arrive at their chosen port in spite of the need to make many changes of course along the way. The same commitment to purpose and vision while constantly monitoring and adapting to the environment is what enables the captains and crews of industry to survive and prosper.

From a culture assessment perspective, the Mission trait includes the enterprise's overall planning and execution process, from individual tasks and responsibilities up through organizational roles to the fundamental purpose of the business and the vision for its long-term future. The Mission trait assesses the degree of employee understanding and buy-in for the organization's efforts to direct its resources toward well-thought-out, defined, and articulated outcomes. It is one thing for the board of directors and top executives to have pondered and decided these things. However, it is the role of the organizational culture to embrace the necessary assumptions and beliefs and to make them an ingrained part of the employees' collective and individual desires, thoughts, and actions.

The degree of variation in understanding the mission is well illustrated in the old story of the three masons who were building a church. They were working side by side doing the same job, but they had entirely different perspectives. When asked what he was doing, the first mason said, "I'm doing the same old stuff I do every day—laying bricks and mortar." The second mason, with a more sophisticated perspective, responded, "I'm building a structure that will last forever." But the third mason was truly focused on the customer when he replied, "I'm building God's waiting room." In many enterprises, people are simply laying bricks and mortar; their work is drudgery, and they have no clue as to what the end result of their efforts will be. Businesses that are high-performing are populated by people who are excited about their work and who know the value they add for clients.

Denison[9] and Fisher[10] have been able to correlate the strength of an organization's Mission trait with the organization's financial and competitive performance as measured by profitability/return on assets, sales and revenue growth, increased market share, higher quality, and greater employee satisfaction.

### The Consistency Trait

Within the context of organization cultures, consistency can be understood to refer to the frequency of replication of the attitudes, values, opinions, behaviors, and actions of the organization's people. In strong cultures, people are very likely to act and behave with great consistency; conversely, in weak cultures, there is little consistency in the way people act and behave. Denison states:

> Building a "strong culture" implies that values and actions are highly consistent. This form of consistency often has been men-

tioned as a source of organizational strength and as a way of improving performance and effectiveness.[11]

An organization's Consistency trait reflects both its internal focus and its ability to establish and maintain a sense of stability. A strong degree of organizational stability instills confidence in the various stakeholders—employees, investors, customers, suppliers, the community, and so on. Stability creates a sense of security and well-being, both of which are important in motivating people to embrace the culture's attitudes, values, and opinions and to behave in ways that benefit the organization.

The internal focus of the organization provides scrutiny and adjustment of how the organization functions to meet the expected outcomes of the stakeholders. The function of the internal focus is to make certain that the organization is doing the right things to ensure its survival and prosperity, much the way an individual's reflection and introspection serve to measure that individual's character and behavior against her or his beliefs and goals. The work done by Fisher[12] and Denison[13] correlates strength in the Consistency trait with higher levels of product and service quality as well as high employee satisfaction.

## The Involvement Trait

A great deal of research has demonstrated that high levels of employee involvement and participation create a strong sense of ownership of and responsibility to the employing organization. A strong sense of ownership by employees imbues a greater commitment to the organization and its goals while reducing the need for hands-on supervision. According to Denison,[14] "Voluntary and implicit normative systems ensure the coordination of behavior, rather than explicit bureaucratic control systems." In other words, providing people with the knowledge, power, and resources to do their job gets better results than command-and-control systems, where knowledge and power are held and distributed by bosses.

In the realm of the Involvement trait, "effectiveness" refers to specific, objective financial and business performance measures—product or service quality and employee satisfaction. Both Denison[15] and Fisher[16] have been able to correlate strength on the Involvement trait with higher levels of product and service quality and employee satisfaction.

An organization's Involvement trait reflects both its internal focus and its ability to create and sustain flexibility. Organizational flexibility facilitates adapting to the internal implications of variables in the external environment, such as customer desires, regulatory changes, and competitor dynamics. Flexibility also enables awareness of and appropriate reactions to internal changes, including changes of leadership and their styles, changes in organizational structure, and changes in technology.

By being aware of, prepared for, and adaptable to the changes inside and outside the organization, the enterprise prepares itself and its stakeholders—employees, investors, customers, suppliers, the community, and others—for events and trends that may threaten its survival or create beneficial opportunities. The vigilance required for organizational flexibility creates a sense of security and well-being, both of which are important in motivating people to embrace the culture's attitudes, values, and opinions and to behave in ways that benefit the enterprise.

The internal focus of the organization serves as ongoing introspection and an ongoing response to the business's performance with respect to its desired outcomes, goals, and standards. Internal focus serves to assure the enterprise's stakeholders that the organization is doing the right things to ensure its survival and prosperity.

## The Adaptability Trait

The Adaptability trait of organization cultures concerns and measures the group's ability to sense the dynamics of its external environment and translate those dynamics into appropriate organizational and operational changes that perpetuate the organization's well-being and success. Organizations can muddle along for quite some time with a poor sense of Mission, a low degree of employee Involvement, and a serious lack of Consistency, but a deficiency in Adaptability puts the death of the organization on the fast track.

The sensory element of adaptability includes an understanding of which environmental variables are important and which are trivial, the most effective way to monitor the important variables, their rate and amount of change, and the benchmarks against which these changes can best be computed. Highly adaptive organizations know what they don't know, and their curiosity goes well beyond simply gathering information to fully understanding the environmental elements that pose danger and/or opportunity. They are constantly gathering and assessing information regarding legal and regulatory changes, new competitors, old competitors with new products, changes in the dynamic world of customers, the supply chain and its variables, and so on.

Adaptability is the critically important link between the flexibility of the organization and its external focus. It is the involvement of everyone in the organization in being aware of, communicating, and responding to the changes that are taking place in the marketplace and with regulators and financial organizations. This focused adaptability in response to the external dynamics maintains the competitiveness needed to perpetuate the success of the enterprise.

Experts[17, 18] have demonstrated a relationship between strength on the Adaptability trait and higher performance on the sales/revenue growth, market share, and product development/innovation financial and competitive measures.

## SUMMARY

Organization culture refers to the underlying values, beliefs, and principles that serve as a foundation for an organization's management system and, when conformed with, provide security, safety, and prosperity for the members of the culture. Cultures have many elements, including the relative strength or weakness of the attitudes, values, and opinions that determine the behaviors of the constituents. Beliefs and assumptions can be negative, as in the case of a snotty waitress, or positive, as when a salesperson goes out of her way to help you. The positive or negative nature of beliefs and assumptions is determined by whether the behaviors help or hinder the organization in achieving its desired outcomes.

Cultures can be flexible or stable, meaning that they can be very adaptive to changes in their environment or very consistent in how they perform their tasks and functions. Cultures also can either focus predominantly on their external environment, such as changes in regulations, customer needs, and technology, or look predominantly internally, at characteristics such as the capability and development of their people, the ongoing validity of their core values, and how they coordinate activities across the organization.

Denison[19] was able to codify the major cultural elements into four traits—Mission, Consistency, Involvement, and Adaptability—and relate each trait to specific financial and competitive performance measures such as profitability, sales/revenue, market share, quality, product development/innovation, and employee satisfaction.

By understanding the nature of organizational cultures and the relationship between cultural traits and objective performance measures, we can develop the foundation for assessing and improving the results of business mergers and acquisitions.

# 5

# HOW TO SEE THE INVISIBLE: THE ART AND SCIENCE OF ORGANIZATION CULTURE ANALYSES

Mergers and acquisitions are usually initiated by the leaders of organizations as ways of growing or becoming more competitive. There is a natural tendency to analyze the merger decision to consider only the primary issues of finance, product, and market mix. Culture may be loosely thought about, but it is only after the merger that it is taken seriously, suggesting that most leaders make the assumption that they can fix cultural problems after the fact. I would argue that leaders must make cultural analysis as central to the initial merger/acquisition decision as the financial, product, or market analysis.[1]

THIS CHAPTER WILL ENABLE the reader to understand the criteria for an objective culture analysis that can improve the results of mergers and acquisitions and to recognize the advantages and limitations of subjective, objective, comparative, and quantitative culture analyses.

## ORGANIZATION CULTURE ANALYSES

In the quotation that opens this chapter, Schein seems to capture the thoughts of many people who are concerned with the success of combinations. There is a profound need to understand the strengths, weaknesses, attitudes, values, opinions, and assumptions and to know the heroes, myths, and artifacts that make up the culture of an organization, and to delineate the differences among these cultures in order to solve the problem of underperforming combinations.

We have learned that organization cultures are developed and used by people in order to survive and succeed. As a species, humans are well equipped to survive, with our physical senses of sight, hearing, touch, taste, and smell and our unique intellectual abilities. We use our senses to detect dangers and respond to opportunities. We measure our environment, including our work environment and other group settings, by using our senses. We use our intelligence to determine the behaviors that are necessary to meet our needs.

Analysis is the process of measurement and decision making. Some analyses are purely subjective, that is, based strictly upon our opinions, such as whether a movie is good or bad. Some analyses are objective in that they are measured against some benchmark, such as how our sense of right and wrong is based on our values. Some of our analyses are comparative, such as when we conclude that one person is taller than another or that we can get across the street before the oncoming car hits us. Some of our measurements and decisions are quantitative in that they use a proven measurement instrument and the results are compared to an established norm, such as when we use a thermometer to determine whether someone has a fever. There are situations in which each type of analysis is appropriate and others in which an analysis with a higher degree of sophistication would be more valuable. For example, we have all learned how inaccurate the back of the hand is when trying to determine whether someone has a fever—the thermometer is a much more accurate and, therefore, more useful measurement tool to decide if someone's well-being is in danger.

Similarly, M&A professionals have at their disposal a wide range of analyses, from subjective to quantitative, to include in the combination process. Each of the analyses has an appropriate use in the combination process. It is important that we get to know each of the culture analyses that are available for use by those of us who are interested in mergers and acquisitions. We need to know their relative strengths and weaknesses and their optimal applications. However, in order to put their characteristics in the proper light in our effort to vastly improve the success of business combinations, we also must understand why each type is limited in its utility. So, before we get into the discussion of the tools we have at our disposal, we need to set a benchmark for the ideal instrument to help us meet our goal of optimized deals based on the best organization culture information possible.

## THE CRITERIA FOR ORGANIZATION CULTURE ANALYSES FOR MORE SUCCESSFUL DUE DILIGENCE AND INTEGRATION PROCESSES

So far, we have made a pretty strong argument for the need for a better understanding of organization cultures in order to improve the chances for success of the decision-making, planning and execution of the due diligence, go/no-go decision, and integration phases of mergers and acquisitions. When defining "need," I like to start with the "perfect world" scenario—that is, if I had all the time, expertise, and resources needed to build the best tool for a particular problem, what would it have to be able to do? Based on my research and experience, the best tool for assessing organization cultures for the purpose of improving the performance of mergers and acquisitions would have to meet the following criteria:

1. The information from the culture assessment must correlate with financial measures and ratios that are familiar and useful to M&A financial professionals so that the information is readily useful in all steps of the typical combination process.
2. The information must provide a valid "snapshot" of the organizations' cultures at the time of the analysis.
3. The survey must provide a basis for prescriptive decisions about what must be done to improve each of the organizations as well as the combined organization if the financial expectations are to be met.

A culture analysis that meets these criteria will add value to each of the steps in the merger and acquisition process and improve the chances that barriers to the success of combinations can be identified and controlled before they impede the success of the deal.

## SUBJECTIVE ORGANIZATION CULTURE ANALYSES

Humans are accustomed to using subjective analyses when we make decisions about our workplace. Recall your last job interview—which, in some very real ways, is similar to a merger due diligence process. Did you "like" the company? Did it look like a "good" place to work? Did the work appear to be "rewarding"? These are all important but subjective decisions, based on our specific personal definitions of "like," "good," and "rewarding," that we make when determining if a company will enable us to survive and succeed and therefore will be our employer of choice.

Even the most disciplined, by the book, objective merger and acquisition professionals use a "smell" test to screen combination opportunities. If you were to press these people on why a company was ruled out early in the deal selection process, they would have difficulty providing a precise answer and would be very likely to say something like, "It just wasn't our kind of a deal. You know, it's not a bad company, but I think we can do better."

Frequently, the basis for subjective organization culture analysis is evidence of the target company's heroes, myths, and artifacts. Some firms with strong, positive cultures have paintings or photos of the firm's heroes, and every employee will know and gladly share the heroes' contribution to the organization. Some firms have mission statements, slogans, and logos prominently displayed. Still others express their strong, positive culture through the demeanor of their employees, such as the "professional" ways in which they dress, speak, and work.

Just because the culture assessment is subjective doesn't mean that the information is invalid or useless. Experts have used subjective analyses to make significant observations on subjects ranging from subatomic particles to the nature of the universe. Relative to our subject, much of the work done by Deal and Kennedy[2] concerning an industry's risk and feedback matrix and its effect on the nature of the businesses' culture is subjective but nonetheless quite valuable. Deal and Bolman[3] developed four "frames" (the factory, the family, the jungle, and the temple) to subjectively describe organization cultures and to define specific ways in which people can "navigate" them in order to achieve personal survival and success. While the "framing" is subjective, the authors provide specific examples of very successful, objective strategies that will enable leaders to prosper in each of the subjectively described environments.

Subjective culture analyses can be powerful and effective ways to screen out the bad deals. The protective instincts that people have used since the dawn of humanity to avoid bad situations can certainly be adapted to provide valuable information about the successful compatibility of two businesses. But subjective analyses certainly don't guarantee successful combinations of companies. Their flaw is that the information is instinctive, almost defying translation into dollars and cents, payback periods, and the financial ratios that the due diligence and integration people need if they are to improve the success rate of their deals. A better analysis method is required to meet the needs of combination professionals and enable them to better understand and articulate the significant differences in the cultures of businesses.

## OBJECTIVE ORGANIZATION CULTURE ANALYSES

The lion's share of merger and acquisition due diligence involves objective analyses. Financial measures such as return on investment, price to equity ratio, and earnings per share are calculated and compared to similar numbers for the industry sector or market.

Likewise, merger and acquisition professionals often perform limited objective analyses of the organizational cultures. For example, the team may look at a target company's employee turnover rate, usually expressed as a percentage of total employment and compared to industry standards available from trade associations. Information gleaned through such objective analyses is important and valuable, but it is not sufficiently sophisticated to rule out the possibility that the numbers are good because of conditions that are not intrinsic to the company. For example, turnover may be low because unemployment in the local economy is high, and the minute the economic circumstances improve, the employees will flee.

Perhaps the most objective analysis of organization cultures and their relationship to the financial performance of the organization was done by Tom Peters and Robert Waterman at McKinsey and later presented in their best-selling 1982 book, *In Search of Excellence*.[4] The authors defined "excellent businesses" as "continuously innovative big companies." As business consultants, they identified six financial measures of long-term superiority for their excellent companies over the 20-year period from 1961 through 1980:

1. Compound asset growth
2. Compound equity growth
3. The average ratio of market value to book value as a measure of wealth creation
4. Average return on total capital
5. Average return on equity
6. Average return on sales

Their goal was to identify significant characteristics of the 62 excellent companies in the sample that would explain their excellence. The authors went on to describe eight attributes that best characterize excellent, innovative companies as follows:

1. *A bias for action*, including the ability to maintain "fleetness of foot" and counter the stultification that almost inevitably comes with size.

2. *Close to the customer*, providing unparalleled quality, service, reliability, and innovation as a result of listening intently and regularly to their customers.

3. *Autonomy and entrepreneurship* by encouraging risk taking and accepting mistakes as an element of innovation.

4. *Productivity through people* by recognizing their people as the "root source of quality and productivity gain."

5. *Hands-on, value-driven* involvement of the management team in the day-to-day operations of the business.

6. *Stick to the knitting* by operating businesses in arenas they thoroughly know and understand.

7. *Simple form, lean staff*—"The underlying structural forms and systems in the excellent companies are elegantly simple."

8. *Simultaneous loose-tight properties*, where autonomy and empowerment have been driven to the shop floor but corporate core values are sacrosanct.

The work done by Peters and Waterman got everybody's attention. Their book became an international best-seller and has been the basis for most of the "humanistic management" thinking since its publication. Many of their theories became the backbone of a generation's management philosophy. They were perhaps the first to familiarize the general public with the relationship between an organization's "soft" characteristics and its financial performance.

The valuable work of experts such as Peters, Drucker, and, more recently, Jim Collins[5] underscores the link between people performance and business performance, which should have a powerful influence on the merger and acquisition process. However, as important and influential as these experts are in most business circles, their influence cannot be found in today's merger and acquisition due diligence, valuation, decision-making, or integration processes.

## COMPARATIVE ORGANIZATION CULTURE ANALYSES

A few years ago, when President Nixon was accused of being a crook, the "duck" analysis emerged. Asked on network television whether or not he believed the president was in on the Watergate break-in, a senator responded, "Back home we say, 'If it looks like a duck, and waddles like a duck, and quacks like a duck, it's probably a duck.' Well, I think the president is a duck." The senator was doing a fine job of describing objective analysis. A duck is a duck because it does what ducks do. Plain, simple, accurate, and true.

Merger and acquisition due diligence often employs similar comparative analyses, such as, "These guys are as buttoned up as IBM" or "This outfit is as customer service driven as Nordstrom's." What makes this type of analysis useful is that a common, mutually understood, but unquantified benchmark serves as a mechanism to compare two sets of information—one known, the other unknown.

The issue of incompatible combinations of uncomplementary cultures has gotten the attention of the consulting arms of some accounting firms, and several objective comparative organization culture analysis tools have been developed over the years. Senn,[6] for example, says:

> The analysis of mergers and acquisitions during due diligence understandably focuses on financial information. But due diligence should also include analysis of human aspects.

To optimize its value to the M&A process, an objective analysis of the "human aspects" of the businesses should include the comparison of relevant documents, policies, and procedures, such as the following:

- Compensation and reward system similarities and differences, including:
  - The nature of compensation, such as salary versus hourly pay, the use of work volume or quality incentives, the use of revenue sharing, and the use of employee stock ownership plans (ESOPs)
  - The nature of benefit systems, such as health and life insurance, vacation, conversion of unused vacation to money, sick leave, maternity/paternity leave, time off for bereavement, incentive and support for the adoption of children, and so on
  - The frequency, style, and objectives of performance review systems, e.g., some companies have the review completed by the employee, while in others the supervisor completes the review
  - How written and implied performance criteria are established, communicated, and enforced
  - Selection criteria and the process for hiring new employees
  - The process and criteria for firing and furloughing employees, along with data indicating the number of dismissals (and their

reasons), the number of voluntary terminations (and their reasons), and any tracking information from exit interviews

- Compare the written artifacts of the businesses, such as:
  - Vision statements
  - Credos and core value statements
  - Mission statements
  - If and how superior performance is recognized for the overall organization, subgroups, and individuals, such as plaques, bulletin boards, trophy cases, and newsletters
  - How performance toward goals is articulated and celebrated, such as charts and banners, respectively
- Compare the investment by the combining businesses in activities that affect the ability of the organization and its people to do well both internally and in the marketplace, such as:
  - The number and organizational levels of attendees at trade shows, conferences, and industry seminars that provide insight into what suppliers, customers, and competitors are doing
  - The number and organizational level of attendees at technical, administrative, and management development training programs
  - The nature, type, number, and extent of use of internal training programs, such as orientation training for new employees, safety training, leadership development, communication skills training, and so on

Such comparative analyses are very effective for gathering data on how the organizations handle certain "people-related" functions and activities. In the end, though, the analyses yield only marginally helpful information, such as "Company A spends more money on training than Company B" or "The company being acquired rewards superior performance with bonuses, while the acquiring company rewards superior performance with a brass plaque and mention in the newsletter."

Some of this information can be factored into the pricing model (e.g., the cost of vesting and liquidating stock options) and into integration planning (e.g., the cost, schedule, and timing of running the employees of the acquired business through the acquirer's orientation program).

Although it is recognized that there are many gaps in these analyses, they provide invaluable insight into the management philosophies and styles of the respective combining organizations. In 1987, Senn and Delaney[7] found that many of the oversights and shortfalls could be addressed by simply identifying an organizational culture characteristic and defining both ends of a graduated, linking continuum. For example, people doing a comparative culture analysis might be interested in the concentration and distribution of functional responsibility and so could develop a criterion such as that shown in Figure 5-1 to measure and compare the combining organizations' approaches.

**Figure 5-1** *Example of a Comparative Culture Analysis*

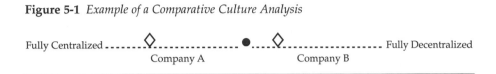

Fully Centralized ------◇---------------●----◇------------------ Fully Decentralized
                          Company A              Company B

There are an unlimited number of cultural characteristics that can be identified and scrutinized using this type of comparative analysis. Some of the more common organizational elements studied this way during mergers and acquisitions are:

- Management style: Autocratic versus participative
- Leadership assumptions: Theory X or Theory Y
- Span of control: Narrow and deep versus wide and shallow
- Pace of change to internal environment: Slow versus fast
- Pace of change to external environment: Slow versus fast
- Flexibility and adaptability versus stability and consistency
- Proactivity versus reactivity for threats and opportunities
- Well-articulated strategies, tactics, and goals versus flying by the seat of the pants
- Internal focus versus external focus
- Long-term focus versus short-term focus
- Build new technology versus buy new technology
- Promote from within versus hire from the outside
- Build competencies internally versus optimize outsourcing of services

These comparative analyses provide a huge improvement in the depth and breadth of understanding of cultural difference in the merger and acquisition process by illustrating the nature and degree of differences in the beliefs and assumptions, attitudes, values and opinions, behaviors, and actions of the combining organizations. And, the use of these tools during the merger or acquisition process provides important information, including a better understanding of the nature and extent of cultural dissimilarities and their impact on the deal and the types of issues that need to be resolved prior to closing in order to make the integration process as fast, efficient, and painless as possible.

These tools have the potential to improve the success of mergers and acquisitions. However, it should be noted that the Senn-Delaney culture profile was developed in 1987. And, in spite of this innovation and other comparative analyses, business combinations continue to fail to meet their financial goals 83 percent of the time. For one reason or another, these tools have not had a significant impact on combination performance. There must be a more effective way to analyze, express, and factor organizational cultures in order to improve merger and acquisition success.

## Alignment Diagnostic Profile

There have been at least two attempts to develop quantitative organization culture analyses. The first is a method of diagnosing the causes of organizational dysfunction. The Alignment Diagnostic Profile[8] was designed to give organizations a visual and quantitative measure of their alignment with respect to strategy, customers, people, and processes. It has been adapted over the years and has been administered to thousands of people at scores of organizations. Each individual is asked to respond to 16 questions regarding the organization's cultural characteristics and to assign a number from 1 through 10 that represents the degree to which they believe that the statement is true of the organization. Examples of these questions are:

- How well the organizational strategy is communicated
- The usefulness of the information that is provided to employees
- How familiar employees are with customer complaints
- The amount of cooperation among people within the organization
- The extent to which processes are reviewed for the sake of improving them

The analysis was an excellent step forward in developing objective, quantitative cultural information that could provide side-by-side comparisons of organizations' cultures and their financial performance. Labovitz and Rosansky[9] studied the pathology of many organizations using the Alignment Diagnostic Profile and then correlated each company's operational performance with its cultural profile. The authors were able to create a typology of alignment pathologies as a vehicle to begin troubleshooting and improving the operations of the organization. Examples of their organizational culture typologies included:

- Market Myopia, with a focus on current clients but out of touch with the overall market
- Dead Man Walking, with a marketing and operational focus on the past
- Strategy Interruptus, where the path going forward has been defined but not implemented

By objectively developing quantitative scores relating to organizational cultures, this process allows the results from two combining companies to be compared and the differences to be factored into the decisions of the merger and acquisition process. This methodology has advanced us toward our goal of developing a tool that can be used to predict and improve the success of mergers and acquisitions, but it is lacking in two important areas. First, the information relates only to the cultures of the specific organizations that were analyzed and is not referenced to a standardized database of pathologies and related operational performance. Second, the correlated profile and performance data are a great resource for organizational development professionals, but the results are not expressed in typical financial measures such as ROI, payback period, and so on. Therefore, their utility for M&A professionals is rather poor and the likelihood that the data will be used during business combinations is small.

## SUMMARY

In this chapter we discussed the advantages and limitations of subjective, objective, comparative, and quantitative culture analyses. Each type of analysis plays an important role in defining certain characteristics of cultures. We use subjective analysis when we decide not to eat in a restaurant because it "doesn't look very clean." Sometimes we combine analyses to make good decisions, such as buying one car rather than another because it has a better safety rating (a combination of comparative and objective analysis). Quantitative analyses relate data to an objective, standardized measurement scale so that the analytical data from one subject, say a business, can be compared to the data from another subject in an apples-to-apples manner.

The cultural analyses we discussed in this chapter provided some value, but none of them met the criteria needed for improving the performance of business combinations, and so the search went on.

# 6
CHAPTER

# THE DENISON
# CULTURE SURVEY

The Denison model offers a tangible, behavioral, business oriented framework to measure, interpret, understand, discuss and
develop organizational cultures in a merger context. Use of the
Denison tools as part of a comprehensive integration plan can
rapidly accelerate the merger process by removing the "assump-
tion-based" confusion, "ordering" the chaos, and structuring the
path toward a mutually beneficial outcome.[1]

A FTER READING THIS CHAPTER, the reader will understand the history,
scientific basis, features, and validity of the Denison Culture Survey
and, therefore, will recognize that the Denison Culture Survey fulfills the
criteria for the optimum tool for improving merger and acquisition performance by providing cultural information in financial terminology.

We have known for quite some time that mismatched cultures lead
to poor financial performance in mergers and acquisitions. The challenge
is to delineate the nature and extent of the cultural problems in terms
that the financial people can understand and factor into their decisions
and calculations for the deal.

The optimum tool for improving the performance of mergers and
acquisitions would be one that gets used because of its functionality,
accuracy, and ease of use. It should gather, analyze, and report information that reflects the cultures' beliefs and assumptions in a very straightforward manner. As discussed in Chapter 5, to be the ideal tool, it should
meet the following functional criteria:

1. The information from the culture assessment must correlate with financial measures and ratios that are familiar and useful to M&A financial professionals so that the information is readily useful for all steps of the typical combination process.
2. The information must provide a valid "snapshot" of the organizations' cultures at the time of the analysis.
3. The survey must provide a basis for prescriptive decisions about what must be done to improve each of the organizations as well as the combined organization if the financial expectations are to be met.

A review of several types of organization cultural analyses, including those that are subjective, objective, and comparative and one that is quantitative, showed that they provide valuable information, but not in a form that financial professionals typically use in their decision-making, valuation, and performance projection activities. Continued pursuit of the optimum tool eventually led me to the Denison Culture Survey and the development of the Quantitative Organization Culture Analysis or QUOCA process.

## QUANTITATIVE ORGANIZATION CULTURE ANALYSES— THE DENISON CULTURE SURVEY

In 1966 Dr. Daniel Denison[2] and his colleagues at the University of Michigan began a series of studies to correlate the characteristics of an organization's culture with the organization's financial performance. The group, under the auspices of the Institute for Social Research, initiated a program of comparative research that they referred to as the Inter-Company Longitudinal Study. The study required the development of an objective, robust data-gathering survey that could be used over an extended period of time and would have validity for a wide variety of business types.

Over the next several years, researchers tested and revised the instrument until the following validated set of indexes and criteria was defined:

*Organization climate*

- *Organization of work.* The degree to which an organization's work methods link the jobs of individuals to organizational objectives
- *Communication flow.* The flow of information, both vertically within the organizational hierarchy and laterally across the organization

- *Emphasis on people*. The interest that the organization displays in the welfare and development of the people who work there
- *Decision-making practices*. The degree to which an organization's decisions involve those who will be affected, are made at the appropriate levels, and are based on widely shared information
- *Influence and control*. The influence of those at the lower levels of the organization
- *Absence of bureaucracy*. The absence of unnecessary administrative constraints in the organization's internal functioning
- *Coordination*. Coordination, cooperation, and problem resolution among organization units

## Job design

- *Job challenge*. Variety, opportunity to learn, and the use of skills and abilities on the job
- *Job reward*. Instrumentality of good job performance with regard to recognition, respect, and getting ahead
- *Job clarity*. Clear and appropriate job expectations

## Supervisory leadership

- *Supervisory support*. The supervisor's attentiveness, approachability, and willingness to listen
- *Supervisory team building*. The supervisor's emphasis on team goals, idea exchange, and working as a team
- *Supervisory goal emphasis*. The supervisor's setting of high standards and encouragement of best efforts
- *Supervisory work facilitation*. The supervisor's helpfulness in improving performance, planning, and problem solving

## Peer leadership

- *Peer support*. Peers' attentiveness, approachability, and willingness to listen
- *Peer team building*. Peers' emphasis on team goals, idea exchange, and working as a team
- *Peer goal emphasis*. Peers' setting of high standards and encouragement of best efforts
- *Peer work facilitation*. Peer help in improving performance, planning, and problem solving

*Behavioral outcomes*

- *Group functioning.* Group members' planning and coordination, decision making and problem solving, knowledge of jobs, trust, and sharing of information
- *Satisfaction.* Seven facets: satisfaction with group members, the supervisor, the job itself, the organization, pay, and current and future career progress
- *Goal integration.* The compatibility of individual and organizational needs

The survey has 60 standard questions and can be customized if the organizations or their industry requires specific tailoring. Denison developed the circumplex (illustrated in Figure 6-1) to function as a high-impact, graphic reporting mechanism for the results of the culture surveys. Data are displayed in the four traits (Mission, Consistency, Involvement, and Adaptability). Traits are subdivided into components indexes (e.g., Mission has traits identified as "Strategic Direction and Intent," "Goals and Objectives," and "Vision"), resulting in twelve bar graphs. Each bar graph represents an organization's relative score for a particular cultural characteristic. Each ring from the center of the circumplex represents a quartile of the score. Exemplary organizations set the standard at the 100th percentile, while lower-functioning organizations are scored both numerically and by the quartile in which they fall. The data from the surveys are quite rich and enable organizations to identify both weaknesses that they need to overcome and strengths that can be used to overcome them.

A parallel challenge for the researchers was to determine financial effectiveness measures to verify and illustrate the correlation between a strong, positive organization culture and the organization's financial effectiveness. To provide information that would be readily accepted and understood by financial professionals, the cultural characteristics had to be unequivocally tied to a well-respected financial data management and assessment resource. The Denison researchers opted to use the most respected resource of the day, COMPUSTAT, Standard & Poor's statistical service, which monitored and analyzed 130 financial measures for 2458 firms that were listed on either the New York Stock Exchange or the American Stock Exchange. For most firms, yearly data for the period from 1961 to 1980 were available, and the goal was to construct a set of annual financial outcome measures for the period extending from the date that the behavioral data for a particular firm were gathered via the questionnaire to 5 years after that date.[3]

**Figure 6-1**   *The Denison Culture Survey Circumplex*

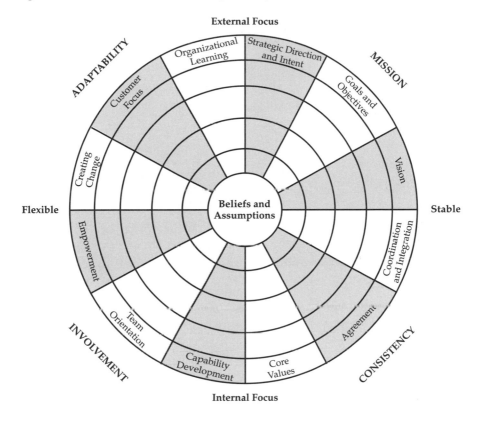

Eleven measures were initially drawn from the COMPUSTAT data to represent both past performance and current organizational health. The measures were:

- Current assets
- Current liabilities
- Long-term debt
- Sales
- Income
- Investment
- Research expenses
- Development expenses
- Earnings per share

- Common equity
- Working capital

Using the data gathered from these measures, six financial ratios were computed:

- Debt to equity ratio
- Current ratio (current assets divided by current liabilities)
- R&D to sales ratio
- Return on sales
- Return on equity
- Return on investment

Analysis of the behavioral data indicated a direct correlation between strong, positive organization cultures and strong financial performance. Further efforts to simplify and add utility to the study determined that two summary ratios can be used to reflect the influence of the organization's culture on its financial performance and effectiveness:[4]

- *Income/sales ratio.* This ratio is a good indicator of the efficiency of a company's operations, showing return on each dollar of sales. This is a good indicator for comparing firms, particularly within the same industry. The ratio is calculated by dividing income by net sales.
- *Income/investment ratio.* This shows the return on each dollar of investment and effectively adds minority interest and long-term debt to the denominator of the income/equity ratio. Thus, it is a measure of return on all sources of investment dollars, not just shareholder's equity. This ratio is calculated by dividing income by total investment.

Researchers soon recognized that because of the cyclical nature of business, the data results had to be standardized for such things as inflation and financial and market trends. The standardization process adjusted each performance element simultaneously for the effects of the industry and for the year.

Denison conducted extensive comparative analyses of 34 companies over a 5-year period and published the results in 1990. In his report, he says:[5]

The quantitative cultural data used in this analysis have been limited, but nonetheless, help in the development of the culture and effectiveness model on which this book is based. The results provide compelling evidence that it is quite possible to use cultural and behavioral measures to predict the (financial) performance and effectiveness of an organization over time.

Since the original research began 20 years ago, the survey and database have consistently demonstrated the correlation between cultural attributes and financial performance for thousands of people and hundreds of companies in virtually every industry sector.

Denison's work was built upon by Fisher[6] in a 1997 paper titled "Corporate Culture and Perceived Business Performances: A Study of the Relationship between the Culture of an Organization and Perceptions of its Financial and Qualitative Performance." In a study of 4750 participants representing 60 companies with between 5 and 300,000 employees in a very broad industry base, Fisher proved correlations between the following financial measures and strength in the cultural traits defined by Denison:

- *Profitability/Return on Assets.* The most general and important measure of a company's financial performance, high profitability as measured by ROA requires an overall balance of internal and external orientation with both stability and flexibility in the operational systems. Denison states that a balance of all four traits (Mission, Involvement, Consistency, and Adaptability) is required in order to enhance profitability/ROA. High profitability/ROA was strongly correlated with strong Mission and Involvement traits.

- *Sales/Revenue Growth.* This is an externally oriented performance factor requiring a combination of stability and flexibility in the operational system. Denison states that a balance between strong Adaptability (external focus; facilitates flexibility) and strong Mission (external focus; facilitates stability) is required in order to enhance sales/revenue growth.

- *Market Share.* This is an externally oriented performance factor requiring a combination of high stability and flexibility in the operational system. Denison states that a balance of Adaptability (external focus; facilitates flexibility) and strong Mission (external focus; facilitates stability) is required in order to enhance market share growth.

- *Quality of Products and Services.* Quality is an internally oriented performance factor requiring a combination of stability and flexibility in the operational system. Denison states that balanced strength in Involvement (internal focus; facilitates flexibility), Consistency (internal focus; facilitates stability), and Mission (external focus; facilitates stability) is required in order to enhance product/service quality.

- *New Product Development/Innovation.* This is an internally oriented performance factor requiring flexibility in the operational system. Denison correlates a balance of strength in Involvement (internal focus; facilitates flexibility) and Adaptability (external focus; facilitates flexibility) with enhanced innovation and product development.

- *Employee Satisfaction.* An internally oriented performance factor, employee satisfaction requires a combination of stability and flexibility within the operational system. Denison links a balance of strength in Involvement (internal focus; facilitates flexibility) and Consistency (internal focus; facilitates stability) to enhanced employee satisfaction.

Fisher's[7] extensive work addressed how cultural strengths (and, conversely, weaknesses) affect the financial performance of organizations, as indicated by traditional measures and ratios; for example:

1. Higher levels of Mission affected, to one degree or another, five of the six performance factors: Profitability/ROA, Sales/Revenue Growth, Market Share, Quality of Products and Services, and Employee Satisfaction.
2. Higher levels of Involvement affected, to one degree or another, four of the six performance factors: Profitability/ROA, New Product Development/Innovation, Quality of Products and Services, and Employee Satisfaction.
3. Higher levels of Adaptability affected, to one degree or another, three of the six performance factors: Sales/Revenue Growth, Market Share, and New Product Development/Innovation.
4. Higher levels of Consistency affected, to one degree or another, two of the six performance factors: Quality of Products and Services and Employee Satisfaction.

From an alternative perspective, Fisher[8] concluded that traditionally "soft" performance factors were directly correlated with "hard" financial performance factors as follows:

1. Quality of Products and Services with Profitability/ROA
2. Quality of Products and Services with Sales/Revenue Growth
3. Employee Satisfaction with Profitability/ROA

4. Employee Satisfaction with Sales/Revenue Growth
5. Employee Satisfaction with Quality of Products and Services

Fisher also found that the Denison Culture Survey results provide both a snapshot of the organization's culture and its relationship to the organization's financial performance *and* a clue to how the organization may perform in the future. She explains:[9]

> Qualitative organizational culture performance factors are manifested in a shorter period of time than financial performance factors . . . thus qualitative factors can provide an intermediary measure of how the organization is doing in a much broader scope. . . . If quality is questionable, innovation is slow, or employee satisfaction is low, a prediction can be made that financial performance, even if currently strong, will erode in the long term.

Through the efforts of Denison and Fisher, an instrument has been developed that has been proven to meet the need for objective analyses of the financial implications of organizational cultures.

1. The information from the culture analysis correlates with financial measures and ratios that are familiar and useful to M&A financial professionals and therefore is readily useful for improving the effectiveness of each step in the typical combination process.
2. The information provides an objective "snapshot" of the combining cultures such that a side-by-side comparison can be made at the time of the deal that will serve as a baseline for the impact of integration and intervention activities.
3. The analysis provides standard financial measures that serve as a basis for prescriptive decisions about what must be done to improve each of the organizations and the combined organization if the performance expectations are to be met.

Thus, we have an instrument that serves our data gathering, analysis, and presentation needs and also serves as the critical objective analysis foundation mechanism for an effective process that can be used by business buyers, business sellers, and related professionals to improve the results of mergers and acquisitions.

## SUMMARY

We began this chapter by describing the need and criteria for an organization culture assessment tool that reflects the organization's characteristics in terms that financial analysts can use to improve mergers and acquisitions. Through the efforts of Denison and his team and the subsequent field analyses by Fisher, we have identified a proven, effective instrument for performing quantitative organization culture analyses that meets our acceptance criteria. The culture analyses have the credibility that comes from having been used to characterize thousands of organizations over more than three decades and having been objectively validated against COMPUSTAT, which is recognized as one of the financial information industry's leading resources for in-depth financial information on publicly traded companies in the United States and around the world. This objective tool provides the basis for a process that can be used to identify and communicate cultural differences in combining organizations in such a way that they can be factored into the M&A selection, decision-making, valuation, and integration steps and improve the likelihood that the deal will be successful.

# QUOCA: QUANTITATIVE ORGANIZATION CULTURE ANALYSES

# 7

# Using Quantitative Organization Culture Analyses to Improve the Financial and Competitive Performance of Mergers and Acquisitions

Organization culture, more than any other factor, will dictate a corporation's ability to survive and thrive in the face of current challenges, which include increased pace of change, heightened technologies, global competition, an increasingly sophisticated workforce, and tougher customer demands. Companies are becoming flatter in an effort to adapt; decisions are being driven to lower levels in an effort to increase speed, to improve quality, and to facilitate responsiveness to the customer. Traditional management techniques such as hierarchical control, rules, policies, and regulations do not work in this new organization. Some contend corporations must now be led and managed through an effective organizational culture. Thus, it is critical that our understanding of culture and its many implications advance.[1]

THE OBJECTIVES OF THIS CHAPTER are for the reader to understand the foundation and workings of the QUOCA process, to know the relationship between weak cultural characteristics and their financial/competitive impacts; and to understand where and how QUOCA can improve the results of the specific steps in the combination process and the overall process as well.

## INTRODUCTION

In my 30 years of business management and consulting experience, I have often observed that executives have a bias toward numbers as the compelling, objective reasoning behind their decisions. Such a bias is understandable. Our language is full of phrases that reinforce the idea that the only valid measurements are those that can be expressed in hard, cold, indisputable numbers, particularly when there is a dollar sign in front. We often hear people say, "The numbers don't lie." Bob Dylan wrote "Money doesn't talk, it screams" and Jerry Maguire's client begged him to "Show me the money!"

And I have frequently run into walls of opposition when I was promoting projects whose outcomes were difficult to quantify in objective terms such as return on investment and payback period. It was frustrating to know in my heart that it was worthwhile to invest time and money in activities with unquantifiable results such as creating a business plan (most small to medium-sized businesses don't have one unless they are seeking funding), doing a market analysis, attending trade shows, or engaging in training and development. Since it was difficult to justify these expenses in objective terms, it was difficult to get funding for them in competition with operational expenditures for equipment upgrades and the latest software version.

In my work, I discovered that there was a need for an objective instrument that would evaluate my clients' organization cultures in a way that provided irrefutable, employee-generated information concerning their attitudes, values, and opinions. I needed a mechanism to define those aspects of the organization that helped people meet their organization's goals, and also the cultural characteristics that impeded them. As an outside consultant, I had the advantage of being able to use my ignorance of the organization's culture to ask tough questions that insiders were extremely unlikely ever to ask. If I developed my own culture survey instrument, I would have some ownership in the process, the data, and the results, and such ownership would be a barrier to my successfully facilitating the change process. Many years of organization development experience had taught me that facilitators are most effective when they use the information they elicit from their group to create ownership of the situation on the part of the group members, allowing them to internalize the desire to change their situation and become empowered to improve it. Several tools were available, but most of them relied on the consultant's observations, which, to my mind, would reduce the effectiveness of the change process. Other instruments used surveys of the culture members, but the results relied too heavily on the consultant for interpretation and presentation of the information, again compromising the effectiveness of the facilitator's role in creating change.

Several years ago I was asked to collaborate on an organization development project for a large pharmaceutical company. My colleagues on the project introduced me to the Denison Culture Survey. Impressed by the vivid display of cultural characteristics provided by the circumplex and the tie-in to the financial implications of the cultural weaknesses, I began using the Denison Culture Survey as the foundation for my clients' culture change processes. The inclusive, participative nature of the survey process and the personal relationship with survey results has proved to be a powerful vehicle for assessing the nature, scope, and significance of cultural issues of organizations and a tool for effectively changing the performance of the organization through ownership of and motivation to overcome its weaknesses.

The discovery of the Denison Culture Survey as a tool for measuring organization culture characteristics and relating the results to financial measures was pivotal. It enabled me to help my clients to develop compelling, objective, number- and dollar-based rationales for prioritizing and gaining support for changing their culture. For example, many companies think that employee knowledge of customer needs is important to only a few key decision makers. But Denison[2] demonstrated that organizations in which all employees have broad, personal knowledge are more adaptable to external dynamics and have higher sales and revenue growth, greater market share, and higher product development and innovation than their counterparts that are weaker in this trait. With this information in hand, the members of my client organizations were better equipped to compare the investment of time and money in these "soft" projects to investments in "hard" projects such as capital improvements because the measurement parameters were the same—numbers, ratios, and dollars. Consequently, they were able to gain their managers' support for soft organization change efforts that improved the financial performance and effectiveness of their organizations.

The survey results were also extremely valuable in developing managers' awareness of and support for their organization's change efforts. For example, an organization that scores in the third and fourth quartile on the Mission, Consistency, and Adaptability traits but in the first quartile on Involvement requires a much more hands-on supervisory team, will have poor collaboration to improve troubled work processes, and will have little bench strength when the capabilities of the workforce are challenged. When Empowerment is low, a much higher burden of responsibility for issues such as quality, cycle-time reduction, and wastage is placed on supervision, thereby directly reducing profitability. Low Team Orientation is statistically tied to the ripple effects of poor work-group coordination, higher-than-average turnover, and inability to adapt to changes in the work environment, all of which affect profitability as well as the ability to adapt to the sudden changes typical of mergers and acquisitions. Low Capability Development is directly tied to the organization's depth of knowledge and flexibility in manpower assignment.

Further, lack of investment in employee knowledge and skills may impair the employees' ability to adapt to the new infrastructure, procedures, and technologies of the acquiring company. Poor Capability Development can have a significant impact on the time required to respond to both internal changes such as new IT systems and external dynamics such as an unexpected demand for a product.

By making managers aware of the financial and competitive implications of their organization's cultural weakness, the survey gives them:

1. Objective, undeniable evidence that the situation exists
2. A powerful financial and competitive motivation to change the way the organization operates
3. Objective baseline data to demonstrate the effectiveness of the change efforts

Consequently, change efforts become focused on issues that had been identified by the organization's constituents as negatively affecting their performance and therefore their sense of security, safety, and prosperity. It is much easier for managers to change the attitudes, assumptions, beliefs, and behaviors of the organization's constituents when the identification of the situation, the ownership of the solution, and the reward for changing is theirs.

The critical ability to objectively analyze and compare cultures demonstrated its value even more profoundly when I began using the Denison Culture Survey as a basis for defining the financial implications of melding two cultures through a business merger or acquisition. Survey scores for the acquiring and the to-be-acquired company can be compared to one another and to the robust database to identify the companies' relative strengths and weaknesses. The survey data become the foundation for Quantitative Organization Culture Analyses, or QUOCA, which link the culture survey scores with their financial and competitive implications that can be effectively used in the combination process to:

- Select the optimum combination partner
- Make logical go/no-go decisions
- Develop more realistic financial and competitive projections and, hence, a more accurate price for the deal
- Improve the effectiveness and reduce the length of time needed to integrate the business operations

## QUOCA IN THE BUSINESS COMBINATION PROCESS

Quantitative Organizational Culture Analyses (QUOCA) can be initiated at several critical points in the typical merger and acquisition process, but the greatest potential for adding value is at the very beginning of thinking about the combination. Figure 7-1 illustrates the steps in the M&A process and indicates those areas where QUOCA adds value to the combination by identifying cultural barriers to the success of the deal.

The required steps in QUOCA are fundamentally the same regardless of when and where in the combination process it is used. Since QUOCA is used as a vehicle for assessing "how things are done" in an organization, it is of paramount importance that the culture analysis process encourages candid, open, honest, uninhibited input. The process must be "owned" by the participants and must be viewed as a collaborative activity that will help both the overall organization and its work groups and individuals. To that end, leaders involved in the process must demonstrate a high degree of support for and involvement in the analysis process and the changes that result from the knowledge of what is working and what is not working within the culture with respect to the organization's vision for the future, strategies, goals, and objectives.

**Figure 7-1**   *The Role of QUOCA in the Merger and Acquisition Process*

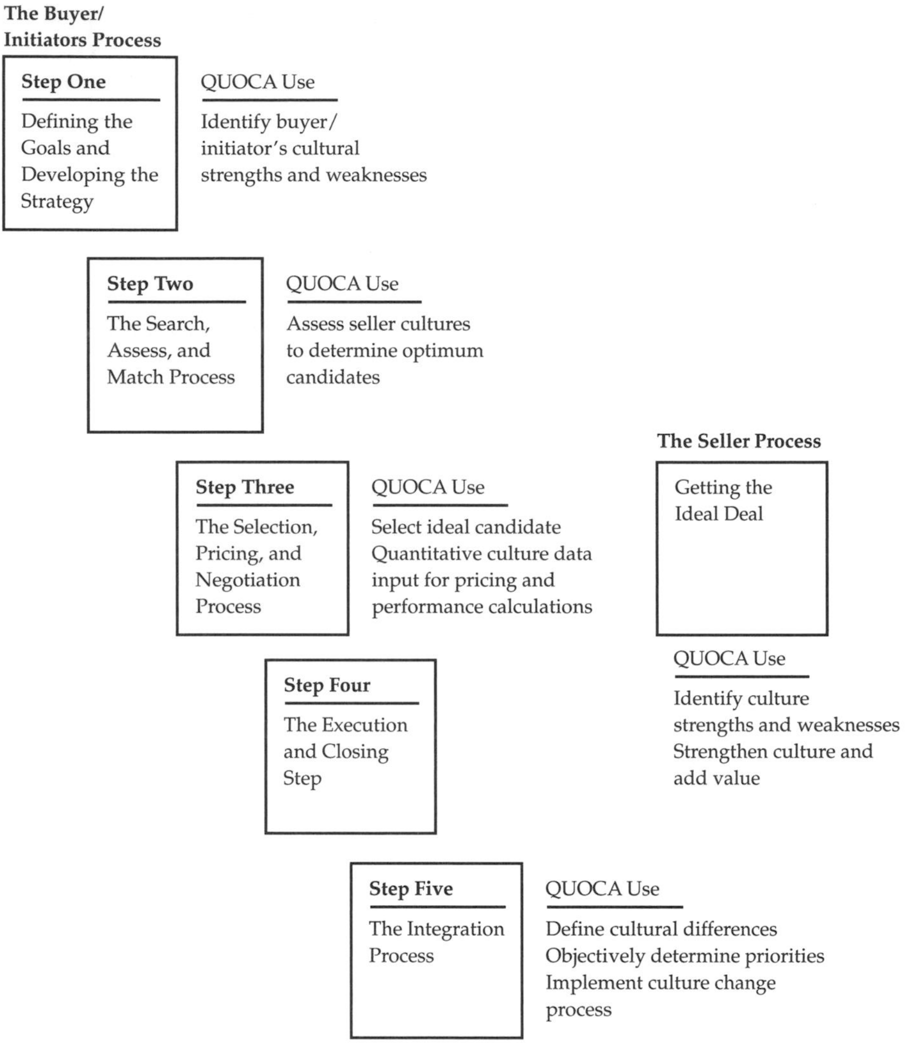

**The Buyer/
Initiators Process**

| Step One | QUOCA Use |
| --- | --- |
| Defining the Goals and Developing the Strategy | Identify buyer/ initiator's cultural strengths and weaknesses |

| Step Two | QUOCA Use |
| --- | --- |
| The Search, Assess, and Match Process | Assess seller cultures to determine optimum candidates |

**The Seller Process**

| Step Three | QUOCA Use | Getting the Ideal Deal |
| --- | --- | --- |
| The Selection, Pricing, and Negotiation Process | Select ideal candidate Quantitative culture data input for pricing and performance calculations | |

QUOCA Use

Identify culture strengths and weaknesses
Strengthen culture and add value

| Step Four | |
| --- | --- |
| The Execution and Closing Step | |

| Step Five | QUOCA Use |
| --- | --- |
| The Integration Process | Define cultural differences Objectively determine priorities Implement culture change process |

The typical Quantitative Organization Culture Analysis is conducted in the following manner:

1. Organization leaders define and agree upon the goals of the analysis.
2. With the goals as the focal point, the appropriate participants are selected, taking into account the need for a statistically valid repre-

sentation of the vertical and horizontal structure of the organization. Participants can be demographically identified while maintaining their anonymity so that the data can be cut several ways to yield an extremely focused and detailed picture of the cultural beliefs and assumptions. Suggestions for appropriate participants in the survey are noted in the discussion of the use of QUOCA during the various combination steps.

3. Participants should be notified of their involvement in the culture analysis process by their organization leaders in a way that articulates the goals and importance of the process, demonstrates the leaders' support for and involvement in the process, and assures the anonymity of the participants' input. Participants should be notified of the time and place for the survey about a week in advance. The usual duration of the survey meeting is half an hour. Supervisors should also be notified to allow for and enable participants' availability.

4. Participants are gathered in a facility with tables, chairs, and pens, to enable completion of the surveys. Leaders should kick off the meeting by reiterating the goals of the process and its importance while demonstrating support for and involvement by the management team and assuring the anonymity of the participants' input.

5. Surveys and envelopes are then distributed and described by the facilitator, who may be an employee or a consultant. Questions are solicited and responded to. Participants complete the survey, place it in the envelope, and seal it before returning it to the facilitator.

6. The surveys are scored and initial results compiled within 10 business days. If necessary, this step can be accelerated to meet the needs of the combination process.

7. Detailed QUOCA is performed to identify the financial and competitive implications of the cultural strengths and weaknesses, including the potential impact of the culture on the merger and acquisition process and its projected outcomes.

8. Potential cultural barriers to the success of the deal are clearly defined and prioritized.

9. Goals, schedules, time frames, and financial projections for the combination are adjusted in light of the potential cultural barriers to success.

10. Intervention strategies and programs are defined to change the organization and its culture in order to improve present and future results.

11. Intervention strategies are implemented.

12. Follow-up QUOCA is performed to assess the effectiveness of the interventions.

13. Steps 1 through 12 are repeated in concert with an overall continuous improvement process.

Although it may not be appropriate for the rank and file of the enterprise to know of an impending acquisition or merger at the time of the initial survey, leaders can accurately frame the culture analysis as a means of improving the organization's results.

## USING QUOCA TO IMPROVE STEP 1 OF THE MERGER AND ACQUISITION PROCESS: THE GOALS AND STRATEGY OF THE DEAL

We discussed the initial step of the combination process in Chapter 2. In this phase of the process, the goals and strategies of the deal are defined. The following is a brief recap of the typical activities involved in this phase of the combination process:

- Develop specific financial and market objectives for the deal.
- Determine the nature of the combination—merger, acquisition, or joint venture.
- Develop a profile for the ideal combination candidate, including such factors as geographic location, products or services offered, current market share, gross sales, and so on.
- Identify deal killers such as debt level or potential liabilities.
- Prepare the due diligence package including materials desired from the acquisition/merger candidate.

Since profit equals revenue less expenses, the fundamental driver for the deal is the desire to increase profits by increasing revenues or decreasing costs. Prospects for business combinations must have the wherewithal to increase revenues through greater market share, broader or deeper client bases, a different demographic or geographic market, or perhaps a combination of two or more of these advantages. Or, the prospect must have a technology, distribution system, book of business, group of long-term contracts, or some other asset or capability that will lower the cost of doing business. The buyer has to remember that its differential advantage works well for *it*, but may not necessarily work so well for the new acquisition's management team or its organizational culture.

## Of All There Is to Know, First of All, Know Yourself

Smart companies know that the best way to find out what they need is to inventory what they already have. QUOCA paints a very clear picture of the culture of the buyer or the company initiating the merger so that it knows its own strengths and weaknesses prior to adding additional assets. If it knows itself, the company can take the time to remedy its deficiencies prior to a deal. And when the conditions are right for a combination, the company can use its cultural knowledge and strength to improve the odds for the deal's success. For most businesses, the following groups should be surveyed to the suggested depth:

- The board of directors: all.
- Corporate officers: CEO, president, CFO, COO, VP-HR, VP-Marketing, VP-Sales, VP-Procurement, VP-IT, and operating division heads.
- A 20 percent vertical sample of operating groups that may interface with the acquired business organization. To clarify, this group should include 20 percent of the supervisors, 20 percent of the line workers, 20 percent of the administrative assistants, and so on.

The QUOCA package provides a separate report and profile for each group as well as an overall report for the business. The reports provide understanding of the organization's strengths and weaknesses, its internal versus external focus, and its flexibility versus adaptability. In addition, the report describes the financial and competitive impacts of the cultural weaknesses and provides a cost/benefit rationale for prioritized culture change initiatives.

For example, an underperforming business in an established and extremely competitive industry was developing its long-term strategy. One of its options was the acquisition of a customer that provided sales and distribution for the products that the company manufactured. A new management team had been brought in, and the new team wanted to make certain that the path forward considered the business's cultural strengths and weaknesses and their direct and ripple effects.

The QUOCA survey and analysis results (Table 7-1) proved to be truly a revelation. An organization whose Coordination and Integration characteristic ranks in the first percentile of all the companies in the database must improve its internal work processes before it has any hope of successfully combining with a newly acquired organization. A ranking in the second percentile on the Creating Change characteristic reveals an organization that is clearly struggling with its existing business dynamics and is certainly not a strong candidate for the challenges of integrating changes in operations, clients, suppliers, reporting relationships, and technologies, which are common with mergers and acquisitions. The financial and competitive implications of these two weak cultural characteristics are widespread and significant—both the Coordination and Integration and the Creating Change characteristics have universal ownership in the organization. Consequently, the required change activities' goals, methods, rewards, and measures will be widespread and will probably require a long-term investment of time and effort.

**Table 7-1**    *Financial and Competitive Implications of Weak Culture Characteristics*

| Denison Culture Survey Characteristic | QUOCA Performance Impact |
|---|---|
| Coordination and Integration, 1st percentile | *Poorer quality:* Leads to reduced sales, lower revenue, reduced market share, higher inventory costs, and higher production costs for scrap and rework |
| | *Lower employee satisfaction:* Leads to higher rates of injury, absenteeism, and grievances; higher turnover; and reduced productivity, efficiency, and effectiveness |
| Creating Change, 2nd percentile | *Reduced product development/innovation:* Leads to slower time to market for new products, loss of market share, higher inventory of passé products |
| | *Lower market share:* Leads to lower revenues and profits, with the associated direct and indirect effects; lower profit margins and less ability to negotiate prices with customers; higher physical inventory and inventory costs; lower production efficiencies from underutilized resources; and reduced buying power/loss of volume discounts |
| | *Lower sales/revenue growth:* Leads to decreased stock price and company valuation; lower availability and higher cost of capital; and reduced profitability, along with its associated direct and indirect effects |
| Vision, 9th percentile | *Reduced profitability:* Leads to lower cash on hand to compensate stakeholders in the form of dividends, bonuses, and salary increases; lower earnings per share, which decrease the stock price and the organization's ability to borrow money at optimum rates; reduced revenues and borrowing ability, which impede the investment in capital improvements that maintain or increase the company's competitive position in the marketplace. Continued low revenues and a high cost of capital can lead to cutbacks in spending |

**Table 7-1**   *Financial and Competitive Implications of Weak Culture Characteristics (Continued)*

| Denison Culture Survey Characteristic | QUOCA Performance Impact |
|---|---|
| Vision, 9th percentile (continued) | for such things as maintenance, marketing, and training, which eventually further affect profitability through unexpected breakdowns, lower market share, and lower employee effectiveness |
| | *Poorer quality:* Leads to reduced sales, lower revenue, reduced market share, higher inventory costs, and higher production costs for scrap and rework |
| | *Lower employee satisfaction:* Leads to higher rates of injury, absenteeism, and grievances; higher turnover; and reduced productivity, efficiency, and effectiveness |
| | *Lower market share:* Leads to lower revenues and profits, with the associated direct and indirect effects; lower profit margins and less ability to negotiate prices with customers; higher physical inventory and inventory costs; lower production efficiencies from underutilized resources; and reduced buying power/loss of volume discounts |
| | *Lower sales/revenue growth:* Decrease in stock price and company valuation; lower availability and higher cost of capital; and reduced profitability along with its associated direct and indirect effects |

An organization with a ninth percentile rank on Vision that is already attempting to change has an opportunity to make relatively quick and cost-effective changes through the efforts of just the executive team. In this case, for example, the executive team was able to implement efforts to improve profitability, quality, revenue growth, and employee satisfaction with the following change initiatives, directed at its weakness on the Vision characteristic:

1. The board of directors and the new executive management team developed a vision statement that clearly expressed their desired future for the business, including the industry and geographic markets that they wanted to serve, their desired competitive position, and their safety, quality, environmental, and productivity goals. The vision statement was officially unveiled and implemented by the new CEO. A copy was provided for each employee with an accompanying letter that committed the company to the long-term success and prosperity of the business. The letter asked for personal

commitments by all employees to make every day a step in the
path to its future.

2. The vision statement was posted on all bulletin boards, the first
   page of the company newsletter, and the home page of the company web site.

3. Progress toward specific goals within the vision statement was tracked
   and displayed next to the vision statements and on the web site.

By analyzing its own internal issues prior to considering an acquisition as a means of improving its financial performance, the company was
able to very cost-effectively acknowledge, prioritize, and address its own
barriers to success. At present, a business combination remains a possible strategy, but overcoming the organization's internal problems is the
first priority in improving results.

## USING QUOCA TO IMPROVE STEP 2 OF THE MERGER AND ACQUISITION PROCESS: THE SEARCH, ASSESS, AND MATCH PROCESS

The critical activity in the second phase of the M&A process occurs when
the initiating company, either directly or indirectly through a broker,
compiles a list of prospective target companies. Prospects for vertical
integration are customers or suppliers with whom the initiator has a successful, mutually beneficial relationship. For horizontal combinations,
lists of competitors can be obtained from sources ranging from simple
local resources such as the Yellow Pages to trade associations and trade
show participants. Target company lists for conglomerate-forming combinations are a little more difficult to put together because the prospects
usually operate outside the acquiring organization's span of familiarity.

An equally important step in this phase of the M&A process is to
assemble a due diligence team to oversee and conduct the deal. The critical competencies of the team are:

- The ability to envision and articulate the optimum combined entity
  and its outcomes
- In-depth knowledge of the combining businesses' markets, their
  dynamics, their variables, and their histories
- In-depth knowledge of the production process for the product or
  service, from R&D through distribution
- The ability to identify and quantify the features of the prospective
  combining businesses into accurate *pro forma* statements so that the

most financially advantageous opportunity is determined and executed

- In-depth familiarity with tax and regulatory issues related to the operations of the individual and combined businesses
- The ability to structure the most advantageous legal relationship between the combining companies
- The ability to source and assemble the most advantageous financial structure for the combination
- Knowledge and sincere appreciation of organization culture fundamentals and the potential impact of cultural mismatches on the success of the deal

Eventually, the prospect list is whittled down to one to three companies, upon which in-depth scrutiny is performed via the due diligence process. In many cases a single critical weakness or uncertainty in a prospect's operations is enough to bump that prospect from the list.

As we have pointed out before, a significant cause of the failure or underperformance of combinations is the mismatch of cultures. The due diligence process, armed with an assessment tool that can objectively determine the best fit of organization cultures and provide enlightened, professional input concerning the financial implications of the cultural differences between the prospective combination candidates, can provide useful information for selecting the optimum prospect.

QUOCA is an extremely valuable and effective resource for objectively determining the best cultural fit between the buyer and the prospective combination candidates. And compared to the agonizing costs of poor deals, the process is extremely cost-effective. The analysis process can be performed in 10 to 15 business days and so can easily be incorporated into the normal due diligence schedule.

Combination prospects may not expect QUOCA to be part of the due diligence process, and so they may need some assurance that the cultural information, like the other operational information that is being shared, will fall under the nondisclosure agreement. I caution deal initiators who are faced with a prospect's resistance to culture analysis to drop that company from consideration. After all, if the prospect declines a culture analysis because it doesn't understand the relevance of cultural information to future operations, it is likely to be unconcerned with its own culture, and as a result that culture probably is not very strong. If the prospect declines because it does know its culture and it doesn't want to reveal that culture to a prospective partner, then the prospect must perceive its culture as a liability to the deal.

The following groups of people within the target company should be surveyed to the suggested depth to adequately assess the culture:

- The board of directors: all
- Corporate officers: CEO, president, CFO, COO, VP-HR, VP-Marketing, VP-Sales, VP-Procurement, VP-IT, and operating division heads
- A 20 percent vertical sample of operating groups that are projected to be significant contributors to the success of the deal

As with the survey analysis for the initiating business, there should be a separate report and profile for each group as well as an overall report for the combination prospect's organization. The survey can be used in the preclosing time frame to stimulate changes in the prospect's organization and operations that will either add value or improve the likelihood of success for the combined businesses. Resistance on the part of the prospective business to making reasonable changes for the sake of the success of the deal should be seen as a red flag warning of resistance to change once the deal is consummated.

There are many benefits for the initiating company from performing QUOCA as an objective means of becoming familiar with its own culture prior to initiating a merger or an acquisition. Of paramount benefit is the opportunity to get its own house in order before beginning the arduous process of integrating the culture of another organization into its operations. Further, if it knows and understands the beliefs and assumptions of its own organization, the initiator can do side-by-side analyses to select the most likely candidate to achieve the desired results of the combination. And once the optimum candidate has been identified, the comparative differences in the organizations' cultures can be instrumental in determining the price of the deal and determining the scope and schedule for integrating the acquired business into the acquirer's operations, as will be extensively discussed in the subsequent chapters.

The reader is strongly encouraged to become thoroughly familiar with the nature and importance of the four cultural traits and the twelve characteristics, discussed in Chapters 8 through 23, in order to understand the nature and importance of the various aspects of organization cultures, since each aspect has the potential for being a tremendous asset or liability to the success of the deal. Each of the chapters describes an organizational culture trait or characteristic, provides an explanation of the financial and competitive implications of strength or weakness in that aspect of the culture, and describes the potential impact on the success of the deal of the relative cultural strength or weakness of the parties. This comparative information resource can be an invaluable asset for a thorough and accurate completion of the due diligence process, particularly for the following steps:

- Identifying showstopper or deal-killer differences in the way the people in the potentially combining businesses think and act
- Determining the nature and extent of complementary and detrimental cultural differences
- Projecting the impact of the culture on the financial performance of the deal, especially the payback period, revenue and expense factors, quality and productivity, return on investment, market share, and time to market of new products
- Including and eventually selecting candidates for the deal based on the likelihood that the combination will achieve the desired outcomes
- Factoring the cultural information and its financial implications into the pricing of the deal
- Identifying the cultural issues that must be addressed before, during, and after the initiation of the integration phase of the combination and the priority and sequence of addressing these issues

## USING QUOCA TO IMPROVE STEP 3 OF THE MERGER AND ACQUISITION PROCESS: THE SELECTION, PRICING, AND NEGOTIATION PROCESS

The determination of the offering price is very involved and is often performed by a team of finance, accounting, and business brokerage experts. As previously discussed, the offer price is influenced by the following factors:

*Revenue factors*

- Combined gross revenues
- Combined market share
- Revenue enhancement by vertical and horizontal market synergies
- Revenue enhancement from bundling products and services
- Product/service leverage, such as follow-on sales

*Expense factors*

- Production and distribution efficiencies
- Marketing and sales efficiencies
- Customer service efficiencies
- Greater purchasing power for supplies, raw materials, utilities, and so on

- Reduction of overhead costs from:
  - Increased leverage in buying and overseeing insurance and benefit programs
  - Combining staff functions such as payroll, accounting, legal services, human resources, organization development, IT, communications, investor relations, facility management and maintenance, and so on
  - Reduction of facility requirements and costs, such as property taxes, energy, insurance, security, and so on, as a result of the combinations
- Transaction costs, including:
  - Attorneys', consultants', accounting, and brokerage fees
  - Licenses, registrations, filings, and so on
  - Shutdown, decommissioning, cleanup, maintenance, caretaking, and so on of redundant facilities
  - Compensation packages and related expenses for redundant personnel
  - Liquidation of equity options in the acquired business
  - Fees and penalties for restructuring existing legal agreements such as contracts and leases

Differences in the cultures of the combining organizations must also be recognized and factored into the future revenues and expenses and, consequently, into the price that the buyer offers to the seller or, in the case of a merger, into the valuation of the deal. It is critically important for the success of the deal to understand that differences in the strength and weakness of cultural traits and characteristics in the combining businesses have been demonstrated to have a significant impact on the long-range success of the deal. Specifically, mismatched cultures can have a negative impact on the following financial measures and operational factors:

- Return on investment (ROI)
- Return on sales (ROS)
- Return on equity (ROE)
- Return on assets (ROA)
- Payback period for the combination
- Market share
- Sales growth
- Product or service quality

- Time to market for new products and services
- Product or service innovation
- Employee satisfaction, turnover, effectiveness, and efficiency

In the past, as we have discussed, there was no mechanism for objectively assessing and quantifying these cultural impacts on business combinations and expressing them in terms that the deal makers recognized, respected, and used. If the strengths and weaknesses of the prospective merger or acquisition candidate both as a stand-alone culture and with respect to the initiating business's culture are measured, the price can be adjusted to reflect a more realistic outcome scenario.

For example, many people measure the performance of mergers and acquisitions in terms of the amount of time it takes to recover the cost of the investment in the deal. Depending on the industry and economic conditions, payback periods for business combinations range from a few years to a decade or longer. The formula for calculating the payback period is as follows:

$$\text{Payback period (in months)} = \frac{\text{cost of the investment (in dollars)}}{\text{net revenue (in dollars per month)}}$$

The formula clearly demonstrates that any aspect of the combination that decreases net revenue or delays its receipt will extend the period of time required for investors, lenders, and other stakeholders to recoup their investment.

## USING QUOCA TO ADJUST PRICE CALCULATIONS FOR BUSINESS COMBINATIONS

The price of the deal should incorporate the impact of cultural weaknesses on the financial calculations that contribute to setting the price for the business combination. The steps involved in incorporating the QUOCA data into the pricing model are:

1. Identify the direct, indirect, and ripple-effect financial implications of weakness on each of the four cultural traits (Table 7-2).
2. Identify specific financial measures/ratios that are affected by a cultural weakness (Table 7-3).
3. Estimate the impact of the cultural weakness on the factors that are used in the financial measures/ratios and competitive measures.
4. Recalculate the measures and ratios using factors adjusted for cultural impacts.

The extent of cultural impacts on the financial measures depends upon the degree of the weakness in each of the combining businesses. Interaction between the deal-initiating team and the organizational culture experts is needed to determine the exact adjustments to be made to each of the affected parameters. The quantitative culture data will be on a par with input from market, operational, accounting, financial, and HR/OD experts and will result in a more complete picture of the likelihood of success for the combination and the barriers to success that must be overcome either prior to or after closing the deal. The impact of QUOCA on the amount of time required to perform the various steps in the combination process should be minimal and the cost should be more than overcome by the improved accuracy of the financial calculations for the price, cost, and returns for the combination.

---

**Table 7-2**   *The Direct, Indirect, and Ripple-Effect Financial Implications of Weakness in the Four Cultural Traits*

*The Mission Trait*

Direct impacts:

- Lower profitability/return on assets
- Slower sales and revenue growth
- Reduced market share
- Poorer product or service quality
- Lower employee satisfaction

*The Involvement Trait*

Direct impacts:

- Lower profitability/return on assets
- Less product development and innovation
- Poorer product or service quality
- Lower employee satisfaction

*The Consistency Trait*

Direct impacts:

- Slower sales and revenue growth
- Reduced market share
- Less product development and innovation

*The Adaptability Trait*

Direct impacts:

- Poorer product or service quality
- Lower employee satisfaction

**Table 7-2**   *The Direct, Indirect, and Ripple-Effect Financial Implications of Weakness in the Four Cultural Traits (Continued)*

*Indirect and Ripple Effects*

Lower profitability/return on assets leads to:

- Lower cash on hand to compensate stakeholders in the form of dividends, bonuses, and salary increases
- Lower earnings per share, which decreases the stock price and the organization's ability to borrow money at optimum rates
- Reduced revenues and borrowing ability, which impede the investment in capital improvements that maintain or increase the company's market share
- Continued low revenues and a high cost of capital can lead to cut-backs in maintenance, marketing, and training, which may further affect profitability through breakdowns, lower market share, and lower employee effectiveness

Slower sales and revenue growth leads to:

- Unmet financial projections and expectations
- Decreased stock price and company valuation
- Lower availability and higher cost of capital
- Reduced profitability, along with its associated indirect effects

Reduced market share leads to:

- Lower revenues and profits, with the associated direct and indirect effects
- Lower profit margins and less ability to negotiate prices with customers
- Higher physical inventory and inventory costs
- Lower production efficiencies from underutilized resources
- Reduced buying power/loss of volume discounts

Less product development and innovation leads to:

- Slower time to market of new products
- Loss of market share
- Higher inventory costs for passé products

Poorer product or service quality leads to:

- Reduced sales
- Lower revenue
- Reduced market share
- Higher inventory costs
- Higher production costs for scrap and rework

Lower employee satisfaction leads to:

- Higher rates of injury, absenteeism, and grievances
- Higher turnover
- Reduced productivity, efficiency, and effectiveness

**Table 7-3**   *Culturally Affected Financial Measures and Ratios*

| | Weak Culture Trait with Negative Direct and Indirect Impact |
|---|---|
| *Balance Sheet Accounts* | |
| Cash | Mission, Consistency, Involvement, Adaptability |
| Accounts receivable | Mission, Consistency, Involvement |
| Inventories | Mission, Consistency, Involvement, Adaptability |
| Current liabilities | Mission, Involvement, Adaptability |
| Long-term debt | Mission, Consistency, Involvement, Adaptability |
| Shareholder's equity | Mission, Consistency, Involvement, Adaptability |
| *Income Statement Entries* | |
| Net sales | Mission, Consistency, Involvement, Adaptability |
| Cost of sales | Mission, Consistency, Involvement, Adaptability |
| Selling, general, and administrative expenses | Mission, Consistency, Involvement, Adaptability |
| Operating income | Mission, Consistency, Involvement, Adaptability |
| Interest | Mission, Consistency, Involvement, Adaptability |
| IBIT | Mission, Consistency, Involvement, Adaptability |
| Preferred dividends | Mission, Consistency, Involvement, Adaptability |
| Net income for common shareholders | Mission, Consistency, Involvement, Adaptability |
| *Ratios* | |
| Current ratio | Mission, Consistency, Involvement |
| Quick ratio | Mission, Consistency, Involvement, Adaptability |
| Total debt to total assets | Mission, Consistency, Involvement |
| Inventory turnover | Mission, Consistency, Involvement, Adaptability |
| Fixed asset turnover | Mission, Consistency, Involvement, Adaptability |
| Total asset turnover | Mission, Consistency, Involvement, Adaptability |
| Profit margin on sales | Mission, Consistency, Involvement |
| Return on total assets | Mission, Consistency, Involvement |
| Return on equity | Mission, Consistency, Involvement |
| Return on assets | Mission, Consistency, Involvement, Adaptability |
| Return on sales | Mission, Consistency, Involvement, Adaptability |
| Return on investment | Mission, Consistency, Involvement, Adaptability |
| Price to earnings | Mission, Consistency, Involvement, Adaptability |

## USING QUOCA TO IMPROVE STEP 4 OF THE MERGER AND ACQUISITION PROCESS: THE CLOSING

We have discussed the unique nature of each merger or acquisition deal closing session. In most cases, all of the legwork and preparation for the closing culminates in the mere formality of the appropriate officers endorsing the required documents. However, the words spoken, the demeanor and body language of the participants, and the expressed and unexpressed spirit of the deal will surely be noted and shared with the people in the combining organizations. Therefore, the depth and degree of feelings of fear, anxiety, and apprehension will be influenced by the public nature of the closing formalities.

For example, an acquired enterprise with weakness in its Adaptability trait can become immobilized by closing comments that imply that big changes are proposed for the acquired organization. Or an acquired organization with a very strong set of values can be traumatized by statements that are insensitive to those cultural beliefs. QUOCA can clearly point out cultural differences that should be addressed in the demeanor of the closing, including press releases and internal communications, in order to avoid lasting barriers to the success of the deal.

## USING QUOCA TO IMPROVE STEP 5 OF THE MERGER AND ACQUISITION PROCESS: THE INTEGRATION OF THE BUSINESS OPERATIONS

QUOCA is an extremely effective tool for recognizing, anticipating, and overcoming the differences in organization cultures that lead to unrealistic expectations, disappointments, inefficiencies, ineffectiveness, dysfunctionality, animosity, poor performance, and potential failure of the deal. Clearly it is preferable to perform the analysis as early in the M&A process as possible. However, the methodology can still make quite a difference in the outcome of the deal even if culture assessments are not employed until the deal has been consummated and the organizations are about to unite.

In every culture analysis I've done, there has been at least one aspect of the organization's culture that has had room for growth, and there have usually been many more. The QUOCA results can be an extremely valuable tool for focusing the integration efforts on the improvement needs of the entire organization. Objective awareness of the contrasting characteristic strengths and weaknesses of the culture traits can be a powerful force enabling the acquiring integration team to recognize and overcome the barriers to success that cultural differences so frequently create.

Our in-depth analysis of the M&A process in Chapter 2 discussed the psychological impact on employees of a change in ownership. Many of the feelings are due to a profound sense of uncertainty and potential loss of the culture that had provided them security and prosperity. This process of mourning is very similar to the loss of a loved one and involves the phases of shock, disbelief or denial, working through the situation, and finally accepting the new reality.

Appropriate intervention during the integration phase of the business combination can do a great deal to minimize or mitigate both the sense of loss and the depth and duration of the mourning phases. The QUOCA results can be used to resolve specific culture weaknesses as the integration phase progresses. In addition, in cases where an acquired company has a very strong culture and is mourning the potential for a profound impact on the postcombination operations, culture analyses can be extremely effective in assuaging fears when the richness of the information is used proactively to:

- Communicate that the motive for and intent of the acquisition is to increase the market position and profitability of the overall organization, thus increasing the security, prosperity, and well-being of the employees.
- Assure the constituents of the acquired company that the acquirer is familiar with and appreciative of the acquired business's strong culture and considers it an important asset in the productive future of the combined business.
- Acknowledge that the acquirer has weaknesses in its own culture that are complemented by the strengths of the acquired company and that the management team is eager to learn from its new partners.
- Explain that all organization cultures have their weaknesses and that the new management team is eager to facilitate the growth of the acquired business's culture in a collaborative manner.

The integration team should also recognize that the business combination may pose a very similar threat to the acquiring company's employees, who may sense that the acquisition could threaten their own security and well-being. Once again, QUOCA can be very effective in overcoming these feelings by providing the basis for integration meetings very similar to those that are held with the acquired business's people.

## AN INTEGRATION EXAMPLE

Let us assume that Company A has a culture that is very strong in its Adaptability trait. The organization is strongly tuned into its clients' needs and is able to quickly convert those needs into new products and services. This strength has helped to carry the business through difficult times. People feel secure in this ever-changing environment because the changes in the past have contributed to their prosperity and well-being.

Company A has done so well that it needs to expand its production capacity. The company decides to acquire a similar business, Company B, because it has always been a tough competitor on price and quality. Company B isn't known as the innovator in the market—that's the role that Company A prides itself on. So on the surface, this looks like a deal made in heaven. After a satisfactory due diligence and easy negotiations, the deal is closed. Experts figure that the investment to buy Company B will be paid back in about 4 years, and they arrange financing for the deal according to their projections.

But Company B's culture is far different from Company A's. Company B is a market follower, which means that while its employees are acutely aware of what's going on in the wants of their customers, they take a wait and see attitude to make certain it's not just a fad. Modifications to products are made reluctantly. The need to change quickly is openly resisted because rash decisions are scary. When the need for new products becomes undeniable, the employees spend a lot of time on research and development. After all, Company B is known for quality—it's their source of security, safety, and well-being.

Company A knows its market and knows that Company B isn't very innovative. "That's great," its managers think. "We'll do the innovation; they'll do the production. This should work out perfectly. And, if by chance they don't like it, tough. After all, we had the wherewithal to buy them, rather than the other way around, so that must put us in the driver's seat." Production and financial projections are based on historical data. Payback in 4 years still looks good. The deal goes through, and the guys from Company A begin to implement their production plan.

And then the problems begin. The B side of Company A+B takes longer to get up to speed on the new products. All they want to do is test, test, test. Operations meetings begin to heat up. The B production line manager left to take a job with another competitor, so A puts one of its guys in his place to show the people from B the right way to do things. Production at B starts to back up, and people resist working overtime to catch up. The A marketing guys who saw the new product opportunity are getting nervous because they can't deliver as promised.

Meanwhile, Company C has sensed the demand for the new product and has jumped on the bandwagon. Oddly enough, the best people from B are going to work for C to make the same thing A wanted to make. A has to raise salaries to attract new people to work at B, which is raising hell with the production people back at A. The downward spiral continues, and the payback period extends well beyond the projected 4 years. The cost to refinance the deal is exorbitant. Shareholders are beginning to put pressure on the board and the officers, complaining that the 1 + 1 = 3 projections for the deal have turned out to be 1 + 1 = 0.8. Pressure mounts to sell B. A finally closes a deal to sell B to C for about half the price that it paid for B in the first place. "Oh, well, good riddance," the people at A think. "Now we can get back to being innovative."

I don't suggest that QUOCA is the silver bullet that will save all deals from the A + B debacle. But let's revisit the scenario equipped with a report that, among other things, identified the fact that A is much stronger in the Adaptability trait than B is. The cultural characteristics that really stood out were B's low scores in Creating Change and Organizational Learning. Deeper analysis indicated that B was particularly weak in its responses to the following cultural elements:

- Responding well to competitors and other changes in the business environment
- Easily adopting new and improved ways of doing things
- Being encouraged and rewarded for taking risks
- Making certain that the right hand knows what the left hand is doing

It was also noted that B is a little weak on the Agreement characteristic, especially when it comes to building consensus on difficult issues.

Company A considers the implications of B's cultural weaknesses. Rather than using B to make new products, it shifts manufacturing of a product that both companies make from A's lines to B's facility. Company A's people invest a lot of time up front in building trust and communications with B's people, praising them for the quality of B's products and emphasizing the need to maintain that high level for the expanded production. The few differences in the products are discussed, and, taking into consideration its resistance to change and challenge in achieving consensus on issues, B is allowed to take a reasonable amount of time to make certain that the differences don't affect quality.

Meanwhile, the highly adaptive people at A are cranking out another new, highly successful product. Market share, customer satisfaction, and gross revenue projections are very close to those calculated when the deal was envisioned. The combination performs as expected, and the capital is paid back as scheduled. Everybody wins.

Of course, life isn't quite that simple and elegant. But QUOCA clearly provides insight into issues that affect the success of M&A deals and, therefore, has the ability to influence the thinking, decisions, and actions of people who want to make those deals work. To some extent, quantitative culture analyses are like seat belts in a car—they are more than just a good idea, they are a way to prevent tragedies.

## SUMMARY

The culture of an organization is a unique and complicated set of behavioral norms that are created, reinforced, and occasionally modified to provide a sense of security and well-being. In organizations with strong cultures, the commitment to the organization's beliefs and assumptions is greater and the behaviors of the constituents are more consistent. Threats to the organization that developed and reinforced the culture are often perceived as threats to the well-being and security of the individuals within that organization, their families, their colleagues, and their community. Widespread knowledge of the failure of mergers and acquisitions and examples of huge layoffs and plant closings are significant threats to an acquired business's culture, and often to that of the acquiring organization as well.

An in-depth understanding of cultural issues can be a significant resource for acknowledging and addressing the cultural issues that can impede meeting the outcomes that were developed and anticipated for the deal.

The rich information gathered through QUOCA can be extremely useful for the initiating organization in the first phase of the M&A process, when the goals and strategy of the deal are being developed. The initiator's greater self-knowledge with regard to its own culture can be critical to wisely determining the nature of the organization that will best complement the initiator and thereby provide a legitimate basis for the goals and strategies of the deal.

Thorough knowledge of its own culture will also assist the initiator in the second phase of the M&A process, when it seeks to find the optimum merger or acquisition prospect. The due diligence process is intended to gather the information required to make a go/no-go decision about the deal, and therefore it is a natural opportunity to gather information about the prospect's culture. QUOCA can be a quick, cost-effective, and extremely informative tool for avoiding cultural mismatches that impede the success of the deal and for planning the eventual integration with the optimum business.

Financial measures such as return on investment, payback period, and time to market of new products and services have been shown to be affected by the strengths and weaknesses of cultures, and can be factored into the financial modeling for the combination. The objective, quantitative information that QUOCA produces is a valuable resource for determining realistic financial projections as input for calculating the price of the deal during this phase of the M&A process.

As the old saying goes, the rubber hits the road when the deal has been completed and the businesses begin to integrate their operations. The sense of apprehension and loss can be profound in both organizations, and the beliefs and assumptions of the organizations' constituents can be either a barrier or an asset for the success of the combination. QUOCA provides the opportunity to mitigate the problems with organization integration by objectively acknowledging the strengths and weaknesses of the cultures and sharing the best characteristics while overcoming the weaknesses. In so doing, the length and effectiveness of the integration phase can be optimized and the likelihood of achieving the envisioned and desired outcomes of the deal can be enhanced.

# 8

CHAPTER

# THE MISSION TRAIT

Every organization has a main thing—the single most powerful expression of what it hopes to accomplish, its instrument for producing growth and profits. Growth and profits are surely the ultimate aim of any business organization, but they are outcomes of succeeding with the main thing.[1]

THE OBJECTIVES FOR THIS CHAPTER are for the reader to understand the cultural purview and characteristics of the Mission trait, understand the external perspective of the Mission trait and its bearing on the stability of the organization, and know the financial and competitive effects of a culture that is weak in the Mission trait.

## THE MISSION TRAIT—THE NEXUS OF STABILITY AND EXTERNAL FOCUS

The Mission trait reflects the organization's beliefs and assumptions regarding its sense of stability and its focus on the external environment. These cultural perspectives play an important role in the enterprise's ability to focus on its long-term vision while at the same time maintaining the flexibility necessary to be relevant and viable in an ever-changing marketplace. A tight-loose relationship between their destination and the path of their journey enables sailors to arrive at their chosen port in spite of the need to make many tacks along the way. The same tough commitment to purpose and vision while constantly monitoring and adapting to the environment enables the captains and crews of industry to survive and succeed.

113

The Mission trait reflects the enterprise's overall planning and execution process, from individual tasks and responsibilities up through organizational roles to the fundamental purpose of the business and the vision for its long-term future. The Mission trait assesses the degree of employee understanding and buy-in for the organization's efforts to direct its resources toward well-thought-out, defined, and articulated outcomes. It is one thing for the board of directors and top executives to have pondered and decided these things. However, it is the role of the organizational culture to embrace the mission and to make it a deeply seated part of the employees' individual desires, thoughts, and actions.

Leaders must consider many aspects of their organization's governance for the present, near future, and long-term success of the business when crafting the statements that direct the thinking and actions of their people. The tight-loose relationship between where the business wants to go and how it is to get there requires a firm, stable definition of the desired outcomes while granting people autonomy and empowerment so that they can accomplish the outcomes in the most efficient and effective way possible. Experts[2] say that leaders must set the direction through clear, concise statements that describe:

- Why the organization exists (purpose)
- What the organization hopes to accomplish (core goals)
- What the organization stands for (core values)
- The basic approach for achieving the organization's purpose (strategy)
- How the organization should be organized (structure)
- How the organization will be operated (systems and business processes)
- The knowledge, skills, and abilities that are needed to accomplish the work (people and skills)
- How the organization expects its people to interact and behave (culture)

We will review the definitions presented in the Introduction to understand the leadership elements of the Mission trait:

- The vision is a statement of the desired future purpose of the organization. It is time-bound at the discretion of the *visionaries*, usually the board of directors, the CEO, and the president of the enterprise. For technology companies, the envisioned future state may be only a few months away; more traditional businesses may set their envisioned future state 5 or more years away.

- The purpose statement describes what the organization does, for whom, where, why, when, and how. Creating this statement, as well as monitoring it and amending it as needed in order to achieve its intent, is the responsibility of the board of directors, the CEO, and the president. The functions of a clearly defined purpose are to:
  1. Articulate and promulgate the theme of the business
  2. Provide a sense of the organization's direction to employees, customers, suppliers, and other stakeholders
  3. Arouse interest, support, and action
  4. Stimulate creativity
  5. Determine and collect the resources required to achieve the purpose

- If properly stated, communicated, and implemented, the purpose statement results in consistency and unity of effort throughout the organization, from the boardroom to the field offices, cubicles, and shop floors.

- Many organizations complement their purpose statement with a formal expression of their core values. These credos or value statements express the specific assumptions, beliefs, and behaviors that people within the organization are to express and employ on behalf of the organization and its stakeholders. Credos often include statements about fair pricing, equal opportunity, community involvement, and so on. They function as a guiding light for the conduct and decision making of the enterprise's people. Although credos are corporate statements, they are created by representatives from all levels and parts of the organization to reflect its overall thinking and to create buy-in and support for the value statements.

- The mission statement refers to the things the organization must do to accomplish its purpose and eventually fulfill its vision. The mission is the time-based link between what the organization wants to do (its purpose) and how the overall group, the hierarchy, and each of the individuals is going to do it via the hierarchy of *goals and objectives*, *strategies*, *tactics*, *jobs*, *duties*, *tasks*, and *assignments*. The mission statement and its accomplishment are the responsibility of the executive management team.

- *Goals and objectives* are prescriptive outcomes accomplished in an appropriate sequence to accomplish the organization's mission and fulfill its purpose. Ideally, goals and objectives are SMART—that is, they are:

Simple, in terms that allow for universal understanding

Measurable, so that achievement and progress toward achievement can be objectively monitored and operational adjustments can be made

Achievable, to build confidence, provide closure, and avoid frustration

Responsibility for achievement is clearly stated and understood

Time-based for accountability, sequencing, and prioritization

- Goals are the responsibility of organization leaders such as division and department heads, with input and coordination from line and staff peers and approval by executive management.

- Strategies are the overarching, broadly descriptive plans and methods for meeting goals and objectives. Strategies are the responsibility of division and department heads, with considerable input from direct subordinates such as line managers and those responsible for organization resources such as manpower, systems, supplies, and budget.

- Strategies are supported and accomplished through *tactics*, which are usually developed and implemented by managers, supervisors, foremen, and group leaders. Like goals and objectives, tactics must be SMART. Tactics are the marching orders for the organization's teams and individual contributors.

- Teams, work groups, task forces, and individuals contribute to the organization's desired outcomes by performing assigned or self-determined *jobs*, *duties*, *tasks*, and *assignments*. These are the day-to-day activities and efforts by people that, in sum, implement the tactics and strategies, achieve the goals and objectives, and fulfill the purpose of the organization. Just as innumerable grains of sand make a beach, the loftiest outcomes of organizations are the composite of routine individual efforts.

## THE CULTURAL CHARACTERISTICS IN THE MISSION TRAIT

The mission culture is characterized by emphasis on a clear vision of the organizations' purpose and on the achievement of goals, such as sales growth, profitability or market share to help achieve the purpose.[3]

High-performing organizations understand the importance of a connection between even the most menial task and the fulfillment of the enterprise's purpose. Every activity in the continuum from jobs, duties, tasks, and assignments to the vision of the enterprise's desired future state is either a step forward or a step backward on the path. High-performing organizations know that activities that are *not* explicitly stated in the planning and execution statements are distractions and, in order to optimize efficiency and effectiveness as well as to improve the odds on the organization's success, *should not be done*. When the organization stays focused on what should be done and rejects distractions, people are given a clear environment in which to operate and to achieve desired organizational outcomes.

The chances for success and survival go way up when resources, particularly human resources in a high-performing culture, are optimized for a specific purpose and pointed in a unified direction. To that end, the Mission trait assesses the culture of an enterprise with regard to three important and illustrative characteristics: Vision, Strategic Direction and Intent, and Goals and Objectives.

### Vision

"In dreams begins responsibility," observed the great Irish poet William Butler Yeats, for he understood that no lasting achievement is possible without vision and no dream can become real without action and responsibility.[4]

The Vision characteristic measures people's beliefs and assumptions about the long-term orientation of the organization. Like the mason laying bricks, people can be so deadened by the monotony of their day-to-day tasks that they lose sight of their contribution to the greater good of the overall organization. When this happens, it is easy to become unfocused, become tolerant of mistakes and problems, and create havoc in downstream activities and outcomes. Soon quality problems pop up, usually at the worst time and place, and focus is shifted from the long-run view of prosperity to short-term fix-its. The elusive vision dangles in front of us like the carrot in front of the horse and in subtle ways encourages us to continue putting one foot in front of the other. Without the vision of a better future, each step becomes drudgery and has no relationship to the rewards for the journey's successful progress.

I once worked for a man who had no vision beyond his daily things-to-do list. Most days were spent dealing with the ripple effects of yesterday's stopgap measures, patch-ups, and jury rigs. Since there was no sense of overall direction, every activity was accomplished for its own sake, performed to its own standard, and done with its own cloistered priority. Soon the thrill of task victories became an end in itself, and the sum of the fixes never resulted in a functional whole. If there had ever been a vision of a desired future state, it had long since been forgotten. Every day was a unique experience that in the aggregate accomplished nothing of significance. As someone who is very goal-oriented, I couldn't get out of there fast enough.

> Vision deals with future uncertainty. It addresses how an organization can survive and grow, given the ability of its employees to think incisively about the future and to harness resources accordingly.[5]

Virtually every successful person begins with a vision of what her or his personal concept of success looks like. Stephen Covey[6] says that we must create things twice: First in our minds and then in reality.  The creation of the ethereal success provides the motivation and drive to create the real success. People in high-performing organizations share a common vision of their future success, rally their contributing efforts to make the vision become reality, and feel rewarded because their efforts are contributing to a long-term, well-planned, desirable outcome.

As a friend described a business he worked with that didn't have a vision for its future, "They were a lot of nice people going nowhere together." Organizations without vision are myopic and stumble over everything that isn't in their immediate field of focus. Without vision, bricks are laid randomly, with no concept of whether the end result will be a cathedral or an outhouse. The sad fact is that an outhouse can be any wall you can briefly hide behind, and that's what usually happens when there is no vision to direct progress. Organizations with little vision will eventually face loss of market share, lower return ratios, inferior quality, and diminished employee satisfaction.

## Strategic Direction and Intent

> Strategy is one's approach to achieving a sense of mission. It's asking: "Now that we know our core goals, how are we going to accomplish them?" Strategy is sometimes defined as the way a company plans to create unique value.[7]

High-performing organizations have a strong sense of where they are going and how they are going to get there. Often they strive to make a mark on their business sector by being known as the innovative market leader. People in such organizations know and accept their role in achieving individual, group, organization, and enterprise success through clear and unambiguous understanding of the strategic direction of the organization and the underlying thinking that developed the strategies. Organization leaders carry out the important tasks of understanding and embracing the enterprise's strategies and communicating those strategies through their words, attitudes, and deeds.

> An organization of leaders, all sharing the same vision and purpose, can be a powerful force.[8]

If the firm wants to be regarded as the leading force in its market, having a strong strategic direction is not enough. It is equally important to make certain that the firm's thinking is appropriate for its market sector and other external environmental dynamics. Organizations that are fortunate enough to have strengths in the Mission and Adaptability traits are able to integrate external dynamics into their defined purpose and the execution of the activities needed to achieve their goals and objectives.

### Goals and Objectives

> If you aim for nothing, that's just about what you'll get. If you aim for a little, you get a little. If you aim for a lot, work hard, and live up to your potential, you achieve a lot. Success, then, is related to setting job objectives. Without objectives there is no success.[9]

A clear set of goals and objectives can be linked to the mission, vision, and strategy and provide everyone with clear direction for his or her work. The noun *objective* means "something toward which effort is directed"[10] and has as its origin the adjective of the same spelling, which means "expressing or involving the use of facts without distortion by personal feelings or prejudices." High-performing organizations use SMART goals and clear objectives as desired outcomes against which performance is measured.

> It is the job of the boss to assure that the objectives are agreed upon and committed to, [in order to] fulfill the requirements of the organization.[11]

Goals and objectives provide the context for the old saying, "Leaders do the right things, managers do things right." Leaders' visions and strategy become accountable actions that lead to desired results through the managers' and supervisors' articulation, monitoring, and adaptation of goals for their people. In high-performing organizations, individuals and their bosses collaborate to ensure mutual understanding of goals, to identify shortfalls in achieving those goals, and to eliminate the root causes of barriers to goal achievement. People understand that they may be building "God's waiting room," as the story goes, but they know that each and every brick must be properly laid if the edifice is to be completed and endure.

Organizations suffer in many ways when they lack goals and objectives or when they have a culture that disregards them. Goals and objectives describe what success looks like and provide a common language for communicating desired outcomes. When these outcomes do not result, goals and objectives provide the benchmark for objectively discussing failures and problems and serve as a reference point for determining whether corrective actions are effective. Organizations that lack well-understood and respected goals and objectives frequently suffer from scheduling and quality problems, low employee satisfaction, and reduced profitability.

## OPERATIONAL AND FINANCIAL IMPLICATIONS OF ORGANIZATIONS WITH A STRONG MISSION TRAIT

The Mission trait defines the direction for the enterprise while allowing it to adapt the path in response to the vagaries of the environment. The organization's vision and purpose provide a clear concept of what long-term success looks like. The credo establishes the code of conduct that will fortify the people in times of doubt and difficulty. Strategic Direction and Intent provide the overarching pathway and guidance to enable people to achieve the desired outcomes. Goals and Objectives are steps and measures of short-term progress toward the long-range vision and purpose of the enterprise. Cultures in which people have clearly defined, shared, and well-understood missions have demonstrated higher performance in terms of profitability, return on investment, sales/revenue growth, market share, perceived quality, and employee satisfaction.

Organizations that enjoy cultural strength on both the Mission and Consistency traits have greater stability and enjoy higher return on assets, return on investment, and return on sales ratios than organizations that are weaker on these two traits. Organizations that have strengths in both Mission and Adaptability focus on the external environment and enjoy greater sales growth and market share as well as higher profitability than culturally weaker groups.

## MISSION TRAIT IMPLICATIONS FOR MERGERS AND ACQUISITIONS

Strength or weakness in Mission can be a major factor in the success of an M&A deal. Combining two enterprises with strong Mission traits should result in agreement on the importance of having a vision, developing goal-oriented strategies, and using objectives as tools for discipline and feedback. However, commitment to the precombination mission and the style for accomplishing desired outcomes may be an obstacle to success. The integration process should clearly state and develop unilateral support for the integrated organization's definitions of vision, mission, and values. There is a greater probability of a solid return on investment and a relatively short payback period in a combination of two strong Mission cultures.

Conversely, combinations involving two organizations that are weak on the Mission traits are likely to have an extended payback period and a disappointing return on investment. However, Quantitative Organizational Culture Analyses can be a powerful tool for illustrating that a new approach is needed in order to develop a unified vision, purpose, and credo with clear strategies, goals, and objectives. The integration team can use the QUOCA results to develop support for unified Mission-related activities and, at the same time, provide meaningful opportunities for communications and relationship development between the combining groups.

# 9

# VISION

Purpose (and vision) statements answer the question, "What are we doing here," at least for now, with respect to the business we are in. What are we up to here? What's the plan? What's in it for "them," the customers, and what's in it for "us," the corporate employees? Where do I fit into the plan? There's an underlying concern in these queries—survival. People want to know not only what top management's explanation of what they're doing, they want to judge for themselves what management's chances are of succeeding at what they're doing."[1]

THE OBJECTIVES FOR THIS CHAPTER are for the reader to be able to identify the key characteristics and strategic advantages of organizations with a well-stated and embraced vision; to develop an understanding of why vision is a critical element for the organization's survival and long-term success; to recognize the financial and competitive business measures that are affected by an organization's strength or weakness in stating and living its vision; to be able to identify the culture characteristics that enable an organization to achieve its vision or retard it from doing so; and to understand how quantitative organizational culture assessments can improve the performance of combinations involving organizations with weak Vision characteristics.

## THE VIRTUES OF VISION

To unite strategy with culture, you first need to develop a vision of the firm's future and then in order to implement strategy for making that vision a reality, you need to nurture a corporate culture that is motivated by and dedicated to the vision.[2]

The company's long-term desires and its culture are inseparable. Without a vision, there is no unifying force for the people. They are a mob rather than a group. The dream of improved security and prosperity unites people for a common cause and promotes cooperation and collaboration. Spirits are buoyed as each step forward brings the vision closer to reality. Each setback inspires greater resolve to make the vision real. The vision exercises tremendous power by capturing the imagination, intellect, and passion of the organization's people.

Imagine that every employee on the lowest tier of the typical organization chart is holding a string that connects him or her to a foreman, who is connected by the multistring twine to her or his supervisor, who is connected by a multitwine line to her or his manager, who is connected by a multiline rope to his or her vice–president, who is connected by her or his hawser to the president, who is directly connected to the board of directors. The direction of force is determined by the board and the president and is communicated through the various connections to each employee. The pulling force comes from the shared desire of everyone in the organization to accomplish its mission and purpose. Every string that isn't being pulled or that is being pulled in the wrong direction reduces the force that is applied in the desired direction. If the hawser end isn't firmly connected with unfrazzled fibers to something that is central to the organization, the pulling power is wasted and the rewards for the effort fall off, as does the effort itself. This metaphor expresses the relationship between the mission and the energy in an organization. The link from the highest level in the organization to the lowest has to be firm if the energy is to translate into action. A shared vision, purpose, and set of beliefs are a powerful force in high-performing organizations.

> As vision moves along the strategy/operations continuum and down through the organization, it takes broad and effective participation to make it come to life. Through it all, vision must be kept clear, specific and simple—simple enough to put into the heads, hearts and hands of the people who make an organization what it is and what it will become.[3]

High-performing organizations have seriously thought about and defined their ideal future, and they candidly share these thoughts with their customers, suppliers, investors, directors, employees, and communities. It is something they are excited about, and they need the support and participation of their stakeholders to make their dream come true. For example, the Gillette vision statement uses less than 50 words to state what it wants to do, how it is going to do it, and the mindset that will get it there:

> The Gillette Company's Vision is to build Total Brand Value by innovating to deliver consumer value and customer leadership faster, better and more completely than our competition. This Vision is supported by two fundamental principles that provide the foundation for all of our activities: Organizational Excellence and Core Values.[4]

Many vision statements are quite succinct but provide accompanying text to elaborate on the statement for stakeholders and other interested parties; an example is the Wells Fargo, Inc., statement:

### The Wells Fargo Vision Statement and Explanation

Every journey has a destination. To get to that destination, you need a vision. Ours is an ambitious one. We want to satisfy all of our customers' financial needs and help them succeed financially, be the premier provider of financial services in every one of our markets, and be known as one of America's great companies. We want to be number one, second to none.

As *team members*, this journey can bring us the satisfaction of being part of one of America's most successful and admired companies. This will result in a higher stock price that will benefit all our team members because virtually all of us own stock and stock options in our company. For our *customers*, who entrust us with more of their business—whether it be retail or commercial—it will mean a financial partnership, sound and professional financial advice, a broader array of products and services, access to any financial channel they choose, more convenience—when, where and how they want to be served, and a better deal and more value for giving us more of their business.

For our *communities*, it means the presence of a leading employer, an active community partner, committed to helping build and sustain a vibrant, prosperous economy in every market in which we do business.

For our *stockholders*, it will mean outstanding financial performance that will produce returns and earnings per share growth among the best for any company, in any industry.[5]

Note that the both the Wells Fargo vision and the elaborative statements address the specific, long-term interests of the company's important stakeholders: employees, who are referred to as "team members";
customers, who are regarded as partners; the communities they serve
and live in; and the stockholders who have trusted the company with
their investments. Each constituent's needs are acknowledged and incorporated in the organization's vision. How would you feel being a stakeholder in Wells Fargo versus being a stakeholder in a company with no
expressed view of its future and no regard for your importance as a
stakeholder in its evolution? The feeling of involvement is a powerful
force. Being part of the dream inspires loyalty, commitment, and action
to transform the vision into reality. The future concept for an organization with no vision statement is tacit acceptance of the status quo in per-
petuity. The absence of a vision statement means that there is
nothing—no dream, no inspiration, no rallying force. And this probably
results in a lower performance than that of competitors who see and are
pursuing a desired future.

> A vision is a mental image of a possible and desirable future state
> of the organization. It expresses the leader's ambitions for the
> organization. The best visions are both ideal and unique. If a vision
> conveys an ideal, it communicates a standard of excellence and a
> clear choice of positive values. If the vision is also unique it com-
> municates and inspires pride in being different from other organi-
> zations. The choice of language is important; the words should
> imply a combination of realism and optimism, an action orienta-
> tion, and resolution and confidence that the vision will be attained.[6]

## THE PRACTICALITIES OF PURPOSE

> Purpose . . . is an organizational glue that binds people together.
> They share a common purpose, with an ensuing set of objectives
> that provide a common base for understanding each other's
> actions.[7]

While the vision statement articulates the desired future for the organization, the purpose statement describes what the organization currently
does, for whom, where, why, when, and how. This is your response to the
cocktail party question, "What does your business do?'

In addition to providing a snappy answer in social circumstances,
the purpose statement has significant power to influence the direction

and effectiveness of the enterprise. If properly developed and fashioned, the purpose statement succinctly:

1. Articulates and promulgates the theme of the business
2. Provides a sense of the organization's direction to employees, customers, suppliers, and other stakeholders
3. Rouses interest, support, and action
4. Stimulates creativity
5. Specifies the resources required to achieve the purpose

The purpose statement develops consistency and unity of effort throughout the organization, from the boardroom to the field offices, cubicles, and shop floors. Many organizations don't have a purpose statement per se, but somewhere in the opening paragraph of company promotional literature, the annual report, or the home page of the web site you can almost always find a self-description of what the enterprise does, for whom, and so on. The following examples come from the web pages of companies that Jim Collins identifies as being "great" in his book, *Good to Great*.[8]

> Pitney Bowes manages change and positions customers for both tactical and long-term success with innovative, cost-effective, end-to-end messaging solutions.[9]

> Nucor is the largest recycler in the United States. Nucor and affiliates are manufacturers of steel products, with operating facilities in ten states. Products produced are: carbon and alloy steel—in bars, beams, sheet, and plate; steel joists and joist girders; steel deck; cold finished steel; steel fasteners; metal building systems; and light gauge steel framing.[10]

> The Kroger Company spans many states with store formats that include *grocery and multi-department stores, convenience stores* and mall jewelry stores. We operate under nearly two dozen banners, all of which share the same belief in building strong local ties and brand loyalty with our customers.[11]

> The Gillette Company is a globally focused consumer products marketer that seeks competitive advantage in quality, value-added personal care and personal use products. We are committed to building shareholder value through sustained profitable growth.[12]

> Building leadership and combining strengths in the areas of *pharmaceuticals, nutritionals, hospital products* and *diagnostics* has enabled Abbott to provide total, integrated solutions across the health care spectrum for some of the world's most prevalent medical conditions, including AIDS, cancer and diabetes. We focus on advancing medical science and the practice of health care with expertise in the therapeutic areas of *diabetes, pain management, respiratory infections, HIV/AIDS, men* and *women's health, pediatrics* and *animal health*.[13]

These concise statements leave no doubt about what the organization does and serve as a guiding force and an expectation for stakeholders of all kinds—customers, prospective and current investors, employees, suppliers, community members, and so on.

## ORGANIZATIONAL CONSCIENCE: CREDOS AND VALUE STATEMENTS

> Ethics is a code of moral principles and values that governs the behaviors of a person or group with respect to what is right or wrong. Ethical values set standards as to what is good or bad in conduct and decision making.[14]

Many high-performing organizations overtly express their philosophy of operation as a value statement, credo, or creed. The words are intended to convey the organizational conscience in such a way that investors and customers have faith in the organization's integrity and that insiders, including directors, officers, and employees, have ethical standards and guidelines for their efforts.

A great deal more will be said on this subject in the discussion of the Consistency trait and its Core Values characteristic. For now, it is important to understand the connection between the vision and purpose of the enterprise and the code of conduct that guides the decisions and actions of the people who work to accomplish those outcomes.

Every culture has a set of articulated and unarticulated standards for acceptable and unacceptable attitudes, values, opinions, and behaviors. Some companies, such as Johnson & Johnson and Walgreens, openly share their philosophy with everyone and often require employees to agree to uphold those principles in both their professional and personal lives as a condition of employment. High-performing organizations regard their values as an important element of how they envision their current operations and as a resource to enable them to create their desired future. Their vision is more than a desired outcome—it is a desired state of being as well. Adherence to the ethical code is an important part of the organization's self-image, self-management, and alignment. Violations of the tenets are not tolerated and often lead to punishment and alienation on the first offense and dismissal for repeat offenses. Recall that the organization's culture functions to provide for the survival and prosperity of the constituents. Threats to the well-being of those constituents are serious offenses, and in a strong culture even dalliances by innocent newcomers will be corrected. Thus, it can easily be understood how the power of the vision combined with personal and organizational values can drive the business to higher rewards than those achieved by organizations with similar resources but unspoken values and dreams.

## THE LEADER'S ROLE IN THE ORGANIZATION'S VISION

A vision allows top management to communicate leadership and drive the organization. In a sense, vision is the starting point for everything that an organization does and how it should do it.[15]

To reiterate part of an old saw, "Leaders do the right thing." The definition of the right thing on a macroscopic scale is not left to chance in high-performing organizations. In fact, it is a common practice today to have employees sign employment contracts and acknowledge that they have read, have understood, and will comply with company policies and statements. In some cases these affirmations are intended to protect the organization from sabotage, espionage, malingering, nonperformance, and ethical misconduct. The higher intent is to explicitly specify the direction in which the organization is headed, its purpose and priorities, and the manner in which it intends to operate.

A vision has two vital functions, and they're more important today than ever before. One is to serve as a source of inspiration. The other is to guide decision making, aligning all the organization's parts so that they work together for a desirable goal.[16]

The mission of the enterprise as communicated by its leaders through the vision, purpose, and values Statements functions as the "true north" for the organization's thinking, planning, decision making, reaction to crises, and routine conduct. Leadership is rewarded by generally higher financial ratios and results such as greater return on assets, superior profitability, greater market share, and higher employee satisfaction.

## THE EMPLOYEE'S ROLE IN THE ORGANIZATION'S VISION

> A truly integrated and permeating vision energizes people and can resurrect disgruntled, routinized, burned-out employees. It provides a true challenge and purpose. It makes each person feel that he or she can make a difference in the world. It becomes a rallying cry for a just cause—their cause.[17]

Statements about how the organization envisions its future, describes its purpose, and articulates its beliefs direct the employees' efforts and motivation toward common outcomes. The statements prescribe what to do and what not to do. Most businesses are careful to state *what* they want without being prescriptive about *how* they expect it to be done. The *how* is the driving force for relentless challenges to the status quo in organizations that are dedicated to continuous improvement. When the destination is clearly stated, well understood, and broadly accepted, people in learning organizations constantly strive for better, faster, higher-quality, more efficient, and more effective ways to get there. The reward for sharing the vision, purpose, and credo with employees is manifold—higher financial rewards, quality, and employee satisfaction.

## RELATED CULTURAL CHARACTERISTICS

Strength on both the Vision and Core Values characteristics is a robust foundation that enables the enterprise to effectively create its defined future through a strong sense of right and wrong. Avoiding problems by removing uncertainties of direction and prescribing appropriate behavior allows the enterprise to walk a straighter path to its desired outcomes. Having fewer value and directional disagreements improves efficiency, increases leadership effectiveness, and elevates employee satisfaction. Time to market for new products is reduced when both values and vision are strong, thereby accelerating the pace at which the high-performing organization can create its desired future.

Organizations that have high results on both Capability Development and Vision are constantly updating their knowledge pool to keep their people on the cutting edge of technical and intellectual developments related to their field of endeavor. High-performing organizations perceive their people's knowledge, skills, and abilities to be a significant competitive advantage and invest the time, money, effort, and availability of their people for the future benefit of being ready for market dynamics and environmental transitions. Once again, such competitive factors as shorter time to market for new products and higher employee satisfaction improve the organizational and financial performance of the enterprise.

Cultural strength on both Vision and Customer Focus ensures that the business is basing its desired future on well-established relationships with clients and insightful anticipation of market trends. The result is the avoidance of the New Coke phenomenon, where the envisioned success is built upon a very shaky understanding of customer needs, desires, and trends. Avoiding bad market decisions is the insufficiently recognized reward for enterprises that include market realities in the formation of their vision.

> This and this alone is the key to the winner's success. They get all their employees in every department or function closely involved in the effort to provide superior customer satisfaction. It's as simple—and as complex—as that. Everything else they do—being obsessive about knowing the customer, setting extremely high standards, designing products that maximize customer satisfaction—is aimed at achieving this one overriding goal.[18]

## FINANCIAL IMPLICATIONS OF THE VISION CHARACTERISTIC

Businesses that are strong on their Vision characteristic often have superior performance as measured by profitability/ROA, sales/revenue growth, market share, quality, and employee satisfaction. Conversely, organizations that are weaker in the behaviors and assumptions that make up their culture's Vision characteristic underperform their stronger counterparts on these measures. The ripple effects of a weak vision are also detrimental to the organization and include:

- *Reduced profitability.* Leads to lower cash on hand to compensate stakeholders in the form of dividends, bonuses, and salary increases; lower earnings per share, which decrease the stock price and the organization's ability to borrow money at optimum rates; reduced revenues and borrowing ability, which impede the investment in capital improvements that maintain or increase the company's competitive position in the marketplace. Continued low revenues and a high cost of capital can lead to cutbacks in spending for such things as maintenance, marketing, and training, which eventually further affect profitability through unexpected breakdowns, lower market share, and lower employee effectiveness.

- *Poorer quality.* Leads to reduced sales, lower revenue, reduced market share, higher inventory costs, and higher production costs for scrap and rework.

- *Lower employee satisfaction.* Leads to higher rates of injury, absenteeism, and grievances; higher turnover; and reduced productivity, efficiency, and effectiveness.

- *Lower market share.* Leads to lower revenues and profits, with the associated direct and indirect effects; lower profit margins and less ability to negotiate prices with customers; higher physical inventory and inventory costs; lower production efficiencies from underutilized resources; and reduced buying power/loss of volume discounts.

- *Lower sales/revenue growth.* Leads to decrease in stock price and company valuation; lower availability and higher cost of capital; and reduced profitability, along with its associated direct and indirect effects.

## THE IMPACTS OF THE VISION CHARACTERISTIC ON MERGERS AND ACQUISITIONS

### Strong Acquirer, Strong Acquired

When two companies that combine both have a strong Vision characteristic, the resulting organization will be blessed with awareness of a desired future and what needs to be done to achieve that vision and so is likely to perform well. One caveat, however: The vision of the combined organization is likely to be different from the visions of the organizations involved in the merger or acquisition. The integration team must understand that while the infrastructure and the willingness to strive toward a vision are in place, successful integration will require the crafting, distribution, and explanation of the new vision of the combined organization and the development of support for that new vision.

### Strong Acquirer, Weak Acquired

An organization that has enjoyed the benefits of a culture with a clear understanding of where the organization wants to go will be unaccustomed to dealing with an organization without a strong sense of vision. The challenge will be to overcome the direct and ripple effects that weak cultures exhibit. Inferior performance as measured by profitability/ROA, sales/revenue growth, market share, quality, and employee satisfaction should be expected and factored into the following combination steps:

- Selection as a viable business partner
- The valuation of the deal, which will need to be based on lower, slower performance
- The length and difficulty of integrating the operations of the organizations

### Weak Acquirer, Strong Acquired

Real problems can occur during the integration step when an acquired organization has greater strength than its acquirer on such an important cultural characteristic as its sense of vision for the future. Since vision is its driving and coordinating force, the acquired business will look to its new leaders for direction. If no direction is given, the organization has two choices: to follow its old vision or to flounder. The objectives of the deal are not likely to be met if the acquired organization is moving in the wrong direction, and they clearly won't be achieved if the business becomes frozen in place by its lack of guidance.

Hopefully, the acquirer has developed a vision for the deal as part of the strategy formation step in the combination process. The integration team should formalize this thinking into a clear, concise vision statement that should be presented, explained, and supported throughout the integration process.

In fact, the initiating company has an opportunity to learn from its new partner by using the vision statement to direct and mobilize its own culture to its desired future state.

### Weak Acquirer, Weak Acquired

The marriage of two organizations that are operating with weak vision characteristics is not as disastrous as shared weakness in other characteristics such as Coordination and Integration or Creating Change. However, it should be understood that neither organization is likely to be functioning to its full capability because of its failure to direct and mobilize its people.

The integration event is a great opportunity to get both halves of the combined business to share a vision for the deal. Higher revenues, market share, quality, employee satisfaction, and revenue growth should result from the investment of time and effort to align people toward the long-range vision for the deal.

## SUMMARY

Vision deals with future uncertainty. It addresses how an organization can survive and grow, given the ability of its employees to think incisively about the future and to harness resources accordingly.[19]

Vision may not be a useful arrow in the quiver to win today's business battles, but it certainly provides a great reason to fight today's battles as hard as possible. Maintaining the status quo is a lousy reward for the risk of battle. Most of us don't fight for the opportunity to have another day of fighting—we fight with the vision of peace and prosperity as the ultimate end. A company without a compelling vision of something great doesn't attract or keep the interest of the best and brightest people. High-performing organizations aim high and stimulate hope, creativity, and empowerment in the people who share the vision.

# 10

# STRATEGIC DIRECTION AND INTENT

Strategic thinking and culture building work in tandem. Actions based on strategic thinking must effectively satisfy customer needs, gain a sustainable advantage over competitors and capitalize on company strengths. Actions aimed at corporate culture building instill a collective commitment to a common purpose, foster distinctive competence among employees to deliver superior performance, and establish a consistency that helps attract, keep and develop leaders at all levels.[1]

THE OBJECTIVES FOR THIS CHAPTER are for the reader to be able to define organizational strategic direction and intent and to understand the role of this cultural characteristic in the financial and competitive performance of the organization; to develop an understanding of leaders' and employees' responsibilities in pursuing the enterprise's strategic direction and intent; to define objective business measures that are affected by an organization's strength or weakness in stating and striving for its strategic direction and intent; and to understand how quantitative organizational culture assessments can improve the performance of combinations involving organizations with weak Strategic Direction and Intent and Goals and Objectives characteristics.

## STRATEGY AND ORGANIZATIONAL CULTURE

Some hard-core, by-the-numbers business minds might wonder about the connection between strategy, which is the realm of MBAs, CEOs, and BODs (and other three-letter acronyms related to black-and-white financial performance) and the soft, mushy organizational culture stuff of HR and OD (only two letters; I wonder if there is a message here?). Actually, what the organization wants to achieve (strategic intent) and "how we do things around here" (the organization's culture) are two peas in the same pod. As Hickman and Silva state:

> Strategy and culture each contribute to the success of any organization. . . . In a few exceptional cases, a strong culture has overcome a stupid strategy, or a smart strategy has prevailed despite a weak culture, but don't count on such exceptions in our increasingly competitive and sophisticated business world.[2]

## STRATEGIC DIRECTION AND INTENT—THE MEANS TO MAKE THE ENTERPRISE'S VISION A REALITY

> A strategic intent is the core of a vision. It is, in essence, the firm's "ambition in life," a central motive designed not only to capture the imagination of the entire organization, but also to extend boundaries within the realm of the possible. Stretch is the sine qua non of strategic intent.[3]

The purpose of an organization is fulfilled through actions. Strategic Direction and Intent channels actions toward the interests and needs of the end users, who reward the enterprise through revenues. As Hickman and Silva say in *Creating Excellence*, "Locating, attracting, and holding customers is the purpose of strategic thinking. Without such a concrete goal, strategic thinking degenerates into an ivory tower experience."[4] So a business's strategic direction and intent is the thinking behind how the enterprise is going to add value for its customers, generate income, and reward its employees, investors, and other stakeholders for their contribution to fulfilling the organization's purpose.

> An organization's strategy is like an architectural blue print: a clearly drawn design that shows what must be done to achieve success.[5]

The high-performing organization focuses its attention on the customers and their needs. It efficiently and effectively assembles and deploys only the resources, talent, processes, and systems that are needed to fulfill the customer's needs—anything extra had better be related to market research or R&D. Any other activity is a distraction from the customers' and the company's best interest. Defining and communicating strategy is a powerful tool for aligning the efforts of the organization toward very clear outcomes.

By developing and executing a customer-driven strategy, you will:

- "Mistake proof" your decision-making process
- Increase your odds for achieving success
- Achieve operational excellence faster
- Obtain more benefits—in quality, flexibility, delivery, cost— along the way[6]

## TYPES OF STRATEGIES

A strategy is a plan for interacting with the competitive environment to achieve organizational goals.[7]

Strategic Direction and Intent is paradoxical in that there are only three basic competitive strategies, but there are an unlimited number of variations on how these strategies can be implemented. The basic strategic alternatives are

- *Low-cost leadership*, in which the company tries to increase market share by emphasizing low cost compared to its competitors
- *Differentiation*, in which the business attempts to distinguish its products and services from others within the industry
- *Focus*, in which the organization concentrates on a specific geographic or demographic marketplace, then deploys *low-cost leadership* or *differentiation* within that chosen market

Once the overall strategy has been established, it must be translated into overarching statements that clearly articulate the intent of the organization to all stakeholders. For example, the following *Good to Great*[8] companies clearly state their strategies on their web pages. The type of strategy is noted in parenthesis.

*Gillette (differentiation).* Transforming innovative ideas into useful daily products sold at a fair price engenders another fundamental Gillette strength—strong and enduring consumer brand loyalty around the world.[9]

*Fannie Mae (low-cost).* Our public mission, and our defining goal, is to help more families achieve the American Dream of homeownership. We do that by providing financial products and services that make it possible for low-, moderate-, and middle-income families to buy homes of their own.[10]

*Kimberly-Clark (differentiation).* We are motivated to continually deliver superior products and exceed the expectations of our shareholders, our customers and ourselves.[11]

*Walgreens' (focus).* To provide consumers with basic goods and services at fair prices.[12]

An expert[13] on business performance once said, "Strategy is sometimes defined as the way a company plans to create unique value." Once the strategy has been established, the enterprise develops Goals and Objectives (see Chapter 11) to translate the desired overarching outcomes into specific performance requirements, responsibilities, datelines, and so on that add unique value to the organization and its stakeholders, particularly its clients. To recall an earlier simile, strategies are the ropes that eventually separate into the strings that tie each individual and his or her activities to the organization's mission, purpose, and vision for the future. In high-performing organizations, virtually everyone can provide a similar, accurate answer to the question, "So what are you doing and why are you doing it?" When the answer is a paraphrase of the organization's unique strategic direction and intent, you can be certain that people have internalized their role in the organization and that they are very likely to be making both a personal and a collective contribution to the success of the enterprise through their focused work.

## THE INDIVIDUAL'S ROLE IN STRATEGIC DIRECTION AND INTENT

Strategy must drive action.[14]

The primary responsibility that any individual has within an organization is to continuously direct her or his creativity, thoughts, actions, and attention toward the strategic intent of the enterprise. Everything else is a distraction, with subtle but significant opportunity costs that impede the success of the intended strategies.

> Strategic leadership gives purpose and meaning to organizations. And in the modern business environment, in which people throughout the organization should think strategically and behave like competent business people, strategic leadership needs to be an activity performed by people throughout the organization, not just by a few people at the top.[15]

When the thinking behind the enterprise's strategy is shared with and understood by the organization's people, those people become active participants in the strategic thinking and implementation processes. High-performing organizations that are committed to continuous improvement empower their employees to be active in shaping their tasks to implement the company's strategies more effectively. After all, who better knows the obstacles to success than the person performing the task?

High-performing organizations know that dealing with reality is critical to success. Greatness is the desired outcome of strategic intent, and, as Collins[16] says, winners recognize that "Good is the enemy of great." When individual contributors, teams, groups, departments, and divisions are experiencing challenges in implementing the organization's strategy, their cultures acknowledge the problem and rally to resolve it.

## THE LEADERS' ROLE IN STRATEGIC DIRECTION AND INTENT

> Once adopted, the strategic intent becomes the rallying point for leadership. It is up to the leadership team to align themselves with the corporate ambition and become the role models of it.[17]

The isolated and biased thinking of top-down management handicaps cultures that do not engage their people in actively understanding and deploying the enterprise's strategic intent. In weak cultures, individual contributors may become barriers to organizational success because their perspective is limited to their own tasks and purview. Since the culture shapes the behaviors of all organizational constituents, the leader's role in communicating the strategic intent of the organization is critical to aligning his or her subordinates' efforts and behaviors toward the enterprise's strategies.

As with any plan, formulating the appropriate strategy is not enough. Strategic managers also must ensure that the new strategies are implemented effectively and efficiently.[18]

Implementation of strategy is critically dependent upon the managers' understanding and embracing the organization's intent, mirroring the behaviors that contribute to the achievement of the strategy, and translating the desired outcomes into team and individual actions and behaviors. By "doing things right" themselves, managers influence the culture's definition of "right," how to do "right," and the consequences of "doing right." The cultural heroes and much of the organization's mythology reflect the challenges, successes, and rewards in pursuing the organizational strategy. The average employee never sees a customer or observes a customer having a need met by the enterprise. The management team has to provide the information link between customers and employees to make certain that the success or failure of the strategy is understood.

The role of culture, you will recall, is to guide the behaviors and actions that provide security and prosperity for the group members. Like Dumbo's feather, Strategic Direction and Intent encourages employees by providing the faith that the group has a viable concept of how it will bring survival and success to the people within the culture. The creation of an enterprise's strategy is the responsibility of executive leadership, but the success of strategic initiatives is dependent upon the active, knowledgeable, collaborative efforts of each individual within the organization. In high-performing organizations, people understand and embrace the functional linkage between their individual role and the strategies designed to achieve success for all stakeholders, from customers to suppliers—including themselves.

## FINANCIAL IMPLICATIONS OF THE STRATEGIC DIRECTION AND INTENT CHARACTERISTIC

Businesses that are strong on their Strategic Direction and Intent characteristic frequently outperform their weaker counterparts on such measures as profitability/ROA, sales/revenue growth, market share, quality, and employee satisfaction. Conversely, organizations that are weaker on their Strategic Direction and Intent characteristic underperform their stronger counterparts on these same measures. The ripple effects of a weak strategy also manifest themselves as:

- *Reduced profitability.* Leads to lower cash on hand to compensate stakeholders in the form of dividends, bonuses, and salary increases; lower earnings per share, which decrease the stock price and the organization's ability to borrow money at optimum rates; reduced revenues and borrowing ability, which impede the investment in capital improvements that maintain or increase the company's competitive position in the marketplace. Continued low revenues and a high cost of capital can lead to cutbacks in spending for such things as maintenance, marketing, and training, which eventually further affect profitability through unexpected breakdowns, lower market share, and lower employee effectiveness.

- *Poorer quality.* Leads to reduced sales, lower revenue, reduced market share, higher inventory costs, and higher production costs for scrap and rework.
- *Lower employee satisfaction.* Leads to higher rates of injury, absenteeism, and grievances; higher turnover; and reduced productivity, efficiency, and effectiveness.
- *Lower market share.* Leads to lower revenues and profits, with the associated direct and indirect effects; lower profit margins and less ability to negotiate prices with customers; higher physical inventory and inventory costs; lower production efficiencies from underutilized resources; and reduced buying power/loss of volume discounts.
- *Lower sales/revenue growth.* Leads to decrease in stock price and company valuation; lower availability and higher cost of capital; and reduced profitability, along with its associated direct and indirect effects.

## CULTURAL CHARACTERISTICS RELATED TO STRATEGIC DIRECTION AND INTENT

Organizations that have high performance on both their Strategic Direction and Intent and their Customer Focus characteristics have a much greater likelihood of developing strategies based on true client needs. Close working relationships between customers and the enterprise provide insight into evolving needs as well as feedback on the performance of the product or service. The effectiveness of the strategy can be assessed and adjusted by continually monitoring and integrating customer input. Business history is rife with stories of products that were developed in a vacuum and expensively promoted in the face of obvious customer apathy. The Edsel, New Coke, Sony BetaMax, and my client's online interactive service were all developed with good intentions but without either a sound strategy or a regard for customer needs.

The combination of cultural strengths on Strategic Direction and Intent and Customer Focus serves as a system of checks and balances to assure that the enterprise's strategy is valid and that its products or services actually meet or create customer demand.

Strength on both the Agreement and the Strategic Direction and Intent cultural characteristics enables high-performing organizations to develop consensus and support for the organization's strategies. High performance on the Agreement trait provides the organization with the openness and candor to challenge strategic thinking for the purpose of confirming its efficacy and motivating the behaviors that will implement the strategies. Active, informed buy-in by the workforce to the organization's approach to meeting client needs improves quality, employee satisfaction, and organizational effectiveness.

Cultural strength on both the Strategic Direction and Intent and the Team Orientation characteristics leads to improved performance through greater collaboration across organizational vertical and horizontal boundaries. When there is an understanding of the connection between the groups' productivity and the organization's overall strategy, interactive organizations tend to work through their differences for the sake of the greater good. Responding to problems that require changes in strategies or in the techniques necessary to meet them faces fewer obstacles and engages creative thinking and greater teamwork throughout the organization.

## M&A IMPLICATIONS OF THE STRATEGIC DIRECTION AND INTENT CHARACTERISTIC

### Strong Acquirer, Strong Acquired

When the combining companies are both strong on the Strategic Direction and Intent characteristic, it is incumbent upon the integration team to acknowledge that each company is very likely to have operated with a substantially different strategy in the past. If the two enterprises are to operate autonomously without changing their strategic directions, then management must be encouraged to support the methodology and practices that have produced this cultural strength and the enterprises' past success.

However, if the organizations are to be integrated into a combined operation with a shared strategy, then in calculating payback period, return on investment, time to market of new products, and collective market share, time must be allowed to enable the new strategic direction to be understood, embraced, and facilitated.

## Strong Acquirer, Weak Acquired

Significant barriers to the success of the combination arise when the acquiring company is stronger on the Strategic Direction and Intent cultural characteristic than the acquired enterprise. Imagine an organization that has prospered in part because it has had a clear understanding of the desired strategic outcomes and shared assumptions concerning what each individual and her or his work group does to further the overall strategy. Now imagine introducing new workmates and colleagues who have never known any strategic direction—who have worked in a knowledge vacuum with regard to what the company intends to do to meet the specific needs of customers in the marketplace. It would be similar to introducing a herd of wild horses into a stable of well-trained pleasure riders. In the mixed herd, a person wouldn't know which horse she could trust to get her where she wanted to go. A great deal of time and effort would have to be invested to get the wild horses to follow the direction of the rider, and in the meanwhile, as John Wayne would say, "They're burnin' daylight." Things that should be done are not getting done, the market is moving, and customers are shifting alliances.

So when a company with a clear Strategic Direction and Intent acquires an enterprise with less appreciation and awareness of its customer strategy, time and money must be invested in changing the culture of the acquired business if the combined operation is to enjoy high performance. The purchase price, the expectations for payback period, and the scope and duration of the integration process should be adjusted in light of the difference in the two organizations' relative scores on the Strategic Direction and Intent culture characteristic.

## Weak Acquirer, Strong Acquired

There is often trouble ahead when a company that is strong in a cultural characteristic comes under the management of a weaker organization. The acquired enterprise will have succeeded in creating value, in part, because of its commitment to its strategic intent. Significant miscommunication, frustration, and inefficiencies can occur when the acquiring enterprise culturally underperforms its new acquisition in terms of its awareness of and commitment to a shared and embraced strategic direction. Unless the acquirer uses the QUOCA results to stimulate and create change in its own organization or chooses to have the organizations operate independently, the cultural differences in the marriage will lead to bickering, dissatisfaction, and poor performance.

**Weak Acquirer, Weak Acquired**

Except in a few commodity markets, coincidental weakness in the Strategic Direction and Intent characteristic of merging organizations can be a significant barrier to the long-range success of the combination. Without a sense of strategy or of the need to have a strategy in order to be certain of market success, the organization will suffer from the business equivalent of Brownian motion—lots of random activity that adds up to no productive outcome. In such deals, the expected payback will be a long time in coming. Combinations involving two cultures that are weak in Strategic Direction and Intent provide an opportunity to use QUOCA to stimulate change. The analysis results can create awareness of the need for a shared strategy and motivate the people to vigorously embrace it for their improved security and success.

## SUMMARY

Business strategy defines the major actions by which an organization builds and strengthens its competitive position in the market place.[19]

Organizations with cultures that foster understanding and support for their strategy for satisfying customer needs typically have higher return on investment, return on sales, and return on asset ratios. Their sales and revenue growth, quality, and employee satisfaction as well as their market share are very likely to be superior to those of enterprises with lower performance on the Strategic Direction and Intent characteristic. There are many compelling reasons for combining organizations to assess and, if needed, invest in improving the Strategic Direction and Intent characteristic of their integrated business culture.

Strategies are the flight plans that guide the company.[20]

C H A P T E R

# GOALS AND OBJECTIVES

Providing work related goals for people is an extremely effective way to stimulate motivation. In fact, it is perhaps the most important, valid and useful single approach to motivating performance.[1]

THE OBJECTIVES FOR THIS CHAPTER are for the reader to understand the role of the Goals and Objectives cultural characteristic in the financial and competitive performance of organizations; to be able to define both the leaders' and the employees' responsibilities in achieving the organization's goals and objectives; and to understand how quantitative organization culture assessments can improve the performance of combinations involving organizations with weak Goals and Objectives characteristics.

## THE ROLES OF GOALS AND OBJECTIVES IN MEETING THE SURVIVAL AND SECURITY NEEDS OF THE ORGANIZATION'S CULTURE

The achievements of an organization are the result of the combined efforts of each individual in the organization working toward common objectives. These objectives should be realistic, should be clearly understood by everyone in the organization, and should reflect the organization's basic character and personality [culture].[2]

Goals and objectives are prescriptive outcomes performed in an appropriate sequence and with an appropriate sense of priority in order to accomplish the organization's mission and fulfill its purpose. Goals[3] are "the end toward which effort is directed." The noun objective[4] means "something toward which effort is directed." These definitions of the two terms are so similar that I'm not going to bother distinguishing between them. For our purpose, goals and objectives are interchangeable, and the terms are used without distinction to indicate the desired outcomes for the organization and its people.

High-performing organizations use goals to express the group's desired outcomes and to measure progress toward them. Clearly stated, agreed-upon, and understood objectives are linked directly to the organization's mission, vision, and strategy and provide everyone with clear direction for his or her work.

> The statement of objectives should include more than financial objectives such as the rate of growth and of profitability. It should also include less tangible objectives such as the rate of technological advance, and the quality of service to customers. . . . A complete statement of objectives is feasible only in a company that has the ability to realize trust, subtlety and intimacy.[5]

Goals and objectives also serve as the yardstick against which the performance of individuals, teams, groups, departments, divisions, and the overall organization is measured. Success or failure in achieving desired results influences the strength of the culture and the morale of the organization. People's faith in the ability of the business to survive and prosper is determined by their sense of the reasonableness of the enterprise's desired outcomes and its ability to achieve them. When the desired outcomes are achieved, people feel more secure, experience greater work satisfaction, and expect their prosperity to remain the same or to improve. Conversely, unmet goals and unfulfilled objectives can reduce the sense of security, job satisfaction, and expectations of continued financial well-being.

The role of the enterprise's culture is to gather, interpret, and share information concerning the performance of the enterprise and its implications vis-à-vis the safety and security of the people. Performance compared to goals serves as a barometer allowing the assessment of the organization's well-being.

> Your organization has many interconnected activities that enable you to reach your goals; these are your business processes.

Inputs (materials, capital, and people) are used, deliverables (products and services) are produced, and customer satisfaction and/or feedback are used to continuously improve things.[6]

Businesses use lots of relative measurements to monitor and determine their performance. Ratios such as return on assets, fractions such as market share, and percentages such as those used to measure product quality all provide valuable information on where the organization stands with regard to desired outcomes, benchmarks, and standards. These numbers are important and serve as parameters for the management information system. However, unless the parameters are well understood and the desired values are clearly communicated to employees as specific objectives, they serve only the leaders of the enterprise.

Leaders should not assume that employees are not interested in or able to interpret outcome measurements. In fact, it has been demonstrated time and again that knowledge about the enterprise's performance leads to greater employee involvement and higher individual performance. As presented earlier, an important role of the culture is to monitor how well the group is doing. Information on performance fulfills the need to assess the environment for threats to the employees' safety and well-being. Measures can be unofficial and subjective, received via the rumor mill, or accurate and objective, received through honest dialogue with leaders. To that end, goals and objectives must have some specific characteristics in order to optimally serve the organization and its people.

What are needed are measures that align everyone with the intentions of the business and with the key goals of their respective departments.[7]

## EFFECTIVE GOALS AND OBJECTIVES

Experts[8] say that key business measures should meet three criteria in order to optimize their effectiveness:

1. They must be broad enough so that everyone in the company can understand her or his individual contribution.
2. They must unify the organization—its culture, systems, processes, and output.
3. They must be future oriented, so that they will still be effective as the company grows.

To be universally understood, as we stated earlier, Goals and Objectives must be SMART to enable the organization and its people to unify their sense of purpose, communicate their expectations for success, and reinforce people's feelings of importance to the enterprise's prosperity.

## TYPES OF GOALS

Goals and objectives can be divided into two general types: strategic and operative. Strategic goals are major targets or end results that relate to the long-term survival, growth, and prosperity of the organization and that support the organization's customer-focused strategies. Executive managers typically establish objective, measurable strategic goals that reflect both effectiveness (providing appropriate outputs) and efficiency (a high ratio of outputs to inputs). Typical strategic goals include various measures of market share, profitability, inventory turnover, quantity and quality of production, and cost of goods sold.[9] Communication of strategic goal measurements to the members of the organization gives them a "big picture" of how well the enterprise is doing with regard to its plan for the future. Meeting and exceeding strategic goals stimulates employees' morale, motivates sustained efforts, and reinforces respect for management's wisdom and skill. Conversely, leaders can use strategic goal shortfalls to rally the troops to greater effort, innovative thinking, and continuous improvement.

Operative goals define the desired outcomes of suborganizations and individuals that are required in order to support and achieve the enterprise's strategic goals. Operative goals are used to describe, communicate, and motivate efforts toward specific measurable outcomes and are often concerned with the short run, such as the current month or quarter. Operative goals and objectives for work groups often include such things as project delivery dates, quotas, quality improvement goals, and sales growth.

Individual objectives specify targets of accountability and responsibility. In some cases, individual goals are built into the performance appraisal system and provide objective, mutually agreed-upon bases for periodic assessment of the individual's performance, determination of raises and bonuses, and the rationale behind the individual's personal development and training program.

Radical change though radical definition holds out a secret satisfaction to the manager who pulls it off. If you can learn to do what other managers in your industry thought to be impossible, you will not only thrive, you will literally redefine the industry.[10]

Another type of objective is what Collins and Porras[11] referred to as a BHAG (big hairy audacious goal), something that is intended to engage people's attention, imagination, and energy—to "reach out and grab them in the gut." BHAGs (pronounced beehag) must be tangible, energizing, and highly focused. People should "get it" right away, with very little or no explanation. According to Collins and Porras:

> Like the moon mission, a true BHAG is clear and compelling and serves as a unifying focal point of efforts—often creating immense team spirit. It has a clear finish line, so the organization can know when it has achieved the goal; people like to shoot for finish lines.[12]

Jack Welch of General Electric challenged his people with a BHAG when he said that GE would be number one or number two in each product line or drop that product line. Imagine being an employee in a GE division that was number three or four in its market, and think about the potential influence that the chairman's statement could have on your performance. People in a weak culture who were given such a challenge would simply give up, allowing the division's performance to slide and management to sell it off to the highest bidder. On the other hand, in a strong culture, people would rally to meet the challenge to their survival and security. The high-performing organization would use its cultural strengths to offset its shortcomings or figure a way to offset its weaknesses. The BHAG would serve its purpose of being compelling, unifying, and energizing.

BHAGs, like favors from friends, cannot become routine or the desired results will diminish. But in high-performing organizations, there is nothing like a stretching, challenging, exciting big hairy audacious goal to bring out the best in people.

## THE INDIVIDUAL'S ROLE IN GOALS AND OBJECTIVES

> Strong lives are motivated by dynamic purposes; lesser ones exist on wishes and inclinations. The most glowing successes are but reflections of an inner fire.[13]

The most significant bond between people and their organization is the sense of symbiotic interdependence that leads to the success of the organization and the continued well-being of the individual. Goals define the role of the individual in the ongoing success of the organization. The need to do something important is what gets the person out of bed every morning and into the company facility.

High-performing organizations recognize, honor, and reward two constituencies—customers and employees—as being critically important to their success. Without goal-achieving employees, there is nothing for the customer to buy. Without customers, there is no reward to share with employees and other stakeholders. Goods and services procured by customers represent the combined goal-oriented output of the employees. Customers may buy the car, but they pay for the designers, the machinists, the accountants, the secretaries, and the custodians. Goals and objectives clarify the role each employee plays in the overall production and provide the basis for rewarding employees for their accomplishments.

## THE LEADERS' ROLE IN GOALS AND OBJECTIVES

> Goals are targets or ends the manager wants to reach. Goals should be specific, challenging and realistic. . . . When appropriate, goals should also be quantified and linked to a time frame. They should be acceptable to managers and employees charged with achieving them, and they should be consistent both within and among work groups.[14]

In high-performing organizations, individuals and their bosses collaborate to assure mutual understanding of goals, to identify shortfalls in achieving those goals, and to eliminate the root causes of barriers to goal achievement. People may understand that they are building "God's waiting room," as the story goes, but each and every brick must be properly laid if the edifice is to be completed and endure.

> A leader is best when people barely know he exists. Not so good when people obey and acclaim him. But of a good leader who talks little when his work is done, his aim fulfilled, they will say, "We did it ourselves."[15]

Perhaps the greatest opportunity to influence the success of their organization and their people that leaders have is the opportunity to demonstrate through their own actions, commitment, innovation, and effort how important the goals are to them and to the organization. Although intense drive and humility seem to be somewhat paradoxical

traits, Collins[16] states that the most effective leaders of long-running successful organizations are tenacious in pursuing their goals but quick to
share the responsibility for attaining them with their fellow employees.
Great leaders demonstrate to their colleagues, coworkers, and subordinates that being the boss doesn't mean that he or she doesn't have to work,
it just means that the work takes on a different form. Look at Herb Kelleher
of Southwest Airlines with his sleeves rolled up, cheerfully talking about
the important relationship between the company's customers and its people. Do you get a sense that he is just another employee, a regular guy who
wants everybody to be happy? You bet! No wonder his organization is
perennially voted as one of the best companies to work for.

Effective leaders not only talk the talk but also walk the walk. They
are genuine in their recognition and respect for goals because they have
their own. Every day they demonstrate their commitment to the organization's desired outcomes through their own personal contribution. By
so doing, they recognize the sanctity of the culture's goals and the relationship between success or failure in meeting those goals and their personal well-being and that of their colleagues.

## THE FINANCIAL IMPLICATIONS OF THE GOALS
## AND OBJECTIVES CHARACTERISTIC

Businesses that are strong on their Goals and Objectives characteristic
frequently outperform their weaker counterparts on such measures as
profitability/ROA, sales/revenue growth, market share, quality, and
employee satisfaction. Conversely, organizations that are weaker on their
Goals and Objectives characteristic underperform their stronger counterparts on these same measures. The ripple effects of a weak Goals and
Objectives characteristic are:

- *Reduced profitability.* Leads to lower cash on hand to compensate
  stakeholders in the form of dividends, bonuses, and salary
  increases; lower earnings per share, which decrease the stock price
  and the organization's ability to borrow money at optimum rates;
  reduced revenues and borrowing ability, which impede the investment in capital improvements that maintain or increase the company's competitive position in the marketplace. Continued low
  revenues and a high cost of capital can lead to cutbacks in spending
  for such things as maintenance, marketing, and training, which
  eventually further affect profitability through unexpected breakdowns, lower market share, and lower employee effectiveness.

- *Poorer quality.* Leads to reduced sales, lower revenue, reduced market share, higher inventory costs, and higher production costs for scrap and rework.

- *Lower employee satisfaction.* Leads to higher rates of injury, absenteeism, and grievances; higher turnover; and reduced productivity, efficiency, and effectiveness.

- *Lower market share.* Leads to lower revenues and profits, with the associated direct and indirect effects; lower profit margins and less ability to negotiate prices with customers; higher physical inventory and inventory costs; lower production efficiencies from underutilized resources; and reduced buying power/loss of volume discounts.

- *Lower sales/revenue growth.* Leads to decrease in stock price and company valuation; lower availability and higher cost of capital; and reduced profitability, along with its associated direct and indirect effects.

## CULTURAL CHARACTERISTICS RELATED TO GOALS AND OBJECTIVES

### Coordination and Integration

> Goal incompatibility is probably the greatest cause of inter-group conflict in organizations. The operative goals of each department reflect the specific objectives members are trying to achieve. The achievement of one department's goals often interferes with another department's goals. . . . Goal incompatibility throws the departments into conflict with one another.[17]

Enterprises that have cultural strength on both their Goals and Objectives and their Coordination and Integration characteristics often have superior performance because of their ability to work out conflicts and differences between work groups for the greater good of the enterprise. Strong, effective cultures keep the big picture in sight and coordinate their efforts across organizational boundaries. Challenges in one area are perceived as threats to everyone's success. People know that a solution to a problem facing one work group that results in a problem for another group has a net zero effect. High-performing organizations understand that the product that goes out the door represents the collaborative effort of all the employees.

## Empowerment

> Allowing people to participate in setting their work goals—as opposed to having the boss set the goals for them—is often a great way to generate goals that people accept and pursue willingly.[18]

High-performing organizations drive the accountability for goal setting and achievement as far down the organization chart as possible. No one knows a job better than the person who is doing it. Barriers to the successful achievement of goals are known to the people who have to achieve those goals. When people are empowered with the responsibility for doing what is necessary to meet their goals, they engage their intellect, creativity, and personal drive when doing their work.

My research indicates that most people contribute only about 20 percent of their capabilities to their work—the rest is available, just not engaged. Organizations that develop mutually agreed-upon goals between leaders and employees, and then empower the individuals to use their intellect to best achieve those goals, engage their employees in something more than just the mechanical performance of their assigned tasks. The increased engagement of knowledge, skills, and abilities in the accomplishment of organizational goals effectively increases the leader's workforce and the successful achievement of the desired outcomes of the organization.

## Organizational Learning

> Goals provide a standard for assessment. The level of organizational performance, whether in terms of profits, units produced or number of complaints, needs a basis for evaluation.[19]

Unlike most baseball coaches I had in my limited playing days, Coach Stiles spent as much time analyzing wins as he did analyzing losses. He recognized that everything was an experience that could provide valuable information both for solving problems and for encouraging more of what worked. He knew that players tend to credit wins to good breeding and losses to bad luck. Coach Stiles was as adept at dissecting wins for things we could do better as he was at assessing losses for things we did right. Enterprises with cultural strengths in both Goals and Objectives and Organizational Learning use shortfalls in achieving desired outcomes as vehicles for learning and for improving the operational performance of the organization. Similarly, successes in meeting or exceeding performance goals are used to optimize systems and procedures so that what works best is done the most.

## M&A IMPLICATIONS OF THE GOALS
## AND OBJECTIVES CHARACTERISTIC

### Strong Acquirer, Strong Acquired

Combining businesses that share cultural strengths in Goals and Objectives will probably result in greater than average return on investment and shorter than average payback periods because of the respect and attention that the organizations and their people give to desired outcomes. Objectives play a powerful role in the success of high-performing enterprises by making organizational expectations clear and important to the individual contributors, their work groups, and the overall organization.

The new organization's management team and the group responsible for integrating the operations of the two organizations will have an easier time rallying people's efforts around the desired outcomes if the objectives are openly stated, shared, and respected in the organizations prior to the deal. The willing and responsive contribution of the work groups and their people to the newly formed organization's desired outcomes should have handsome rewards in the form of faster and greater profitability, quicker time to market for new products and services, and continued employee satisfaction, which is likely to reduce the personnel turnover that is typical of acquisitions.

### Strong Acquirer, Weak Acquired

When an organization that is strong on its Goals and Objectives culture characteristic acquires an enterprise that is weak in this area, it will be frustrated by the lack of responsiveness of the new managers and workers to its directives. Low-performing organizations will not understand that goals are actually performance contracts between the enterprise's leaders and its people that ensure collaborative efforts and shared success.

The return on investment and payback period are likely to be disappointing when a strong acquirer buys an enterprise that has low regard for Goals and Objectives. Time to market for new products and services will be retarded, combined market share may actually decrease rather than represent the sum of the shares of the individual companies, and the productive generation of quality products and services may decline as a result of the frustrations and inefficiencies caused by dissimilar regard for desired outcomes in the combined organization.

### Weak Acquirer, Strong Acquired

Disaster can be anticipated when a business that ranks low on Goals and Objectives acquires one that is accustomed to having clearly articulated and respected goals. There is a very good chance that the acquired business was attractive to the acquirer because of its financial performance, and the financial performance may in fact be high because of the enterprise's ability to set and meet goals.

If the acquirer imposes its management style and relatively weaker method for defining and achieving goals, the acquired organization will flounder and fail to produce the value envisioned for the combination.

This is clearly a situation in which QUOCA can save a deal. By knowing the weaknesses of its own culture, the acquirer can capitalize on the intangible assets of its acquisition and use the organizational dynamics of the acquisition to improve its own operations.

**Weak Acquirer, Weak Acquired**

Coincidental weakness on the Goals and Objectives characteristic may be a better situation than one in which either the acquirer or the acquired is stronger than the other party to the deal. When neither of the combining companies recognizes the need for and advantages of clear Goals and Objectives, and yet the two have succeeded to the point where one of them has the wherewithal to acquire another company and the other has become attractive enough to be acquired, some cultural characteristic must be compensating for the weakness.

Once again, QUOCA can be extremely effective in creating an understanding of the value of a strong Goals and Objectives characteristic and creating organizational change that will lead toward improved performance through better goal setting and achievement.

## SUMMARY

Organizations that do not have Goals and Objectives, or whose culture for one reason or another disregards them, suffer in many ways. Specified desired outcomes describe what success looks like and provide a common language for communicating what is needed if the individual, group, and organization are to prosper. Well-articulated goals provide a benchmark for objectively discussing failures and serve as a reference point to determine if corrective actions are effective. It is understandable that organizations that lack well-understood and respected goals and objectives frequently suffer from scheduling and quality problems, low employee satisfaction, and reduced profitability. Conversely, high-performing organizations, in terms of high profits, productivity, and employee satisfaction, can attribute a significant portion of their success to clearly expressed and enthusiastically pursued Goals and Objectives.

# 12

# THE CONSISTENCY TRAIT

Organization culture is the set of important assumptions about the organization and its goals and its practices that members of the company share. It is a system of shared values about what is important and beliefs about how the world works. In this way, a company's culture provides a framework that organizes and directs people's behavior on the job. That's the essence of control.[1]

THE OBJECTIVES FOR THIS CHAPTER are for the reader to understand the cultural purview and characteristics of the Consistency trait; to understand the internal perspective of the Consistency trait and its bearing on the stability of the organization; to know the financial and competitive effects of a culture that is weak in the Consistency Trait; and to understand how quantitative organization culture assessments can improve the performance of combinations involving organizations with weak consistency characteristics.

## A CONSISTENCY STORY

The tale of the tragic death of high-wire legend Karl Wallenda has a fascinating moral. Wallenda was the patriarch of an amazing family of acrobats, jugglers, clowns, aerialists, and animal trainers that had performed throughout the world since the 1700s. Karl had completed breathtaking "Sky Walks" between buildings and across stadiums, including Busch, Veterans, JFK, Three Rivers, and the Astrodome, among others. His most famous walk was a 1200-foot-long trek across the Tallulah Falls Gorge in

Georgia, where 30,000 people watched as this 65-year-old legend performed two separate headstands at a height of over 700 feet in the air.

It was during a promotional walk in San Juan, Puerto Rico, in March 1978 that the leader of the Great Wallendas fell to his death at age 73. The fatal stunt, only a few hundred feet above the ground and a relatively short walk between the wings of a hotel, was not nearly as challenging as many of his fabulous death-defying adventures. Nonetheless, the great Karl Wallenda did fall to his death.

Fans from around the world were stunned, and the accident received worldwide publicity. An investigative reporter decided to analyze the circumstances of the fall and conducted several interviews with crew members and the Wallenda family to see why Wallenda had failed to perform a relatively minor stunt after having done so many much more challenging tightrope acts.

A theme emerged in the course of the interviews. In every preceding, successful walk, the 70-year circus veteran had concentrated all of his attention and efforts on the objective of "making the walk." But things were different this time. Wallenda personally checked the ropes and knots and rigging. He seemed preoccupied with the weather conditions. He applied and reapplied talc to his shoes. But in spite of all of this extra attention to details, he plummeted to his death.

His wife, it is reported, made the comment that best expressed what was different that day and how it led to the tragedy when she said, "Every other time, he concentrated on the goal of 'making the walk' across the rope. That one day, instead, he concentrated on 'not falling,' and look what happened—he fell."

Consistency had been the secret of his success—having a goal in mind, trusting the system of coordination and integration of the various activities that went into doing things properly, having a set of core values that directed the attention of the team and gave them confidence, and trusting everyone to do the right thing in a collaborative way that would bring success. But on the one occasion when disaster occurred, his performance was inconsistent with the past practices that had led to his survival, success, and prosperity. The focus had shifted from achieving the goal to not failing, and the mindset, the faith and confidence, and the outcome changed, too.

## CONSISTENCY AND ORGANIZATIONAL CULTURES

Most managers would agree that they want to create a strong culture that encourages and supports goals and useful behaviors that will make the company more effective.[2]

*Consistency* is defined[3] as the "condition of adhering together," "firmness of constitution and character," "agreement or harmony of parts to one another or a whole," and "harmony of conduct or profession without contradiction." In organization cultures, consistency can be understood to refer to the frequency of replication of the attitudes, values, opinions, behaviors, and actions of the constituent people. In cultures that are strong on this trait, people are very likely to act with great consistency; conversely, in weak cultures, there is little consistency in the way people behave. Denison states:

> Building a "strong culture" implies that values and actions are highly consistent. This form of consistency often has been mentioned as a source of organizational strength and as a way of improving performance and effectiveness.[4]

Other experts agree that strong cultures have a positive impact on an organization's effectiveness because a shared system of beliefs, values, and symbols that are widely understood by the organization's members has a positive impact on the organization's ability to achieve consensus and carry out coordinated actions. The logic behind this belief is the idea that implicit control systems, such as a strongly shared culture based on the internalized values of the constituents, are a superior means of achieving agreement and coordination of activities as compared to command-and-control systems, which rely on specific directions, strict oversight of activities, and explicit rules and regulations with threats of punishment as the impetus for compliance.

> In contrast to strong cultures, weak cultures have the following characteristics: Different people hold different values, there is confusion about corporate goals, and it is not clear from one day to the next what principles should guide decisions. As you can guess, such culture fosters confusion, conflict and poor performance.[5]

## THE CONSISTENCY TRAIT

An organization's consistency reflects both its internal focus and its ability to establish and maintain a sense of stability. A strong degree of organizational stability provides the various stakeholders—employees, investors, customers, suppliers, the community, and others—with confidence that the business will be there for them. Stability creates a sense of security and well-being, both of which are important in motivating people to embrace the culture's attitudes, values, and opinions and to behave in ways that benefit the organization.

The internal focus of the organization provides scrutiny and adjustment of how the organization functions in its efforts to meet the expected outcomes of its stakeholders. The function of the internal focus is to make certain that the organization is doing the right things to ensure its survival and prosperity, much the way an individual's reflection and introspection serve to measure that individual's character and behavior against her or his beliefs and goals.

Of course, if we spend all of our time in reflection, we can have no actions to evaluate, and if we are too stable, we may not evolve appropriately for our ever-changing environment. That is why high-performing organizations balance their internal focus with an external focus and their stability with flexibility. Like Karl Wallenda, it takes a lot of balance and focus for an organization to survive.

There are three culture characteristics that are measured to determine the strength of the organization's Consistency Trait: Coordination and Integration, Agreement, and Core Values. Coordination and Integration measures the extent to which the organization's culture is able to look within itself for problem solving and prevention as well as for providing a sense of predictability and continuity in the way the organization goes about doing its work.

> Cooperation is the result of common culture values and reflects the need for harmony and cooperation among a diverse set of people.[6]

High-performing organizations are adept at putting aside turf issues and "not my job" attitudes in order to effect collaborative outcomes that are in the best interests of the overall business. They share the common perspective that it is through complementary efforts by coordinated work groups that the company's desired outcomes are realized. In high-performing organizations, cross-organizational efforts toward goal achievement enjoy relative ease in reaching agreement and collaboration.

The Agreement characteristic reflects how well the organization is able to confront its inevitable conflicts and problems in a way that meets the needs of its stakeholders. High-performing organizations have developed and embraced one or more effective ways of bringing conflict to the surface, acknowledging it, and resolving it in a manner that sustains or improves the well-being of the individuals, teams, groups, and overall business. The ability to effectively convert conflict into agreement is a powerful force in establishing and maintaining organizational equilibrium in the face of problems, changes, challenges, errors, and adaptation. It is easy to see why organizations that have a strong Agreement characteristic outperform those that are comparatively weaker on this characteristic.

> The standards for ethically or socially responsible conduct are embodied within each employee as well as within the organization itself.[7]

The essence of an organization's culture is its Core Values. When we talk about strong and weak cultures, to a very large extent we are talking about the commitment that group members have to the organization's code of values, ethics, and behaviors. An important role of the organization's culture is to provide almost sacrosanct guidance for its members' work-related behaviors. The Core Values characteristic provides an assessment and evaluation of the strength of the organization's commitment to its values and ethics as a way to provide consistency of behaviors and sustain the success of the organization.

## FINANCIAL AND OPERATIONAL IMPLICATIONS OF THE CONSISTENCY TRAIT

It should be no surprise that the aspects of the organization culture that concern such important attributes as the ability to achieve agreement on issues, the capacity to coordinate the activities of disparate work groups and disciplines, and the core values that guide behaviors and decision making have a significant impact on the performance of the enterprise. As noted previously, when organizations are weak on the Consistency trait, they are subject to confusion, conflict, and poor performance.

Fisher's[8] research identifies two specific performance measures that are negatively affected by a weak Consistency trait: the quality of products and services and the degree of employee satisfaction.

The financial and performance implications of poor quality are significant and widespread. From a marketing and revenue perspective, it is difficult to maintain customer loyalty and market share with inferior quality. Sales volume and gross income are sure to suffer in today's competitive environment. Production will also suffer as a result of waste, rework, and disruptions. Production costs can escalate when overtime and additional shifts are required in order to create acceptable outputs. Efficiencies drop because the volume of inputs needed to produce acceptable outputs must increase. Both shipping and handling costs and inventory costs escalate as a result of returns and reshipments. As income drops and costs increase, profitability is reduced, lowering the amount of working capital available for investment in maintenance and capital improvements. The cost of money increases as debt ratings drop as a result of lower return on sales, income, and equity. As with the king who lost his kingdom for the want of a nail, poor quality can be the first step on the downward spiral that ends in the death of the business.

Low levels of employee satisfaction can have a similar impact on the success and survival of a business. Disgruntled employees:

- Are less productive
- Are less creative
- File more grievances
- Have higher absenteeism
- Require more employee assistance because they have more family problems and higher rates of substance abuse
- Have more on-the-job accidents
- Produce lower-quality products and services
- Are much more likely to leave the company, taking their knowledge and experience with them—often to a competitor

The financial and operational ripple effects of dissatisfied employees are equally extensive, including all of the implications of poor quality plus much higher labor costs to offset low productivity and absenteeism, the costs of replacing employees and training the new employees, and the inefficiencies resulting from vacant positions.

Like a seaworthy ship with a mission, a business requires a rudder to set its direction (Core Values), a functional crew (Coordination and Integration) to effectively keep it moving, and a destination (Agreement) to strive for. No matter how windy the environment is (market demand), the ship will make very little headway if it doesn't know where it is going, can't effectively deploy the crew, or is unable to be steered.

OK, that's enough metaphor. Simply put, weak cultures significantly handicap the enterprise's ability to be competitive and survive.

## CONSISTENCY TRAIT IMPLICATIONS FOR MERGERS AND ACQUISITIONS

The following chapters will go into significant detail about the implications of combining cultures with strength or weakness in the characteristics that make up the Consistency trait. For now, it is important to understand that combining two organizations with anything less than a strong Consistency trait can be risky because of their weak commitment to core values, their inability to collaboratively resolve conflicts and solve problems, and their difficulty in coordinating activities within their respective organizations. For example, if an acquiring business's culture is weak in the Coordination and Integration characteristic, it means that the company has significant problems in working well across organizational boundaries, such as marketing and manufacturing. If the business can't coordinate and collaborate well with its own people, imagine how hard it's going to be for that business to negotiate and close a deal and then integrate operations with a different culture.

Next we will learn to identify, mitigate, respond to, or avoid problems that arise when combining businesses with less than stellar Consistency traits. For now, please recognize that in order for the *emptor* to use the *caveat*, the *emptor* needs the best possible vision.

# 13

# COORDINATION AND INTEGRATION

A strong culture . . . has a much greater potential for implicit coordination and control of behavior. A strong culture, with well-socialized members, improves effectiveness because it facilitates the exchange of information and the coordination of behavior.[1]

THE OBJECTIVES OF THIS CHAPTER are to understand the contribution that the Coordination and Integration cultural characteristic makes to the operational and financial performance of the enterprise; to value the leaders' and employees' responsibilities in coordination and integration efforts within the organization; to appreciate the financial implications of combining organizations with various strengths and weaknesses in their Coordination and Integration characteristic; and to understand how quantitative organization culture assessments can improve the perform-ance of combinations involving organizations with weak Coordination and Integration characteristics.

## COORDINATION AND INTEGRATION—ACCOMPLISHING COMPANY GOALS THROUGH CROSS-ORGANIZATIONAL COLLABORATION

Integration is the quality of collaboration among departments.[2]

The Coordination and Integration culture characteristic reflects the abil-ity of the functional groups and hierarchical strata within the organization to work together to accomplish the enterprise's goals and objectives. Organization development experts[3] state that integration is achieved through structural mechanisms that enhance collaboration and coordination. Any job activity that links different work units performs an integrative function.

The Coordination and Integration characteristic is in the Consistency organizational culture trait, which measures the overall strength of the culture by looking at the degree of shared attitudes, values, opinions, and behaviors and their effect on the well-being of the individuals and their organization.

Like the other Consistency characteristics, Agreement and Core Values, Coordination and Integration reflects the relative stability and internal focus of the enterprise when compared to other enterprises and their financial performance. Coordination and Integration measures the extent to which the organization's culture is able to look within itself for problem solving and prevention as well as for providing a sense of predictability and continuity in the way it goes about doing its work.

High-performing organizations are adept at putting aside turf issues and "not my job" attitudes to develop collaborative outcomes that are in the best interests of the overall business. They share the common perspective that it is through complementary efforts by coordinated work groups that the company's desired outcomes will be realized. In high-performing organizations, cross-organizational efforts toward goal achievement enjoy relative ease in reaching agreement and collaboration.

> If a group is to accomplish tasks that enable it to adapt to its external environment, it must be able to develop and maintain a set of internal relationships among its members. The processes that build and develop the group occur at the same time as the processes of problem solving and task accomplishment.[4]

Another important aspect of high-performing organization cultures is their ability to rally cooperative, cross-organizational efforts in response to challenges from the marketplace. Like the Three Musketeers, who vow to be "All for one and one for all," well-integrated organizations unite their intellect and innovation to overcome the real threats to their well-being: competitors, customer dynamics, regulatory changes, and other such factors. Effective coordination and integration can be a significant strategic advantage in rapidly changing markets. The respected culture expert Edgar Schein states:

Most companies today are trying to speed up the process of designing, manufacturing, and delivering new products to customers. They are increasingly discovering that the coordination of the marketing, engineering, manufacturing, distribution, and sales groups will require more than good will, good intentions, and a few management incentives. To achieve the necessary integration requires understanding the subcultures of each of these functions and the design of intergroup processes that allow communication and collaboration across sometimes strong sub-cultural boundaries.[5]

An enterprise can develop a significant competitive advantage by aligning the full intellectual capabilities and innovation of the organization, regardless of department or work group affiliation, to achieve the enterprise's goals and overcome the barriers to success. When this occurs, people become engaged in the successful outcome of the organization and develop an upward-spiraling sense of importance that contributes to their own success, survival, and well-being as well as that of their group and the overall organization. People begin to see coordination and integration of inter- and intraorganizational activities as rewarding and beneficial. Without a great deal of resources other than facilitation and support, Coordination and Integration can become a gift that keeps on giving. The viral emulation of successful coordinated activities is one of the few cultural changes that can take place in a relatively short period of time.

## THE ROLES OF COORDINATION AND INTEGRATION IN STRENGTHENING THE PERFORMANCE OF THE ORGANIZATION

Integration, and its related concept, coordination, refers to the procedures that link the various part of the organization to achieve the organization's overall mission.[6]

Strong organization cultures have widely shared and deeply held beliefs and assumptions regarding the attitudes, values, opinions, and behaviors that contribute to or threaten the security and well-being of the organization's constituents. The group members value the ability to successfully coordinate and integrate individual, team, group, and department activities because it improves their effectiveness and, consequently, the odds in favor of their current and ongoing prosperity.

The more highly differentiated your firm, the greater the need for integration.[7]

It is relatively easy for a human with one of each to have the right hand aware of what the left hand is doing, but this is not so simple for a centipede. A significant potential barrier to the effective coordination and integration of activities is the size and complexity of the organization. Clearly the greater the number of people, the more personalities, communication glitches, distractions, schedules, and so on impede perfect integration of activities and efforts. The diversity and specialization of different work groups and the volume of work done by each further complicate the perfect coordination of efforts.

High-performing companies are able to optimize their coordination and integration by knowing and exploiting their organization's most effective methods for:

- Gaining people's awareness, attention, and interest
- Providing relevant knowledge and information
- Creating motivation and incentive
- Rewarding the achievement of desired outcomes

Creating awareness of activities that may affect other groups within the organization—the left hand knowing what the right hand is doing sort of thing—can often be handled by traditional communication vehicles such as newsletters, memos, meetings, or emails, depending on the importance and immediacy of sharing the information. It was for this specific reason that the Internet was originally developed—i.e., to network various government research and university labs. Clearly, if the federal government can share information on thousands of projects, breakthroughs, discoveries, and innovations in a myriad of disciplines and studies among hundreds of labs with many scientists and technologists, a for-profit business ought to be able to figure out some way to coordinate and integrate its activities.

## THE INDIVIDUAL'S ROLE IN THE COORDINATION AND INTEGRATION CHARACTERISTIC

The system by which the goals of the employee are integrated with goals of the organization is the basis not only for individual personal growth but also for supplying the talent for higher-level responsibility.[8]

People are generally quick to recognize, accept, and emulate behaviors that benefit them. In the case of coordination and integration, leaders have the responsibility for "leading their horses to water"; the "horses" have the responsibility for recognizing that the water is good for them and taking the metaphorical drink.

It is nearly impossible for bosses to force people to cooperate with one another—personal barriers to cooperation are easy to create and impossible to disprove. The logical alternative is for leaders to stimulate cooperative behaviors by providing motivation and rewards for people who engage in them. Often the incentive for an individual is shared success in achieving the enterprise's outcomes—job security, continued compensation, perhaps a raise or a bonus. On other occasions, the reward may simply be a task that can be performed more easily, higher productivity, or less rework. Ripple effects are exposure of the collaborative individual to a broader network of people, the opportunity to demonstrate creative and cooperative skills, a deeper understanding of the company's business, and greater potential for advancement within the organization.

## THE LEADERS' ROLE IN THE COORDINATION AND INTEGRATION CHARACTERISTIC

> Ironically, the simplest and most effective approach to coordination may just be to have independent parties talk to one another. Coordination by mutual adjustment involves feedback and discussions to jointly figure out how to approach problems and devise solutions that are agreeable to everyone.[9]

The most important step in using coordination and integration to improve organizational effectiveness is for leaders to embrace and support the concept through early successes. People are often eager to accept practices that contribute to their well-being. By initiating, facilitating, encouraging, and rewarding the successful coordination and integration of cross-organization activities, leaders can develop a self-sustaining informal coordination system that very effectively complements the leaders' more formal integration efforts.

> Rites of integration (such as the office Christmas party) create common bonds and good feelings among employees and increase commitment to the organization.[10]

The keys to successful coordination and integration efforts are widespread interpersonal relationships and effective communication channels. Both can be developed and sustained in a number of ways, including:

- Intranet chat groups
- Brown-bag and after-hours seminars
- Formal technical and administrative training programs
- Company-sponsored sports teams and interest groups
- Holiday parties and picnics

The nature, cost, and complexity of the interactive events are far less critical than the simple existence of occasions for people to meet and develop relationships that encourage familiarity and communication. As noted in Chapter 14, where the Agreement characteristic is discussed, personal acquaintance with people from other work groups within an organization effectively reduces the "us and them" barriers to collaboration. The development and use of effective individual networks that transcend organizational boundaries enable high-performing organizations to avoid the "us and them" syndrome, which, in turn, makes it much easier to successfully perform tasks that involve people from different organizations.

## FINANCIAL IMPLICATIONS OF THE COORDINATION AND INTEGRATION CHARACTERISTIC

Organization cultures with high performance on the Cooperation and Integration characteristic have higher-quality products and services than their lower-performing counterparts.[11] It makes sense that a benefit of cross-organizational cooperation would be improved means of recognizing, confronting, and successfully dealing with problems that affect quality. Higher-quality products and services, in turn, improve profitability through reduced scrap and rework, higher production efficiencies from better use of resources, and reduced inventories. The company's reputation, market share, and sales volume are also favorably affected by higher quality.

Cultures with high performance on the Coordination and Integration characteristic also have higher employee satisfaction, which improves productivity and reduces personnel turnover. Improved productivity leads to lower cost of sales and higher net profits. Low personnel turnover reduces the cost of hiring and training replacement people as well as the usual decrease in productivity that results from the absence of the experienced people who have departed.

Conversely, cultures that are weak on the Coordination and Integration characteristic underperform stronger cultures in their level of quality and degree of employee satisfaction. The direct effects of poor quality are lower profitability, increased costs of scrap and rework, lower production efficiencies, and the higher costs of increased inventories. Ripple effects include lower company reputation, market share, and sales volume.

Low levels of employee satisfaction can have a direct effect on the quality and quantity of the employees' work; the results can include lost time accidents and situations that lead to higher turnover, such as malingering, theft, and absenteeism, as well as reduced efficiencies.

## CULTURAL CHARACTERISTICS RELATED TO COORDINATION AND INTEGRATION

Highly effective organizations complement their cultural strength on the Coordination and Integration characteristic with strength on the Goals and Objectives, Team Orientation, and Creating Change characteristics. The combination of operational strengths on both Coordination and Integration and Goals and Objectives provides focus on the desired end results for collaborative efforts across vertical and horizontal organizational boundaries as well as providing the cooperative relationships that contribute to the organization's success.

Combining the Team Orientation and Coordination and Integration cultural strengths enables groups of people from disparate organizations to collaborate effectively. Organizations that use task forces, ad hoc teams, and matrix organizations for specific activities benefit from these cultural strengths through their ability to get people from different work groups to work productively together. The common result is faster time to market for new products and services, which can lead to higher revenues and market share as well as faster, more effective problem resolution that reduces inefficiencies and opportunity costs.

Organizations whose cultures have strengths on their Coordination and Integration and Creating Change characteristics are able to quickly determine and implement needed adjustments to their goals and work processes. The organization will benefit financially from its nimbleness combined with its cross-boundary collaboration in several ways. Swift redirection of talent and resources to new or modified objectives and techniques improves efficiencies and reduces time to market of new products or services. This enables the business to increase its revenues and make changes that reduce costs and improve profitability.

# M&A IMPLICATIONS OF THE COORDINATION AND INTEGRATION CHARACTERISTIC

## Strong Acquirer, Strong Acquired

For a number of sound reasons, the odds that a deal will be successful improve when the deal has the good fortune of bringing together enterprises that are both strong on the Coordination and Integration cultural characteristic. First, both parties should be able to capitalize on this strong cultural attribute as a means of effectively working their individual and collective way through the due diligence, negotiation, and closing phases of the deal. Next, organizations that are high performing on this characteristics have the mindsets, processes, and relationships that enable them to successfully resolve conflicts, handle change, resolve problems, and overcome challenges—each of which is a natural element of the integration phase of business combinations. The integration process should be easier, quicker, and more amicable, which should reward the parties with:

- Fewer disagreements
- Early opportunities to develop collaborative relationships and examples for the evolving culture
- Higher quality of products and services
- Reduced impact on the morale, performance, and employee satisfaction of the acquired business's people
- Greater retention of talented people in the combined organization

The financial reward for combining companies that share strength on their cultures' Coordination and Integration attribute (barring other significant cultural weaknesses) should be returns that are close to the usually optimistic forecasts for market share, return on investment, and payback period.

## Strong Acquirer, Weak Acquired

In contrast to the improved chances for success of deals involving two organizations that are both strong on the Coordination and Integration characteristic, combinations in which the acquirer is significantly stronger than the acquired business in its ability to successfully work across organizational boundaries will face immediate challenges. The early M&A phases, such as due diligence, negotiation, and closing, will be an eye-opener for the acquiring business as it realizes that its methods of achieving coordination are foreign to and unappreciated by its new partners.

High-performing Coordination and Integration companies should be able to capitalize on their strength to smooth the combination process. Investing the time necessary to familiarize the people in the acquired organization with the acquirer's style for reaching agreement through collaboration should avoid some problems in the combination process and set the stage for smoother integration and long-term operations.

Deals involving a company that is stronger on Coordination and Integration buying an enterprise with relative weakness on this cultural attribute have the potential to meet the projected outcomes *if* the buyer is willing and able to use its organizational asset to improve the attitudes and behaviors of the acquired business. If it can do so, the deal should come close to meeting the projections of the buying team for return on investment and payback period. If it cannot, the deal may suffer from extended integration, lower profits, reduced combined market share, high employee turnover among people on both sides of the deal, and reduced product or service quality.

## Weak Acquirer, Strong Acquired

Combinations involving an acquired business that is stronger on this cultural characteristic than its acquirer are often problematic because the people in the purchased business recognize early on that they are the more effective in their ability to coordinate their activities. They often feel as if heathens have overrun them. The people in the acquired enterprise will quickly learn that their effective efforts to resolve cross-organizational issues are not recognized or are turned aside by the acquirer. Unfortunately, this is a self-compounding problem because its very existence inhibits its resolution, and so the relationship can easily go to hell in a handbasket in very short order.

Cultures that are strong on the Coordination and Integration characteristic typically outperform their weaker counterparts in quality of products and services.[12] It will be difficult to retain this strength in the acquired organization if the new bosses do not emulate and reward the behavior. Quality may suffer, with ripple effects of lower revenues from:

- Reduced market share
- Higher production costs
- Lower production efficiencies
- Longer time to market for new products and services

Additionally, the reward of higher employee satisfaction may dissipate along with the decline in the Coordination and Integration attribute, resulting in:

- An increasing number of unresolved cross-boundary issues
- Lower morale, increased grievances, and more EAP issues
- Higher turnover, with associated increased costs for replacement and training of human resources

The financial implications of a combination of a culturally weaker acquirer with a stronger acquired business may be significantly disappointing because of the acquirer's inability to coordinate and integrate cross-organizational issues. Profitability as measured by return on investment and the period of time required to pay for the acquisition may be poor. The use of QUOCA to identify the potential implications of the acquiring company's being culturally weaker in this area would be an extremely cost-effective way to mitigate problems of this nature. In this case, incorporating the acquired company's effective Coordination and Integration techniques into the buyer's culture during the early M&A phases of due diligence and negotiation could significantly improve the relationship between the parties and, consequently, the performance of the deal.

### Weak Acquirer, Weak Acquired
A weak Coordination and Integration cultural characteristic on both sides of a combination can be a significant barrier to the success of the negotiation and closing phases of the deal because neither business will have the understanding or the resources to create win-win outcomes across organization boundaries. These issues will loom even larger should the combination survive the closing of the deal and move on to integration of operations. The performance issues described earlier—poor quality and low employee satisfaction—are likely to plague the deal and cause an extended (perhaps infinitely so) payback period and a low or negative return on investment.

## SUMMARY

The Coordination and Integration cultural characteristic assesses and reflects the overall organization's ability to work together to accomplish the enterprise's goals and objectives. Coordination and Integration measures the extent to which the organization's culture is able to look within itself for problem solving and prevention as well as for providing a sense of predictability and continuity in the way it goes about doing its work.

High-performing organizations have developed effective techniques for putting aside turf issues and "not my job" attitudes in order to produce

collaborative outcomes that are in the best interests of the overall enterprise. Such cultures share the common perspective that it is through complementary efforts by coordinated work groups that the company's
desired outcomes are realized. As a result, cross-organizational efforts can
relatively easily lead to agreement and collaboration for goal achievement.

# 14

# AGREEMENT

Contrary to popular myth, great teams are not characterized by an absence of conflict. On the contrary, one of the most reliable indicators of a team that is continually learning is the visible conflict of ideas. In great teams conflict becomes productive. . . . The free flow of conflicting ideas is critical for creative thinking, for discovering new solutions no one individual would have come to on his own.[1]

THE OBJECTIVES FOR THIS CHAPTER are for the reader to understand the nature of the Agreement cultural characteristic; to be able to link cultures that are weak on their Agreement characteristic to financial and competitive underperformance; to define the leaders' and employees' responsibilities for creating a culture that is strong in Agreement; and to understand how quantitative organization culture assessments can improve the performance of combinations involving organizations with weak Agreement characteristics.

## AGREEMENT AND DISAGREEMENT: THE ABILITY OF THE ORGANIZATION TO EMPLOY DIFFERING IDEAS

Total and consistent agreement among group members can be destructive. It can lead to groupthink, uncreative solutions, and a waste of knowledge and diverse viewpoints that individuals bring to the group. Thus, a certain amount of constructive conflict should exist.[2]

The Agreement characteristic reflects the organization's ability to effectively resolve problems and reconcile differences. Organizations that are culturally strong on the Agreement characteristic are not populated by automatons who look and act alike as they bob along in functional lockstep. Cultures in which people have a strong understanding of the organization's goals and a strong buy-in to those goals are willing to work for "the greater good" and collaborate to solve problems. The process of achieving such agreement also creates employee commitment to the necessary action to achieve the goal.

Command-and-control decision making enforced by the power of the hierarchy is fine for surgical operating rooms and military actions. However, most successful enterprises rely on the ability of people to:

- Think problems through in light of their objectives
- Identify root causes
- Develop action plans that resolve the problems without creating new ones
- Stimulate the desire to take action for the good of the organization

A unique aspect of each organization's culture is how agreement is reached and what techniques are used to develop a sense of unity and support for the organization's decisions. The unique knowledge, skills, and abilities of the employees; a sincere commitment to the goals of the organization; and a strong desire for continuous improvement contribute to a culture with a strong Agreement characteristic.

It is tempting to think that the opposite of agreement is conflict. In fact, conflict is merely one method of engaging people's creative thinking in order to achieve agreement. Other methods used by some organizations to achieve agreement on their desired outcomes and the processes to be used to achieve them are confrontation, consensus building, and humor.

A noteworthy aspect of the Agreement characteristic is that it straddles organizational stability and internal focus. Agreement helps to provide constituents with a reference point and an ongoing example of how challenges will be resolved and problems overcome. The Agreement aspect of a culture is part of the woodwork—a tried-and-true way for the organization to perpetuate its survival and success by appropriately addressing its issues. Organizations that are successful in creating agreement enjoy more employee satisfaction, higher product or service quality, and stronger financial and competitive performance than their counterparts who are weaker on this cultural attribute.

## CONFLICT AND AGREEMENT

Conflicts in the workplace are unavoidable. A conflict can be constructive in signaling a need for change, clarifying expectations
(contingencies), preventing serious interpersonal deadlocks,
building cohesiveness and creating a problem-solving climate.[3]

High-performing organizations realistically accept conflict as a means of
acknowledging and resolving problems. In fact, the word *agreement* has
no meaning when conflict is absent. If the word is defined as "harmony
of opinion, action or character,"[4] the definition itself infers that such harmony did not exist at another time. So the Agreement attribute of an
organization's culture addresses how well the group deals with the
inevitable conflicts that arise in the internal and external dynamics of the
business environment.

A great deal has been written about non-zero-sum conflict outcomes,
where one party prevails at the expense of another party. Since, in the
case of conflicts within an enterprise, both "parties" belong to the same
organization, there is no overall benefit to such an agreement. High-performing organizations strive for win-win outcomes, in which collaboration prevails in the quest to find a resolution that either benefits both
parties or at least does no harm to one or the other. In reality, these are
win-win-win outcomes because the overall organization benefits from
the constructive resolution to the conflict.

High-performing organizations have developed and embraced one
or more effective ways to bring conflict to the surface, acknowledge it,
and resolve it in a manner that sustains or improves the well-being of the
individuals, teams, groups, and overall business. The ability to effectively convert conflict into agreement is a powerful force in developing
organizational equilibrium in the face of problems, changes, challenges,
errors, and adaptation. It is easy to see why organizations that have a
strong Agreement characteristic outperform those that are comparatively
weaker on this characteristic.

## THE NATURE OF ORGANIZATIONAL CONFLICT

Intergroup conflict can be defined as the behavior that occurs
among organizational groups when participants identify with
one group and perceive that other groups may block their
group's goal achievement or expectations.[5]

There are two types of intra-organizational conflict. *Horizontal conflict* occurs among groups or departments at the same level in the hierarchy, such as between line and staff.[6] Conflict can also arise vertically among hierarchical levels. *Vertical conflict* arises over issues of control, power, goals, and wages and benefits.[7]

Horizontal conflict can occur between rival individuals, teams, groups, departments, or divisions. In many cases, such conflicts are power struggles aimed at ensuring the well-being of the parties in conflict. High-performing organizations are able to take a step back from such issues and consider them from the perspective of the best interests of the organization. People in these organizations are able to metaphorically move from a situation in which the problem lies between them to one in which the people are on the same side of the table and the problem is on the other side. Together they are able to "what if" their way through a collaboratively developed list of alternatives until one is accepted as being "win-win." In the process, their relationship is strengthened and their problem-solving abilities are improved.

Vertical conflicts are often made more difficult by the inherent difference in power caused by the hierarchical standing of the parties. There can be a tremendous barrier to collaboration when one party holds sway over the size of the other's raise or bonus, the other's reputation within the organization, and so on. The onus is on the more senior person to create an environment that openly and honestly identifies the core conflict and encourages candor and sincerity in the efforts to resolve it. More will be said on this later in the section discussing the leaders' role in optimizing the Agreement characteristic.

If the organization's overall culture is weak in its ability to create agreement, the chances are slim that either the superior or the subordinate will proactively and collaboratively address the conflict before it has reached a crisis. Such is the penalty for not having a vehicle to direct energies toward the issues rather than the people with the issues.

A strong Agreement trait puts aside vertical confrontation issues concerning differences in organizational rank, the personal nature of the situation, or implications concerning compensation for the "greater good" of the enterprise.

## CONFRONTATION AS A MEANS FOR AGREEMENT

Confrontation involves making problems or events explicit so that the persons involved will recognize what is happening.

Attention is given to issues and behavior that the individual or organization has been avoiding.[8]

On March 28, 1979, I was teaching nuclear power plant operations and maintenance techniques to people who had been hired to staff the Midland, Michigan, facility that was being built by Consumers Power Company. The date is significant because some 500 miles away from my classroom, near Middletown, Pennsylvania, a disaster was in progress at Three Mile Island, our sister plant. Beginning at about 2:00 A.M., people much like my students and me were frantically trying to figure out why alarm lights on the control panels kept going off. Each alarm was individually acknowledged by one of the two Nuclear Regulatory Commission–licensed reactor operators or their boss, the shift supervisor, who held NRC's senior reactor operator license.

At that time, Consumers Power Company was investing somewhere around $500,000 to train someone to become a licensed operator and upwards of $750,000 to train someone for a senior license. The people running around in the TMI control room represented about $2 million and six person-years of technical training on how to run a reactor. Not a nickel had been spent on teaching them how to collaborate on problem solving. They had been trained to pass a test that gave them the right to run a power plant. They knew that when this alarm goes off, you turn that switch, and they turned the switches very well that terrible night. But the core (no pun intended) problem wasn't acknowledged and solved until someone from outside of the group of three was able to objectively assess the overall event, confront the root cause, and suggest a solution. By then, the reaction (again no pun intended) to all of the symptoms was too late. Resolving the root cause at that point was like cleaning the lenses on the Titanic's binoculars after the iceberg had been hit.

> Cooperation and collaboration are still the most civilized ways of getting where you want to go, and the people who choose to fight first and talk later usually end up broken or dead. By finding common areas of agreement and seeking unity of effort, you can avoid the damage that usually accompanies head-on battles.[9]

It takes a culture that is strong in agreement to avoid the temptation of jumping to solutions when the first sign of a problem occurs. Collaborative organizations know that knee-jerk responses seldom address the root cause and may, in fact, make the problem worse by delaying the real solution, alienating colleagues and other fellow stakeholders, creating pandemonium, and sending ripple effects throughout the enterprise.

It is understandable that confrontation is most useful in dealing with troubles, problems, and challenges. It is usually counterproductive in dealing with people.[10] I strongly believe that most problems, even those in which an individual is clearly responsible for the immediate issue, are caused by faulty or inappropriate organizational systems, processes, and procedures. Look at it this way for a moment. If a person makes a mistake, it is usually because he or she doesn't know or doesn't care—or both. If the person doesn't know, it's a matter of the organization's not having hired the right person or not having trained her or him to be competent. If the person doesn't care, the organization has failed to provide the proper motivation for acceptable performance. If the person both doesn't know and doesn't care, the organization has doubly failed him or her. It is only when the person is competent and properly motivated and still fails that the onus for failure falls solely on the person's shoulders.

When people approach performance problems from the perspective of confronting the root cause rather than identifying the culprit, problems are more quickly and agreeably resolved. High-performing organizations know that confronting the problem assumes that everyone shares the same desired outcomes for the organization. They also assume that the person who is most directly related to a problem or an issue has both the greatest familiarity with the circumstances and the most to gain from its resolution. True win-win situations occur through engaging the involved individuals as a resource in the confrontation and resolution of the problem.

## CONSENSUS AND AGREEMENT

> Consensual decision making both provides the direct values of information and value sharing and at the same time openly signals the commitment of the organization to those values. When people get together in one room to discuss a problem or to make a decision, that meeting is often noticed and even talked about: it is a highly visible form of commitment to working together.[11]

The Japanese management system, which was the rage for a number of years, relied heavily on the consensus of all of the involved individuals to resolve conflicts, solve problems, and forge agreement. Contrary to the conventional American interpretation of "consensus" as meaning that people hash things out until everyone agrees, the Japanese interpreted the term to mean that everyone was given an opportunity to voice an opinion concerning the situation or the proposed solution. Usually, a manager listened to all of the perspectives and either made a command decision or supported the direction of the democratic majority. Generally speaking, the problem-related outcome of the consensus effort was situational and utilitarian. But the process-related outcome was a sense of importance, respect, and consideration on the part of the stakeholders. In many cases, individuals came away from the process with an acceptable but less than ideal solution—and the assurance that the process would sooner or later provide an optimum solution for them.

There are two types of consensus: a "focusing down" type of consensus that seeks the common denominator among multiple individual views, and an "opening up" type of consensus that seeks a picture that is larger than any one person's point of view. The first type of consensus builds from the content of the individual views—discovering what part of an individual's view is shared by the other members of the involved group. This is the common ground upon which all constituents can agree. The second type of consensus builds more from the idea that we each have our own interpretation of reality.[12] For example, when everyone in a circular stadium takes a picture of the object directly across from him or her, the assembled photos provide a panorama of the entire constituency and environment. By sharing the views and assembling them into an aggregate, we create a complete picture, and we can use the information to accurately confront the situation and develop agreement concerning the resolution.

> *Ringi*, or consensus building, a unique and heralded feature of Japanese style management, is finally beginning to be cumbersome in the present age of high technology. The process precludes snap decisions and dilutes responsibilities.[13]

While consensus is a much-heralded approach to developing agreement, it does have its drawbacks. First, it can be extremely time-intensive because of the requirement that all the involved people participate and because of the iterative nature of arriving at a mutually agreed-upon outcome. Second, the final resolution often ends up being the lowest common denominator, rather than optimizing the end result for the overall organization. High-performing organizations have a working knowledge and command of a repertoire of agreement-building techniques and use these techniques as appropriate to arrive at the best solution for the situation.

# USING HUMOR TO DEVELOP AGREEMENT

A company in which laughter is encouraged is a very different place to work than one in which humor is discouraged or merely tolerated. A workplace stimulated by laughter tends to score higher in marks in job satisfaction and productivity. Communication, creativity, and morale are all affected by the amount and type of humor sanctioned by an organization. A corporate culture with a "sense of humor" is likely to be more open and responsive.[14]

As you might guess, I am a real fan of objective cultural analysis. Bob Dylan impressed me when he said, "Money doesn't talk—it screams." If you want to get a businessperson's attention, you must converse in his or her language—how does the problem affect the bottom line? With that said, there is still a very special place in my culture-tuned eye for subjectively assessing how people in an organization work together, such as:

- Is there reserved parking for the muckety-mucks, or is it first come, first served?
- Are they chummy or a little formal when they talk?
- Is there a newsletter heralding birth dates and bowling scores?
- How hard do you have to look to find a *Dilbert* or *Far Side* clipping?

When I was in the Navy, two shipmates were always trying to one-up the other, to the merriment of the guys in the department. We were practicing battle situations in the Caribbean during the summer. All the vents and hatches were sealed, and the air conditioning was shut down to ward off potential biological or nuclear hazards inflicted by the simulated enemy. What might have been observed from afar as a gentle sea caused a slow, monotonous rolling of the ship. We were the "repel boarders team," and we were decked out in full combat gear to fight anyone who attempted to overtake the ship. We were in stand-by, below decks. Even the saltiest of the sailors was close to becoming seasick.

Suddenly, Robinson, always the antagonist, noticed that Bossart (his usual foil) was wearing a brand-new black leather belt with the ship's name and hull number elaborately stitched in gold thread. After some intense reflection, Robbie said, "Hey, Boss. How much didja pay for that snappy new belt?" Bossart proudly replied, "Ten dollars American." After some more heavy thought, Robinson said, "Well, I betcha ten I can rip it in two in less than a minute." Bossart eagerly accepted the bet. Being somewhat trustworthy, I held the bets, and Bossart unbuckled his belt, removed it, inspected it, and gave it to Robbie, who also spent a minute or two studying the form and assembly of the accessory. Robbie folded the stiff new belt so that both hands could comfortably fit on the inside of the loop. He nodded to Boss to start the clock and began twisting the belt like he was ringing out a towel. Round and round he twisted the belt and the leather squeaked in protest. In just a few seconds, a weak spot gave way and Robbie held a piece of the belt in each hand. I matter-of-factly gave the winnings to Robinson, who graciously returned the remnants to Bossart with the comment, "Well, now you got a twenty-dollar belt you can't wear!" The comment and the look it created on Bossart's face turned our miserable situation into such a funny moment that I haven't forgotten it in 35 years. Suddenly, our hot, stifling, miserable situation wasn't so bad.

Humor defuses tension and brings a lighter heart and sharper mind to bear on life's problems. Organizations that make room for the joyful dimension of their people also encourage the enjoyment of their work and a better perspective on the true size of problems. High-performing organizations get the most out of their people by making work fun and transforming problems into challenges that people are encouraged to address. Humor can go a long way in making fear, anxiety, tedium, and drudgery fade away.

## THE ROLES OF AGREEMENT IN STRENGTHENING THE PERFORMANCE OF THE ORGANIZATION

Many management teams have too little conflict; their culture is one in which the boss dominates or crushes dissension, or in which people urge one another to be agreeable or teams inevitably face conflicts and must decide how to manage them. The aim should be to make the conflict productive, which is for those involved to believe they have benefited rather than lost from the conflict. People believe that they have benefited from a conflict when 1) a new solution has been implemented; and 2) work relationships have been strengthened and people believe they can work together productively in the future.[15]

It has been said that success begets success, and the same is true with agreement begetting more agreement. A certain amount of contagiousness occurs when people directly participate in or observe a cultural phenomenon working for the betterment of the individuals and their organization. The organizational grapevine and emulation are two very powerful factors in the adaptability and evolution of business cultures.

People are generally not fools—they know that conflict in the workplace is inevitable. But when the organizational culture fails them by allowing conflict to get out of hand, disrupt operations, or threaten their sense of well-being, they begin to doubt the mental health of the organization. Failure also begets failure when nothing is done to curtail it. The very powerful role of agreement within an organization is to provide the example, techniques, ground rules, and confidence to enable the group members to confront and successfully tackle their conflicts, disagreements, and problems.

## THE INDIVIDUAL'S ROLE IN THE AGREEMENT CHARACTERISTIC

High-performing organizations empower each individual to be an important element in the ongoing effort to continuously improve quality, productivity, and job satisfaction. The roles of the individual as a participant in the organization's agreement process are threefold.[16] First, individuals must recognize that conflicts and problems are common in all organizations and embrace agreement as a beneficial mechanism for resolving them. Second, individuals must eagerly and openly participate in the agreement process. And finally, everyone in the organization must reinforce, strengthen, and perpetuate the agreement process by indoctrinating new employees, sharing successes, and insisting on the continuous improvement of work processes through ongoing collaborative efforts.

## THE TEAM'S ROLE IN AGREEMENT

The film *Twelve Angry Men* is the finest representation I have ever seen of how people can work their way through their personal baggage, put aside their prejudices, and truly listen as well as be heard, in an effort to come to an agreement on an issue. The film concerns a jury that has been sequestered in order to determine whether a young man is guilty or innocent of the murder of his father. The roles of the jurors (many played by very recognizable award-winning actors) are almost stereotypical—a world-weary senior citizen; a young hotshot; an academician; someone who doesn't care about the quality of the outcome as long as the process doesn't take too long; a very bitter, closed-minded man; an average Joe; a man who feels superior to the process and his peers; a timid wallflower; a guy with all the answers; someone who is very fickle and "goes with the flow"; a jokester; and a person who is dedicated to arriving at a just result no matter what it takes (played by our hero, Henry Fonda). At the outset of the film, the outcome appears to be cut and dried—guilty. But Fonda has some doubts. The next hour and a half is high drama as the group of individuals wrestle with their prejudices and opinions. But the turning point is the key to my point and the movie. In spite of all of the acrimony and personal differences, a sudden subtle change occurs when they unite for the purpose of making the *right* decision. Suddenly, the old man becomes animated, the hotshot becomes a more humble participant, the timid guy becomes assertive—each person in his own way becomes a peer among peers in search of the right answer.

In the end, they all agree that the young man couldn't and didn't kill his father. Henry Fonda turns as he leaves the room and humbly smiles as he thinks of how the self-consumed individuals had become an effective team that was able to come up with the right decision.

> Companies must develop what we like to call "coherence" among the many disparate and far-flung parts of the company. By this, we mean establishing a potent binding force and sense of direction and purpose for the organization. . . . By achieving coherence, each part of the company and each and every individual will be better able to drive purposefully toward a common goal that is clear, communicated and understood by everyone.[17]

It is difficult to articulate what happens when a number of people unite for the greater good of the group. Kurt Lewin[18] described it as a tension that develops in individuals for the purpose of a positive sensation when it is released through the successful achievement of a goal. The point is, of course, that there is an elevation of energy, creativity, and productivity when people unite for a common purpose. The role of teams in achieving agreement for the recognition and resolution of conflict is to enable their members to shed their personal baggage for the sake of the greater good—a collaborative solution with net positive results in which as many stakeholders as possible win and those who don't win are, at the least, not harmed. Once again, high-performing organizations openly value and encourage participative problem solving because they know that quality, fairness, utility, buy-in, and employee satisfaction all benefit from the process.

## THE LEADERS' ROLE IN THE AGREEMENT CHARACTERISTIC

> Conflicts per se are not a problem: the problem is how to manage them.[19]

According to Daniel Goleman,[20] competent leaders who have mastered the art of negotiating and resolving conflicts are able to:

- Handle difficult people and tense situations with diplomacy and tact
- Spot potential conflict, bring disagreements into the open, and help de-escalate the conflict
- Encourage debate and open discussion
- Orchestrate win-win solutions

One of the competent leader's greatest responsibilities is recognizing, confronting, and resolving conflicts within the organization. As the person responsible for the results of the group, the leader is frequently the first person to become aware of disappointing outcomes. Similarly, when individuals cannot resolve problems, they turn to their leader for help. The leader's first responsibility is to deal with the problem—acknowledge it, determine the relative priority of the situation, assess the impact of doing nothing, and, if and when appropriate, resolve the conflict her- or himself or put together a team to tackle it. By confronting and responding to the problem, the leader reinforces the beliefs and behaviors of the culture by demonstrating sensitivity to issues and showing the ability and willingness to act appropriately by doing what is necessary to achieve the desired outcomes of the organization.

> Successful organizations must find healthy ways to confront and resolve conflict. Managers champion a *cooperative model* of organization, meaning they foster cooperation and don't stimulate competition or conflict, which work against the achievement of overall company goals.[21]

Leaders play an important role in strengthening the organization's cultural approach to reaching agreement by being an effective advocate during both vertical and horizontal conflicts. The leader solidifies her or his reputation within the group by championing the interests of the organization during cross-boundary conflicts. The leader has a powerful influence on subordinates as well as peers by striving for agreement that supports the group's interests while contributing to the organization's desired outcomes.

# FINANCIAL IMPLICATIONS OF THE AGREEMENT CHARACTERISTIC

> Conflict and competition should be directed toward other organizations. This approach increases cohesion, satisfaction, and performance for the organization as a whole.[22]

Organizations that are strong on the Agreement characteristic outperform their weaker counterparts on a number of business measures. The quality of products and services is understandably higher in organizations that are adept at developing win-win solutions for their conflicts and whose cultures clearly have a sense of the right and wrong ways to do things. Higher quality yields more efficient operations and greater profitability through less rework, easier and more accurate planning, reduced inventories, and higher customer satisfaction.

Further, a strong Agreement cultural attribute correlates strongly with high employee satisfaction. Happier employees have been shown to be more productive, to have less absenteeism, to file fewer grievances, and to be less likely to leave their job. The financial rewards of the higher employee satisfaction resulting from stronger Agreement are lower operating costs, higher product or service quality, and the avoidance of costs for replacing and training employees.

Organizations that have a high degree of Agreement also enjoy the hidden cost savings of more prompt recognition and resolution of problems. It is nearly impossible to calculate the cost savings that result when disasters don't occur or conflicts don't arise. As when a person stops to smell the roses along the way, the luxurious aroma of the flower is far superior to the smog of a traffic jam. The difference is simply priceless.

# CULTURAL CHARACTERISTICS RELATED TO AGREEMENT

High-performing organizations complement their strength on the Agreement characteristic with strengths on the Capability Development characteristic for the technical and task-related competencies of their people, the Strategic Direction and Intent characteristic for defining and motivating people to achieve the organization's desired outcomes, and the Organizational Learning and Creating Change characteristics to enable the organization to adapt its functional processes to both internal and external dynamics.

## Capability Development

Enterprises that are strong on both Agreement and Capability Development nurture well-rounded employees who are both competent at their specific responsibilities and able to grasp the notion that their work is only an element of the greater whole. By being able to collaborate with colleagues to avoid and resolve conflicts and problems, the people in strong cultures improve their own job performance and satisfaction while aiding their coworkers in achieving the same rewards. Investment of time, money, and opportunity costs to develop employees' capabilities better prepares them to effectively handle both routine work and problems that involve other people and work groups. In the end, these cultural strengths result in reduced costs for errors and process problems, higher-quality products and services, lower personnel turnover, and higher employee satisfaction.

## Strategic Direction and Intent

Strategic Direction and Intent is the thinking behind how the enterprise is going to add value for its customers, generate income, and reward its employees, investors, and other stakeholders for their contribution to fulfilling the organization's purpose. People, as the primary resource of an organization, provide the brains and the brawn to perform the tasks that result in the value that is purchased by the clients and customers. When an organizational culture is clearly focused on the organization's Strategic Direction and Intent and has a strong ability to achieve Agreement, conflicts and problems that affect the quality of the product or service are either prevented, effectively mitigated, or quickly resolved.

As Stephen Covey[23] says, we must "begin with the end in mind" and then commit our resources to doing everything that can be done to achieve the desired end result. High-performing organizations that are strong on their Strategic Direction and Intent and their ability to reach Agreement on their issues are better able to consistently, efficiently, and effectively provide quality products and services than are organizations that are weaker on these cultural attributes.

## Organizational Learning and Creating Change

Strength on two important organizational culture characteristics within the Adaptability trait, Organizational Learning and Creating Change, complement strength on Agreement by facilitating the organization's learning and accepting new ways of doing things. Without the coincidental Adaptability characteristic strengths, Agreement may be easily achieved, but the things that are agreed upon may prove difficult to implement as a result of resistance and a reluctance or inability to learn new systems and techniques.

As a result, businesses whose cultures have coincidental strengths in these three characteristics are better prepared to effectively and efficiently employ new strategies, tactics, processes, and procedures.

## M&A IMPLICATIONS OF THE AGREEMENT CHARACTERISTIC

### Strong Acquirer, Strong Acquired

When two organizations that are both strong on the Agreement characteristic combine through merger or acquisition, the likelihood of the combination's success is greatly enhanced because of their cultures' ability to effectively confront challenges and resolve conflicts. The use of QUOCA during the due diligence process to identify these and other cultural strengths and weaknesses would provide a powerful resource for the integration team. By capitalizing on the abilities of the respective organizations to adeptly seek and achieve agreement on issues, the integration process should be shortened.

The financial implications of this coincidental, shared cultural strength can be significant. Financial measures such as payback period, return on investment, and aggregate market share should be favorably influenced by the combined organizations' ability to address and resolve the challenges of uniting their organizations.

### Strong Acquirer, Weak Acquired

When an organization that is adept at confronting and resolving conflict and developing agreement on its issues acquires an organization that is weak in these capabilities, the integration process can be difficult and protracted. Under the best of circumstances, there are few business challenges as daunting as being merged or acquired. An acquired organization with a culture that is average or poor in its ability to confront issues and collaborate for the successful resolution of those issues will be handicapped unless the acquirer's integration team astutely recognizes this cultural weakness.

In this circumstance, QUOCA identifies a situation that is ripe for the acquirer to use its cultural strength to work with the acquired organization during the integration process. When this happens, the acquired organization is exposed to and benefits from a strong cultural characteristic of the acquiring company. The short-term result should be a smoother and possibly shorter integration process, with the accompanying financial savings and rewards—reduced payback period; faster, higher return on investment; and retention of the aggregate market share. In the long term, the spread of Agreement strength through the acquired organization's culture should both improve the quality of the organization's products and services and improve employee satisfaction and retention, with the accompanying economic rewards of reduced production and administrative costs.

### Weak Acquirer, Strong Acquired

It won't take long for the deal to become shaky when an organization blessed with a culture that is strong in its ability to confront and resolve problems is being acquired by a business that is weak in the Agreement characteristic. The first signs of problems will probably occur during the negotiation step, when the enterprise that is being acquired attempts to resolve an issue using its effective techniques and is trampled by whatever ineffective agreement process the acquiring company tolerates.

In such circumstances, the cultural strength that has carried the acquired company through its travails will be abandoned in the face of the undisciplined problem-solving tactics used by the acquirer. A suitable metaphor would be a successful amateur boxer who has won many battles in the closely refereed ring being thrown into a Tough Man contest with few rules and no one to enforce them. It won't take long for the amateur to forget his sophisticated techniques and do whatever it takes to survive. The acquired company will feel threatened by the culture of the acquiring organization and will either fight or flee. In either case, the integration of the two organizations will be negatively affected. The acquired business's productive employees will either leave or abandon the culture that enabled them to be satisfied and productive. Their high-quality products or services will suffer from the distraction and confusion resulting from the loss or dilution of their Agreement capability.

The financial implications of such a combination are significant and very straightforward:

- An extended integration period
- Reduced, if any, return on investment
- Payback period extended, perhaps indefinitely
- Ripple effects of all of these results for the life of the deal, such as bitterness, acrimony, and an inability to reach Agreement

### Weak Acquirer, Weak Acquired

Deals are difficult to complete when both of the combining organizations are weak on the ability to achieve agreement. Unresolved conflicts will arise in both organizations as they attempt to resolve conflicts with their prospective business partner. Negotiations will be like the blind leading the blind through a field of land mines and barbed wire. If the deal can be closed, integration of the organizations is very likely to be long and difficult. Unresolved conflicts may linger for quite some time, and, since both organizations are poor at reaching equitable agreements, acrimony and poor communications, coordination, and integration are likely to prevail.

Once the deal is done and problems have been allowed to sort themselves out (a euphemism for "I don't know what to do, so I'll do nothing"), people will return to their accustomed ineffective way of dealing or not dealing with issues. In the long run, the combination of two organizations that are weak in the Agreement characteristic may outperform a combination in which one of the enterprises is stronger than the other because their shared dysfunction sidestepped the acrimony of one party "getting it" and the other not knowing what "it" is.

A deal between two cultures that are weak on the Agreement characteristic will suffer from an inability to resolve issues both within and across the respective organizations. Financial performance, such as ROI and payback period, is likely to be disappointingly less than projected, and the combined organization is likely to suffer from its inability to recognize, confront, and resolve problems, with all of the accompanying financial implications.

## SUMMARY

The Agreement characteristic is central to the organization's cultural stability and internal focus. Organizations that are strong on Agreement provide their people with the desire and ability to confront their challenges in a manner that meets the needs of the organization. The positive consequence for enterprises that are successful in creating Agreement is greater employee satisfaction, higher product or service quality, and stronger financial/competitive performance than are achieved by their counterparts who are weaker on this characteristic.

# 15
C H A P T E R

# CORE VALUES

Ethics is a code of moral principles and values that governs the behaviors of a person or group with respect to what is right or wrong. Ethical values set standards as to what is good or bad in conduct and decision making.[1]

THE OBJECTIVES OF THIS CHAPTER are for the reader to understand the role of the Core Values cultural characteristic in the financial and competitive performance of the organization; to define both the leaders' and the employees' responsibilities in living the organization's Core Values; and to understand how quantitative organization culture assessments can improve the performance of combinations involving organizations with weak consistency characteristics.

## ORGANIZATIONAL CONSCIENCE—CREDOS AND VALUE STATEMENTS

Openly stated, endorsed, enforced, and well-understood core values serve as the conscience of the organization by creating a sense of organizational identity and a clear set of expectations about behaviors that are right and wrong. The "core" aspect connotes the idea that the values are the essence of the organizational being—how its people will conduct themselves in both normal and adverse circumstances. The dictionary draws distinctions between the terms *values*, *integrity*, *ethics*, *moral principles*, and *beliefs*. I have chosen to use these terms interchangeably to mean "The moral identity and driving force within the organization that guides and influences ethical behavior within the context of the work environment."

The essence of an organization's culture is its core values. When we talk about strong and weak cultures, to a very large extent we are talking about the people's commitment to the group's code of values, ethics, and behaviors. Core values are the core of the organizational culture. An extremely important role of the organization's culture is to provide nearly sacrosanct guidance for its constituents' work-related behaviors.

Most ethics codes address subjects such as employee conduct, community and environment, shareholders, customers, suppliers and contractors, political activity and technology.[2]

Many high-performing organizations openly express their philosophy of operation as a value statement, credo, or creed. The words are intended to convey the organizational conscience in such a way that outsiders such as the community, suppliers, investors, and customers have faith in the organization's integrity and that insiders, including directors, officers, and employees, have ethical standards and guidelines for their behaviors. Within the organization, the core values and the code of conduct guide the decisions and actions of the people as they work to accomplish the vision and purpose of the enterprise.

Some organizations have very pointed, succinct statements that are usually attributed to a cultural hero, such as the founder or a past executive who led the organization through a defining moment. For example, Sam Walton made no bones about Wal-Mart's primary value when he said:

We put the customer ahead of everything else. . . . If you are not serving the customer or supporting the folks who do, then we don't need you.[3]

Hewlett-Packard's former CEO summed up his organization's core values by saying:

The HP Way basically means respect and concern for the individual; it says, "Do unto others as you would have them do unto you."[4]

Johnson & Johnson is famous for the influence that its credo had on the decisions of the business during the Tylenol poisonings in the 1980s, even though J&J's founders wrote the statement nearly 150 years ago. Value statements are hard to write, but they certainly make critical and routine decisions easier and more consistent across the organization and through its history. Note the power of the Walgreens creed, which has served to express the business's values for more than one hundred years (see Figure 15-1). No wonder the company is one of the most respected in its market, in the country, and in the world. Can you imagine anyone not wanting to work for a business that openly says that it likes to laugh, be kind, and be generous? Can you imagine the impact of such a statement on the culture—the "how we do things around here"—of the organization and the type of work environment it must nurture?

---

**Figure 15-1**   *The Walgreens Creed*

We believe in the goods we merchandise, in ourselves and in our ability to render satisfaction.

We believe that honest goods can be sold to honest people by honest methods.

We believe in working, not waiting; in laughing, not weeping; in boosting, not knocking; and in the pleasure of selling our products.

We believe that we can get what we go after, and that we are not down and out until we have lost faith in ourselves.

We believe in today and the work we are doing, in tomorrow and the work we hope to do, and in the sure reward the future holds.

We believe in courtesy, in kindness, in generosity, in cheer, in friendship, and in honest competition.

*Source:* Walgreens, Inc., web site.

## THE CAUSE FOR CORPORATE VALUE STATEMENTS

Failing to respect the values of people of both sexes, and of all ages, races and ethnic backgrounds will lead to serious problems for the organization in terms of job performance as well as labor relations and in meeting the requirements of Equal Employment Opportunity laws.[5]

Corporate ethics or values statements are much more common today than they used to be. They became popular in the 1980s in the face of such industry and corporate challenges as the accident at Three Mile Island, the incident at Bhopal, and the issues involved in dealing with a dramatically changing workforce. These issues led to a new focus on the concept of corporate citizenship and, conversely, liability. Tough new federal sentencing guidelines in 1991 increased fines for illegal activities, but specified more lenient fines for those companies that had an ethics statement in place.[6] Many organizations looked at enterprises that had earned the respect of both the public and regulators as inspiration for their code of ethics. Others sought consultants who had expertise in the area to craft their statements. One such expert stated that the elements of an integrity strategy included the following:

1. The guiding values are shared and clearly understood by everyone.
2. Company leaders are personally committed to the values and willing to take actions on them.
3. The values are considered in decision making and reflected in all important decisions.
4. Information systems, reporting relationships and perform-ance appraisals support and reinforce the values.
5. People at all levels have the skills and knowledge to make ethically sound decisions on a daily basis.[7]

In some cases, organizations had to go on record to establish or reiterate an ethical tenet. For example, following an employee discrimination lawsuit, Kroger publicly stated its position on the subject as follows:

> Kroger's policy is clear: We are committed to providing a work-place free from unlawful discrimination, which includes sexual harassment and other forms of harassment because of one's race, color, religion, gender, national origin, age, disability or sexual orientation. Any form of harassment undermines the Company's insistence upon employee integrity and is considered serious misconduct.[8]

If the reader is skeptical about the reach and importance of an orga-nization's stated and unstated values, the following story may be illus-trative. I was working with a group of relatively young and junior Merrill Lynch financial services professionals during the Orange County portfolio debacle a number of years ago. I could tell at the outset of a group facilitation session that something was quite wrong, and I asked what was going on that had caused several participants to be so somber. One of the people spoke up and said how disappointed he was that sev-eral Merrill employees had been found culpable in the Orange County situation. He went on to explain how, as a Merrill Lynch employee, he felt betrayed and embarrassed by the actions of his colleagues, even though he did not personally know them. He felt that the respect that he got from people outside the organization would be lessened by the con-duct of these strangers. He said that he had been indoctrinated with the belief that Merrill Lynch people would universally and uncompromisingly conduct themselves with the highest integrity. His colleagues agreed, and one of them said, "There is no excuse for that kind of stuff."

I tossed my agenda in the trashcan, and we spent the next 2 hours talking about the role of values in the daily conduct of Merrill Lynch's people. The organizational core values that people felt had been violated were:

- Trust
- Professionalism
- Integrity
- Selflessness

I was not surprised that subsequent Quantitative Organizational Culture Analyses results indicated that the Merrill Lynch group was in the highest quartile on its Core Values characteristic. When people can articulate specific cultural values and can express discomfort, embarrassment, and anger over violations of their code of ethics, the group has a powerful tool for promoting behaviors that benefit the individuals, the group, and the overall organization.

## THE ROLES OF CORE VALUES IN MEETING THE SURVIVAL AND SECURITY NEEDS OF THE ORGANIZATIONAL CULTURE

Values define the firm's *non-negotiable behaviors*, as well as provide the guideposts for navigating through gray areas. They set forth the "do's" and "don'ts", the "always, under any circumstances" and the "never, under any circumstances." They are the essence of the corporate culture.[9]

I love watching the Discovery Channel, particularly when the subject is the behaviors of the few aboriginal cultures that still exist. In a recent program, many of the subject group's cultural activities revolved around the gathering, preparing, and consumption of the traditional foods. Each person had an ornately decorated, handcrafted bowl that was used for all food and drink. The clan gathered for its meals around the communal fireplace in the center of the circled shelters. Children crawled from lap to lap, and food was shared in a joyful way. During the program, a clan member violated a taboo. The elders met to discuss his fate, and the entire clan assembled around the fire pit to witness the elders' judgment on the culprit. The council discussed the person and his violation and the impact of that violation on the group, and then listened to his pleadings for leniency.

The lead elder, perhaps the chief, listened and then ruled. He explained that the clan would be weaker with the absence of the young man, who was an accomplished hunter. The chief went on to say that the clan was very old and had survived many ordeals. It had preserved and perpetuated its way and its people through its beliefs in the honor of the tribe. Its customs and beliefs had allowed it to survive while other tribes had been wiped out. The chief ordered the offending man to hand him his bowl. When he did so, the chief smashed it and threw the shards into the fire. Without a word from anyone, the young man left the fire to live alone in the wild.

Strong cultures serve their constituents and their organization by providing a sense of values that are more important than the people themselves. When people have a generally agreed-upon code of conduct, they are not distracted by the need to consider how to act in the maelstrom of situations that confront them. Core values are clear, unambiguous, instructive, and nonnegotiable, such as:

"Always do your best."
"In all things use good judgment."
"Do unto others as you would have them do unto you."
"The customer always comes first."
"Quality is job one."

Strong cultures are often said to help business performance because they create an unusual level of motivation in employees. Sometimes the assertion is made that shared values and behaviors make people feel good about working for a firm; that feeling of commitment or loyalty is then said to make people strive harder.[10]

Walk into any Home Depot, Wal-Mart, or Nordstrom's and ask the first employee you see to help you find any product in the store. The individual behavior of 50,000 or more people can be easily predicted—the employee will honor you and your question. If the employee is already helping someone else, he or she will let you know that and will promise to be right with you; when the first customer is fully served, the employee will give you his or her undivided attention until you are fully served. Why? Because the culture dictates that this is the only acceptable way to treat a customer. If an employee doesn't want to do it the organizational way, that employee's bowl is broken and he or she is driven away from the community.

When our core values are poorly defined or disregarded, we betray others and ourselves in ways that cause harm.[11]

Uncompromising behavioral standards may appear to be harsh to someone who has not worked in a strong culture, but to the members of the culture themselves, the core values are a comfort. They are a unifying force and a means for reducing conflict and ambiguity in the organization. High-performing organizations don't have to redefine themselves every time a challenge pops up. The members of these organizations feel good about their values—if they don't, they leave or are driven away. The ethos of the group gives them comfort, strength, and motivation. They know right from wrong, and they don't have to spend a lot of valuable time making judgment calls. They say, "North is where we are going and North is thataway. Head 'em up, move 'em out."

> Values keep the company together and give it resilience. They are expressions of its "personality," determining its attractiveness to employees, customers, and all others who have a say in whether the firm will prosper.[12]

Which company do you think attracts the best and the brightest job applicants—one of the Top One Hundred Most Respected Companies or one of its direct competitors? Companies that gain the respect of critics and sages do not do so because their financial performance allows them the luxury of taking the time and effort to set and then follow values. They capture attention and admiration because of the manner in which they approach their customers, employees, suppliers, communities, stockholders, and other stakeholders.

> Core values are what the organization stands for, holds dear. Values are the heart and soul of an organization. They are the fundamental notions of ideal behavior, the set of beliefs upon which decisions are made and actions are taken.[13]

The book *Good to Great*[14] studied some 1435 *Fortune* 500 companies over a 30-year period to find the secret of the very few (11) that prospered. Think about this for a minute—1435 *Fortune* 500 companies. Hmmmm. There had to be a lot of companies coming and going for 1435 companies all, at one time or another, to be on a list that has only 500 company names on it each year. What were the key differences between the companies that had sustained success (distinctive profitability for 15 consecutive years or more) and those that were high flyers at one time, like Chrysler, Rubbermaid, and Burroughs? One of the key differentiating attributes of the 11 companies with sustained success was *a culture of discipline* that gave people a great deal of freedom and responsibility within the framework of a highly developed system. People within the elite companies were often described as being *disciplined, rigorous, determined, dogged, diligent, precise, fastidious, systematic, methodical, workmanlike, demanding, consistent, focused, accountable,* and *responsible.* These characteristics pointed to cultural values that led to the success and prosperity of the organization and to the survival, security, and well-being of the people who functioned within the defined system of disciplined behaviors. You can bet that cultural nonconformers had their bowls broken and were quickly driven away.

These companies were able to create and sustain success because they were self-aligning. They didn't need outside experts to tell them when they had deviated from their own standards of behavior. They knew themselves first and foremost, and they were able to use their system of discipline to get back on their desired course. The culture of a high-performing company serves as a gyroscope, always adjusting the trim but never varying the direction of movement.

## THE ROLE OF CORE VALUES IN ORIENTING
## NEW EMPLOYEES TO THE ORGANIZATIONAL CULTURE

> Strictly speaking, values are the "what's really important" in an organization, and newcomers soon learn the values simply by observing behavior.[15]

This quote reminds us that the words and actions of incumbent employees have a great influence on the indoctrination of new employees in the core values of the organization. Even when an organization has earned renown as a great place to work or has provided the new person with a copy of the written credo, the actual behaviors of the new person's peers, supervisors, and subordinates and the officers of the organization during his or her formative acclimation period will imbue him or her with a lasting sense of the nature and extent of the organization's truly accepted values and behaviors. If the company espouses a commitment to unwavering customer service but an old-timer mistreats a client, then no matter what the karat of the gold in which the value statement is written, this glimpse of contrary behavior will hold sway in the formation of the recruit's behavior.

A phenomenon that I observed when developing qualification standards for nuclear power plant personnel after the accident at Three Mile

Island concerned a flaw in on-the-job training: The long-standing practice of assigning a new person to a veteran to learn plant equipment and
systems had an intrinsic defect. No matter how well an operator or tech-
nician knew the power plant, he or she inevitably had a blind spot that
he or she would surely have corrected had he or she been aware of it. But
the problem with blind spots is that we are ignorant of them and we have
learned to compensate for them or work our way around them. Thus, if
an operator happens to be weak in how to manually start up a pump, his
trainees and those who are eventually trained by his trainees will all be
weak in their knowledge of how to start the pump. Such defects self-
perpetuate in organizations where objective self-criticism and self-
correction are not part of the culture.

## THE INDIVIDUAL'S ROLE IN CORE VALUES

In a visionary company, the core values need no rationale or
external justification. Nor do they sway with the trends or fads of
the day. Nor even do they shift in response to changing market
conditions.[16]

There are two critical roles that the individual must perform if the organization is to have a strong and enduring commitment to its core values.
The first is a personal commitment to living the values that the company
embraces. If an employee cannot bring him- or herself to conform to the
set of behaviors expected by the organization, that employee should
either find another job with more suitable expectations or work within
the system to change the values while conforming to the existing values.

Second, employees have the responsibility to help colleagues to be
aware of the problem when their behaviors run counter to the culture's
values. This self-aligning action strengthens the culture and confirms the
importance of the core values. It is noteworthy that a strong culture has a
built-in mechanism to enhance and continue its value system, while weak
cultures perpetuate their weakness by virtue of a dearth of self-alignment.

## THE LEADERS' ROLE IN CORE VALUES

Organizational values are developed and strengthened primarily
through *value based leadership*, a relationship between a leader
and followers that is based on shared, strongly internalized values that are advocated and acted upon by the leader. Leaders
influence cultural and ethical values by clearly articulating a

vision for organizational values that employees can believe in, communicating the vision throughout the organization, and institutionalizing the vision through everyday behavior, rituals, ceremonies, and symbols, as well as through organizational systems and policies.[17]

A great quote needs little embellishment to get its point across—and this quote is a great one. Leaders do far more than give orders, monitor progress, and solve problems. Great leaders set the example for future great leaders through the values and behaviors that they use when dealing with their bosses, peers, direct reports, customers, and suppliers. Great leaders effortlessly carry the burden of perpetuating the organization's culture.

## FINANCIAL IMPLICATIONS OF THE CORE VALUES CHARACTERISTIC

Direct results always come first. In the care and feeding of an organization, they play the role calories play in nutrition of the human body. But any organization also needs a commitment to values and their constant reaffirmation, as a human body needs vitamins and minerals.  There has to be something "this organization stands for" or else it degenerates into disorganization, confusion and paralysis.[18]

In general, the Consistency trait has been correlated with organizational product or service quality and employee satisfaction. These cultural aspects affect the enterprise's profitability in subtle but substantial ways. For example, when the culture is weak on Core Values and the resulting poor product or service quality comes to the attention of customers and clients, the firm's short-term profitability is affected by the unnecessary costs and increased expenses connected with handling and replacing returned merchandise, rework of products, increased inventory, and reperforming work on a nonbillable basis. In the longer run, poor quality inevitably affects client loyalty, market share, and competitive position. If uncorrected, reduced product quality will challenge the organization's viability and impose significant financial losses, opportunity costs, and the distraction of leadership on remedial issues rather than perpetuating and preparing for continued success.

Enterprises with cultures that are weak on the Core Values characteristic often suffer from poor employee satisfaction, which, in turn, may lead to apathy, reduced professionalism, higher absenteeism, more grievances, and greater employee turnover. The financial ripple effects of these symptoms often are first reflected in unsatisfactory product or service quality. If unabated, poor employee satisfaction can significantly increase production or service costs through higher overtime labor costs and increased recruiting and employee development expenses.  In tight labor markets, where prospective employees have the leverage in hiring decisions, employee satisfaction can be a silent, powerful force in attracting or repelling the talent needed to perform the enterprise's work.

If you had a choice, where would you prefer to work—in an organization that has clear, unambiguous values that aid in decision making, provides consistency in dealing with colleagues and clients, and evolves its cultural values through self-alignment, or in an organization that is in search of itself, relying on situational ethics to resolve a constant onslaught of challenges to an unestablished self-definition and a fluid set of values.

One caveat: Please do not confuse core values with inflexibility or cultlike absolutism. Hockey has lots of rules, both written and implied, for the behavior of its players, yet it flourishes as a sport because of its dynamics. No two games are ever alike, yet the code of conduct is basically consistent from minute to minute, game to game, and season to season.  The momentum of the game is never stopped to create a new rule or to drop an old one. The excitement of the game is the unpredictability of the contest within the rules.

Similarly, organizations that are strong on their Core Values free the attention and creativity of their constituents to work within the rules. An organization with weak, misunderstood, or inconsistent Core Values is like a bunch of people who want to play a game that doesn't yet have any rules—almost all of the effort goes into arguments about what is right and wrong, good and bad, fair and unfair. Very little time is spent playing the game. The bottom line is that Core Values set the boundaries of freedom and serve to avoid chaos.

## CULTURAL CHARACTERISTICS RELATED TO CORE VALUES

Like the other organization culture characteristics, the Core Values of a group can be enhanced or retarded by strengths or weaknesses on other cultural characteristics. For example, when an organization is strong on both Core Values and Vision, that organization will enjoy both a long-term end result and an unwavering code of conduct that will lead its people through the journey. Lacking one or both of these cultural characteristics is tantamount to a very convoluted, undisciplined hike to an unspecified place—frustrating, demoralizing, and inefficient.

Organizations with cultures that are strong on both Creating Change and Core Values are able to easily adapt the *how* of their work processes within the boundaries of their *why* value system. Thus, changing the way a job is done is encouraged and embraced as long as values are not compromised. So, for example, employees at Ford (where "Quality is Job One") are encouraged to seek and implement auto manufacturing and assembly processes that improve efficiency and reduce costs as long as the core value of a quality product is not compromised.

On the other hand, organizations that are weak on either or both of these culture characteristics are at a disadvantage relative to their culturally stronger competitors. An enterprise that is strong on Creating Change but weak on Core Values may kill the goose while trying to make better eggs. An organization that is strong on Core Values but unable to adroitly institute adaptive changes will be like a champion driver hampered in a race by a car that doesn't steer well. Of course, an organization that is weak on both its ability to Create Change and its Core Values will be like a carload of people staying on the wrong road—they may be lost, but they're making good time.

Compared to an organization with a strong internal compass and the ability to quickly adapt to its external environment, weaker cultures will suffer by having poorer quality and lower employee satisfaction as well as the ripple effects of these weaknesses.

Strengths on Empowerment and Core Values enable the organization to create its vision of the future more effectively by having indisputable ground rules on how that vision is to be created. Empowering individuals to engage all of their resources in order to achieve their very best is made easier by having unambiguous ethical principles to direct their energies and efforts.

Enterprises that are strong on Core Values but weak on Empowerment may suffer in a couple of ways from having powerful organizational ethics but poor trust in individuals. First, people may sense that the core beliefs are being imposed on them rather than being entrusted to them, and therefore they may feel estranged from the real organizational essence instead of being part of it. Second, the lack of empowerment gives employees little incentive or leverage to participate in how values are translated to individual and group tasks and activities.

Organizations that are high on Empowerment but weak on Core Values may have delegated their value systems and related decision making to people who do not understand or appreciate the need for consistent values and ethical behaviors across vertical and horizontal organizational lines. Situational or even individual values and behaviors will prevail in the decisions and actions of employees, creating confusion and chaos. A friend in Brussels once described NATO as the most inefficient organization he had ever seen. When asked to explain, he said that leaders could never be sure who was available to do what on any given day because everyone was allowed to celebrate the religious and national holidays of his or her home country. Imagine running a company like that—not knowing who was doing what at any given time because there were no set guidelines on how things were to be done. The tie between Empowerment and Core Values is a powerful one in which coincidental strengths provide a competitive edge and weakness in either one can seriously impede success.

## M&A IMPLICATIONS OF THE CORE VALUES CHARACTERISTIC

### Strong Acquirer, Strong Acquired

When two cultures with strong Core Values combine to form a single, unified operation, the integration team should brace itself for challenges concerning the inevitable differences in those core values. In fact, such deeply held and consistently reinforced cultural elements as what is "right" and "wrong," what "good judgment" entails, what "a fair day's work" looks like, and so on are bound to be interpreted differently and to cause huge chasms between "them" and "us."

Quantitative Organization Culture Analyses can be quite an effective tool for articulating the specific differences between the values, attitudes, beliefs, and assumptions of the combining organizations; defining and explaining the bases for the differences; and preparing a foundation for an integrated value system. At the least, the integration should underscore the ethical intent of the combined businesses and promote understanding and acceptance of the differences between the organizations' core values. Ideally, however, the integration team will use its skill and resources such as QUOCA to craft integrated core values that both sides can embrace for the greater good of all stakeholders. This process can be quite long—after all, we are talking about changing peoples' value systems—but in the long run the combined organization will avoid losing top-level performers because of frustration and dissatisfaction and losing customers because of a decline in product or service quality.

The financial implications of such a combination are likely to be an extended payback period, reduced return on investment, extended time to achieve projected synergies, and so on, until the core values are defined and accepted by both parties to the deal. Up to the point where the combined organization begins clicking on all value-based cylinders, financial and competitive performance will suffer. But once shared beliefs and assumptions are developed, the combined organization will have an extremely powerful foundation from which to operate and compete.

## Strong Acquirer, Weak Acquired or Weak Acquirer, Strong Acquired

As a friend once said, "It should be obvious to the most casual observer" that a combination of two organizations with dissimilar strengths on a cultural characteristic as fundamental as Core Values may have some challenges in achieving the desired success of combined operations. Like someone trying to explain baseball to an alien or Christianity to the lost tribes of the Amazon, the organization with the strong sense of Core Values will be at a loss in figuring out where to begin. If the acquiring company has the stronger value system, at least it can use its power as buyer to impose its beliefs on the acquired organization.

They paved paradise and put up a parking lot.[19]

However, should the acquired enterprise have a stronger sense of Core Values than the acquiring company, stakeholders should brace themselves for a real battle. Perhaps the very ethics that led to the acquired company's success and subsequent attraction to the buyer will become the wedge that blocks cooperation between the organizations and inhibits the envisioned success. At any rate, when the inevitable conflict arises between the organizations in which Core Values determine the resolution, the acquired company must be on its guard to see how the situation will be handled. Should its deeply held values and beliefs be violated, the stage may be set for a battle of wills between those who have a value system and those who wonder, "What's wrong with those guys?"

The organization with a weak or absent value system is like the person who smokes and whose sense of smell is thus tainted, and so he or she is unable to perceive the offensive odor of his or her habit. The person wonders what all the fuss is about while the nonsmokers gag. People from a culture with low performance on the Core Values cultural characteristic have no basis for appreciating the importance of beliefs to their newly acquired organization and so are likely to proceed with blissful ignorance to trample something that took years to create. The cost of their ignorance is likely to be the best and the brightest people and the engine that made the deal attractive in the first place.

Here is another opportunity to use QUOCA to recognize and resolve a potentially disastrous combination between vastly different organizational cultures. The analysis will graphically reveal the difference between the two cultures and can serve as the basis for designing an integration plan that develops the Core Values characteristic of the acquiring company and provides a common language and a set of common beliefs for cooperative planning and conflict resolution. The result will be a sense of appreciation for the Core Values of the acquired organization and avoidance of the loss of key people and the beliefs that led them to their success.

### Weak Acquirer, Weak Acquired

Combining two organizations that are both weak on the Core Values characteristic is actually second best to the combination of two enterprises that are strong on this characteristic. The reason for this is that the occasion of the combination provides an opportunity for the respective organizations to collaborate in creating value systems that will help drive them to the success they envision. A QUOCA process will reveal the shared cultural weakness and provide the basis for considering how the organization will handle ethical challenges and consequently develop a credo or value statement that will serve the needs of the organization and create common core values throughout the newly formed organization.

## SUMMARY

Core values (are) the organization's essential and enduring tenets—a small set of general guiding principles; not to be confused with specific or operating practices; not to be compromised for financial gain or short-term expediency.[20]

There is good reason why this is the one of the longest of the chapters discussing the organizational culture characteristics and their impact on the success of business combinations. The culture dictates "the way we do things around here"—the beliefs and assumptions people have that provide a sense of security and safety for themselves, their personal stakeholders, and their coworkers. Core values indicate how people are to react to certain situations, provide the basis for decisions and actions, and serve as a benchmark for interpreting and judging the behaviors of other people both within and outside the organization.

Organizations that are weak on or lack commitment to Core Values are ethically adrift, dependent upon leaders and supervisors to make judgment calls. Empowerment of individuals is almost impossible without Core Values because every individual has a different set of principles to separate right from wrong and good from bad. Consequently, supervisors won't be able to trust their people with empowerment. And, very likely, the lack of shared Core Values will inhibit managers from empowering supervisors, executives from empowering managers, and directors from empowering executives. It is no wonder that an organization with a weak Core Values cultural characteristic suffers from poorer product or service quality and lower employee satisfaction. Without shared values, what can the organization provide the individual in terms of safety and security? How can people work together to create quality?

The essence of an organization's culture is its core values. When we talk about strong and weak cultures, to a very large extent we are talking about the commitment the constituents of a group have toward its code of values, ethics, and behaviors. Core values are the core of the organizational culture.

For a quick assessment of the values of an organization, look no further than the behaviors of the president or CEO. Leaders set the standards for the core values by establishing, enforcing, and emulating the acceptable behaviors of the organization. Just as parents exert the strongest influence on the development of values in children, so leaders exert the strongest influence in a company. They are an integral component of the cultural imprint that can make or break a company.[21]

# 16

# THE INVOLVEMENT TRAIT

Virtually all companies say the right things about how they treat their people. The winners will be the ones who not only say it, but do it. They'll be the companies where people not only work hard but enjoy their work; where each person is treated not as a commodity but with respect and dignity and as part of the team; where people are valued for their minds as well as their hands; where people are empowered to make decisions to improve products and processes; where the company's people are viewed as the most important competitive resource.[1]

THE OBJECTIVES OF THIS CHAPTER are for the reader to understand the cultural purview and characteristics of the Involvement trait; to understand the internal perspective of the Involvement trait and its bearing on the flexibility of the organization; to know the financial and competitive impacts of a culture that is weak in the Involvement trait; and to understand how quantitative organization culture assessments can improve the performance of combinations involving organizations with weak Involvement characteristics.

## THE INVOLVEMENT TRAIT

Research shows that a high level of employee involvement creates a strong sense of ownership in the employing organization. The sense of ownership imbues employees with a greater commitment to the enterprise and its goals while reducing the need for hands-on supervision. According to Denison, "Voluntary and implicit normative systems ensure the coordination of behavior, rather than explicit bureaucratic control systems."[2] In other words, providing people with the knowledge, power, and resources to do their job gets better results than command-and-control systems where knowledge and power are held and distributed by bosses.

In the realm of the Involvement cultural trait, "effectiveness" refers to specific, objective financial and competitive performance measures—product or service quality and employee satisfaction. Both Denison and Fisher[3] have been able to correlate strength on the Involvement trait and its three component cultural characteristics—Capability Development, Team Orientation, and Empowerment—with higher levels of quality and employee satisfaction. The implications of these correlations will be discussed here and the chapter dedicated to each characteristic.

An organization's Involvement reflects both its internal focus and its ability to create and sustain flexibility. Organizational flexibility promotes acknowledgement of and adaptation to the internal implications of changes in the external environment, such as:

- Ever-evolving consumer/customer demands
- Regulatory changes
- Dynamics in financial and economic factors

Flexibility also enables awareness of and appropriate reactions to internal changes, including:

- Leaders and their leadership styles
- Organization structure
- Strategic direction
- Goals and objectives
- Individual roles and responsibilities
- Production technologies
- Information and communication systems

By being aware of, prepared for, and adaptable to the changes that are taking place inside and outside the organization, the enterprise prepares itself and its stakeholders for events and trends that may threaten its survival or create beneficial opportunities. Flexibility creates a sense of security and well-being, which are important motivators for people to embrace the culture's attitudes, values, and opinions and to behave in ways that benefit the enterprise.

The internal focus of the organization serves as ongoing introspection on and response to the business's performance with respect to its desired outcomes, goals, and standards. Internal focus serves to assure the enterprise's stakeholders that the organization is doing the right things to ensure its survival and prosperity.

Just as high-performing organizations must balance their internal focus with an eye on the dynamics of the external environment, they must also balance their flexibility with a certain amount of stability. High-performing organizations have a "tight-loose" relationship between stability through commitment to a vision, mission, and core values and being flexible with regard to the means, methods, and mechanisms to achieve the desired results.

## AN OVERVIEW OF THE INVOLVEMENT TRAIT

There are three culture characteristics in the Involvement trait: Team Orientation, Capability Development, and Empowerment. Team Orientation measures the extent to which the organization's culture leverages its human resources through cooperative and collaborative activities to achieve common goals. Organizations with strength on Team Orientation have more creativity, adaptability, and proactivity. The financial and competitive performance benefits related to these abilities are higher-quality work and greater employee satisfaction.

An organization's Involvement trait also reflects the degree to which employees are given the authority, responsibility, and autonomy to accomplish their tasks via the Empowerment characteristic. High-performing organizations reap the benefits from empowering their people through quicker recognition and solution of problems and more innovative ways to do work. Empowerment of employees rewards the organization by providing it with happier, more loyal, and more greatly involved people who produce superior products and services for both internal and external customers.

Enterprises with strength on the Involvement trait also invest in the knowledge, skills, and abilities of their people as a means of improving their people's performance and the quality of their work. Capability Development often translates into a differentiating advantage in the market. As the old saying goes, "People who know 'how' will always have a job; people who know 'why' will have a career." Businesses that invest in the capability development of their employees provide a sustaining and prosperous environment for the long-term, continued success of their employees and the other stakeholders of the enterprise.

A paradox of culture change leadership is that the leader must be able not only to lead but also to listen, to emotionally involve the group in achieving its own insights into its cultural dilemmas, and to be genuinely participative in his or her approach to learning and change.[4]

Because Involvement is on the "flexible" half of the organization's attention focus, it is an important part of the enterprise's ability to change and adapt in order to do well.

Leaders must be able to give away power in order to receive the benefit of empowerment. They must be willing to invest the time, money, and opportunity costs required by Capability Development to build a springboard for future creativity and improved efficiency. And leaders must be willing to both empower and develop teams to facilitate growth, learning, creativity, innovation, coordination, relationship building, and cross-boundary collaboration.

In strong Involvement cultures, leaders are freed from the burdens of overseeing the mundane, resolving the repetitious problems, and prodding the employees for more productivity. Leaders are themselves empowered to fulfill their highest-order function—to lead their organization on its most promising path through goal setting, planning, and delegation.

## FINANCIAL AND OPERATIONAL IMPLICATIONS OF THE INVOLVEMENT TRAIT

The Team Orientation, Capability Development, and Empowerment characteristics have been correlated with the enterprise's ability to:

- Produce high-quality products and services
- Generate higher profits as measured by return on assets
- Stimulate greater product development and innovation
- Produce higher levels of employee satisfaction[5]

The financial implications of higher quality are significant. From a production cost perspective, higher initial quality of products and services reduces wasted resources, including materials for scrap and labor for wasted production time and rework. Higher quality has significant marketing implications, too. It is much easier to win new customers with a high-quality reputation, and it is far more efficient to keep old clients who are happy than to win back disgruntled customers.

High levels of employee satisfaction can have a similar impact on the success and survival of a business. Happy employees:

- Are more productive and more creative and produce higher-quality products and services
- File fewer grievances, have lower absenteeism, have fewer on-the-job accidents, and require less employee assistance due to family problems and substance abuse
- Are much less likely to leave the company, thereby producing a more stable workforce and greater aggregate competency

Greater, faster product development is a significant benefit of cultures with a strong Involvement trait. This enables the enterprise to:

- Create customer demand, capture new markets, and develop new clients
- Better serve existing "early adaptor" customers
- React more quickly to external environmental factors such as regulatory changes, the availability of new materials and products, and the greater or reduced availability of capital
- Lead the pack of competitors rather than simply following the developments of other businesses

Of course, the most eye-catching benefit of businesses with strong Involvement cultural traits is the greater profitability and higher return on assets than are experienced by their competitors with weaker Involvement. It stands to reason that organizations with greater team involvement, more empowered employees, and high capability development will outperform their weaker competitors. That's exactly why the investment of time, money, and effort is made by high-performing enterprises.

Empowered employees are more likely to recognize and resolve problems before they become significant. They have a great deal of incentive and authority to make their work as efficient as possible. Empowered employees know where the barriers to success and the opportunities for improvement are, and they have the responsibility, accountability, and desire to respond appropriately.

Strength on the Team Orientation and Capability Development characteristics rewards employers with higher profitability by providing them with the intellectual capital for challenging the status quo, creating new products and services, and adroitly solving and preventing problems. Organizations with stronger Involvement trait cultures have the ability and the wherewithal to generate and sustain higher revenues, reduce costs, and keep more profit than their competitors.

## INVOLVEMENT TRAIT IMPLICATIONS FOR
## MERGERS AND ACQUISITIONS

In the ideal world, the two parties in a business acquisition deal will be able to integrate their operations profitably, quickly and easily because of their individual and collective culture strengths on the Involvement trait. The high degrees of empowerment, the investment in capability development, and the strong team orientation will enable businesses to accept and embrace the logic of the combination as well as the new strategies, goals, systems, and organization.

The real challenge comes when one or both of the combining enterprises are weak on the Involvement culture trait. Undeveloped people will be disadvantaged when working with their more developed counterparts and may resent those counterparts' stronger abilities. Organizations that use teamwork effectively may bewilder counterparts who lack such an enabling strength. People who have never known autonomy, accountability, and responsibility for their decisions and actions and the satisfaction of empowerment will quickly feel the difference when they are exposed to an empowered workforce.

The difference in the strength of the organizations on one or more of these cultural characteristics will certainly have a negative impact on the short- and long-term success of the combination. From the outset, due diligence is likely to take longer than expected because of the challenge the weak organizations will face in efficiently understanding and executing the unfamiliar activities related to information gathering and presentation. Negotiations may be extended as people have difficulty understanding and extrapolating the valuation, terms and conditions, and so on, of the initial deal and subsequent counterproposals. Closing may or may not be aggravated by weak Involvement, but the integration and postintegration phases of the deal will certainly be complicated and extended by the less-than-optimum capabilities, teamwork, and empowerment of the people in the combining companies.

The following chapters will discuss the characteristics that measure and reflect the Involvement trait and also the appropriate use of Quantitative Organizational Culture Analyses to identify, mitigate, respond to, or avoid problems when combining businesses with differences in their cultural strength in Capability Development, Team Orientation, and Empowerment.

# 17

# EMPOWERMENT

At all levels, companies need people who can deliver at the frontier of performance. They must understand where the company is going and be able to influence its path. They must share in its fortunes and be motivated for greater achievements. They are the ones ultimately entrusted with the competitiveness of the corporation. They are the repositories of much of the knowledge and skill base that makes the firm competitive. No company can be successful with a detached and unmotivated work force.[1]

THE OBJECTIVES OF THIS CHAPTER are for the reader to understand the performance advantages of an organization with empowered people; to recognize what leaders and employees must do to make empowerment work in an organization; and to understand how quantitative organizational culture assessments can improve the performance of combinations involving organizations with weak Empowerment characteristics.

## POWER TO THE PEOPLE!—AND RESULTS FOR THE STAKEHOLDERS

The old paradigm that exalted control, order, and predictability has given way to a nonhierarchical order in which all employees' contributions are solicited and acknowledged and in which creativity is valued over blind loyalty. Sheer self-interest motivated the change. Organizations that encourage broad participation, even dissent, make better decisions.[2]

The times they are a-changin'. Never before have individuals had more clout. Technology has connected everyone to sources of knowledge and power that were once the domain of kings and barons of business. Business cycles have swung so far, so fast that companies that had prided themselves on stability and mastery of their universe now feel like the tail of the dog. Jobs for life have been replaced by lives with a job. Even in a weak economy the unemployment rate is low, and people are nomads seeking self-fulfillment and power over their own lives rather than the first job they are offered. Anyone with a library card has access to the Internet and more job opportunities, market knowledge, and buying power than at any other time in history. With all of this personal power, people expect to be treated professionally, with intellectual respect. The days of command and control are over. It's time for power to the people! And if this is done right, it may be the best thing that has ever happened for the long-term success, profitability, and prosperity of business.

Empowerment can be defined as the sharing of power with employees for the purpose of enhancing their confidence in their ability to do their jobs and their belief that they are influential contributors to the business. People are given the power, authority, autonomy, and rewards to:

• Effectively make decisions
• Create their own methods of performing their work
• Develop and apply their innovativeness
• Proactively define and remove barriers to their success

Empowerment involves the sense people have that they are at the center of things, rather than on the periphery. In an effectively led organization, everyone feels that he or she is contributing to the organization's success. Empowered individuals believe that what they do has significance and meaning.

Empowerment of people in the workplace is a strong cultural indicator of the degree of trust the organization has in its employees—and in itself. Businesses are able to significantly reduce their costs by providing individuals with the knowledge, power, discretion, perspective, and rewards to make decisions on how best to do their work. An empowered workforce reduces costs because fewer people are needed to supervise, monitor, and coordinate the people who do the work.[3] Empowerment improves quality and service, because high performance is inspired at the source—the people who do the work. It also allows quick action because people who are on the spot see problems, solutions, and opportunities for innovation on which they are empowered to act. The direct and ripple-effect benefits can be significant:

- Faster, more efficient communications with fewer misunderstandings and resulting inefficiencies
- More immediate recognition and resolution of problems
- Increased efficiencies from people providing their own direction rather than waiting for instructions from a boss
- Continuous engagement of intellect in process improvements
- Increased pride, ownership, responsibility, and accountability
- More direct relationships between behavior and reward

Denison[4] has also shown that the greater the degree of empowerment of the people within the organization, the greater the benefits in the form of both product and service quality and employee satisfaction. High-performing organizations on the Empowerment cultural characteristic are easy to identify. Effective empowerment of people creates a business environment in which:

- People are directly or indirectly involved in the development of desired outcomes
- Employees feel highly involved in their work
- People believe that they have a great deal of power and influence over their work
- Decisions are made at the organizational level where the best information is readily available
- Information systems effectively ensure that people have the knowledge they need when they need it

The rewards are significant, but the path to empowerment can be arduous. The organizational changes needed to successfully create an empowered workforce require great courage, as they require letting go of traditional roles and power distributions.

## THE ELEMENTS OF AN EMPOWERED CULTURE

Increasingly, managers are discovering that control systems based solely on bureaucratic and market mechanisms are insufficient for directing today's workforce because:

- The nature of work is evolving to more intellectual activities, such as reasoning and decision making, making standardization and close supervision inappropriate.
- The nature of management has changed, so that managers are no longer likely to be experienced or expert in the tasks performed by their people.
- The employment relationship has changed to one in which compensation is overshadowed by the need to feel challenged, important, and respected.[5]

As a result of these unstoppable trends and dynamics, the reasons for empowerment are threefold.[6] First, empowerment is a means for the continuous improvement of products and services and the processes that create them, with the benefit of greater innovation, reduced costs, and optimized income. Second, competitors are effectively using it to improve their operations and competitive position. When it comes to trends in the competitive environment, the old saying goes, "If you snooze, you lose." Third, it allows you to create a unique organization with optimized use of human and other resources that has the optimum performance capabilities for the mission and vision of the business.

> You've got to trust the workforce. If you don't you've done an awfully bad job.[7]

Leaders are being forced to respond to these workplace dynamics by sharing power, responsibility, and accountability with the people they had traditionally commanded and controlled. In fact, when an organization has been fully empowered, leaders become peers of those they have traditionally led, with the important role of coordinating the group's efforts and integrating them with the rest of the enterprise. Empowering employees means that the traditional managers, supervisors, foremen, and group leaders must give their people four elements that enable them to act more autonomously in accomplishing their jobs:[8]

1. Information about company, work group, and individual performance objectives and their meaning and consequences
2. The knowledge and skills necessary to develop personal mastery of their tasks and the importance of those tasks in the linear process of achieving the organization's desired outcomes
3. Power to make decisions and do the things needed to be successful in their role

4. Rewards commensurate with their contribution to the success of the organization, such as profit sharing and stock ownership

In addressing the role of leaders in the development of an employee-empowered organization, Peter Senge states:

> They [must] work relentlessly to foster a climate in which the principles of personal mastery are practiced in daily life. That means building an organization where it is safe for people to create visions, where inquiry and commitment to the truth are the norm, and where challenging the status quo is expected—especially when the status quo includes obscuring aspects of the current reality that people seek to avoid.[9]

Thus, in an organization that has embraced empowerment of all its people, including the management team, the focus of the leader's efforts shifts from:

- Supervision to facilitation
- Leverage of power to distribution of power
- Being a technical expert for everything his or her people must know to being a process expert for everything his or her people need
- Being the keeper of knowledge as to the goals and direction of the company to being an ally of the people whose efforts achieve the desired outcomes
- Being the boss to being the coach

> The key to organizational success today is getting the people to want to own the responsibility for their own performance.[10]

The cultural impact of empowerment in a high-performing organization is the encouragement and support of the following beliefs and assumptions among employees:

- *Meaning.* People believe that their job fits their values and attitudes
- *Competency.* People feel that they are performing their work with skill and capability
- *Self-determination.* People feel that they have choices in how they perform their job and their pace of work
- *Impact.* People feel that they have influence over important decisions and outcomes for the enterprise[11]

As noted previously and elaborated on later in this chapter, the organization's rewards for the beliefs and assumptions of its people are reduced fixed and variable costs, much higher quality of products and services, and significantly greater employee satisfaction.

## THE INDIVIDUAL'S ROLE IN EMPOWERMENT

The best person to be responsible for the job is the person doing the job. Since the person doing the job is the expert in that job, he or she is the one who should make the decision about how the work can best be done. In the intellectual capitalism model, that's the person with the ultimate power, anyway.[12]

To a large extent the individual's role in the success of empowerment as a vehicle for expanded, continued success of the organization is to pick up the gauntlet that has been thrown at her or his feet. The environmental and technological dynamics that make empowerment attractive to organizations and many of their people may not necessarily be all that attractive to everyone. Some individuals may lack the self-confidence, motivation, initiative, and desire for autonomy. Others may regard their work as mechanical rather than cerebral. The challenge for leaders is to choose an approach to these individuals that also serves the needs of the organization and the people who are willing to accept empowerment and autonomy. Options for the employees who decline an empowered role include:

- Training to remedy knowledge, skill, and ability deficiencies
- Coaching to remedy confidence, initiative, and motivation deficiencies
- Dismissal

Training workers to understand the business and giving them the power to make decisions based on what they know helps to create a sense of ownership and pride among employees.[13]

For individuals and their organization to receive the benefits and rewards of an empowered workforce, they must understand and comply with several critical success factors:

- A thorough understanding of the vision, mission, strategies, goals, and objectives of the overall business
- The specific role of their organization (e.g., department, work group, team) in meeting the desired outcomes of the overall business

- The specific goals and objectives of their organization, including objective measures, time frames, and feedback methods for monitoring and adjusting goals and work processes
- The individual's specific role in accomplishing the organization's goals, including measures, time frames, and feedback methods
- The individual's limits of responsibility, authority, autonomy, and decision making
- Resources available to aid the individual in his or her success, including training, coaching, knowledge sources, technology, and collaboration

With proper understanding and the needed resources, the role of the individual becomes one of effectively employing her or his empowerment. There may be an integration period needed to optimize the effectiveness of empowerment in enterprises that are making the transition from a traditional command-and-control management style. Leaders, in addition to their own adaptation to the new management style, often have to coach their subordinates through the transition period.

> Empowered people have both discretions and obligations. They live in a culture of respect where they can actually do things without getting permission first from some parent figure. Empowered organizations are characterized by trust and system-wide communication.[14]

## THE LEADER'S ROLE IN EMPOWERMENT

> To make empowerment work, recognize that it's a two way street. First, bosses need to spell out the boundaries within which the employees can make their own decisions. Second, employees need to assure bosses that they can make their own decisions.[15]

Leaders in empowered organizations have a far different role to play in the success of their people and organization from that played by those who manage traditional command-and-control systems. The leader of an empowered group differs in the nature and scope of his or her activities and responsibilities in many ways—he or she is:

- A facilitator rather than a supervisor
- A distributor of power rather than the seat of power

- A process expert for the needs of his or her people rather than a content expert for the aggregate knowledge, skills, and abilities of all his or her people
- An ally and resource to the people whose efforts achieve the desired outcome, rather than the keeper of knowledge regarding the goals and direction of the company
- A coach and counselor rather than the boss

Empowerers proactively empower: asking questions, organizing data to confront people with reality, bringing customers and performers together to discuss standards of great performance and feedback on actual performance against those standards.[16]

Because of their nontraditional role, leaders in empowered organizations must have different skill sets from those of typical command-and-control leaders. They must be:

- Better communicators
- Expert in providing constructive feedback on the performance of their people
- Able to effectively set, communicate, monitor, and provide feedback on performance goals
- Able to track the performance of individuals against their goals and reward them accordingly
- More empathetic in understanding the needs of their people
- Tolerant of well-intended errors
- More trusting of their people's commitment, drive, initiative, capabilities, and decisions
- Skilled at creating an environment of cooperation, collaboration, and integration of people's efforts
- More able to determine individual strengths and weaknesses and assign work accordingly
- Expert at being empowered members of the workforce themselves so that they optimize their own performance and set an example for their people

The role of leadership is to forge points of connectivity by redefining roles and responsibilities, driving communications, rewarding achievement and allowing penalty free failures.[17]

The critical competencies for leaders in cultures with high degrees of empowerment are interpersonal skills rather than technical superiority.

To some extent, the effective use of power in command-and-control organizations must be supplanted by the effective use of psychology. One expert comment on how to effectively oversee empowered groups states:

> The most constructive action for improving productivity is for managers to figure out why people behave the way they do and to shape their management systems into patterns, which will result in people wanting to produce more.[18]

To that end, effective leaders must keep the goals of their group at the forefront of their minds and make the facilitation of the collective success of their people their highest priority. Acceptance, encouragement, and support of individuals' creativity, given the diversity of the individuals' experience, knowledge, and skills, will liberate the tremendous capability of people to do their work more effectively, efficiently, creatively, and with greater initiative and satisfaction.

## THE FINANCIAL IMPLICATIONS OF AN EMPOWERED ORGANIZATION

> Empowerment results in changes in employee's beliefs—from feeling powerless to believing strongly in their own personal effectiveness. The result is that people take more initiative and persevere in achieving their goals and their leaders vision even in the face of obstacles.[19]

When we think about the increased sense of job ownership and the direct relationship between performance and reward, it is not surprising that organizations with strength on the Empowerment characteristic have both a higher quality of products and services and greater employee satisfaction.[20] Businesses with highly empowered leaders and individual contributors are better at defining, resolving, and promulgating solutions to problems that affect quality because the people are close to the problems and familiar with the sources and causes of problems. As discussed earlier, higher quality of products and services leads to greater profitability and market advantages as a result of:

- Less scrap and rework
- Higher production efficiencies from better use of resources
- Reduced inventories
- Improved company reputation
- Higher market share and sales volume

Cultures that are strong on the Empowerment characteristic enjoy a higher degree of employee satisfaction than their competitors who are weaker in this aspect of their culture. Higher employee satisfaction from empowered people translates into:

- Higher productivity
- Greater innovation
- Faster problem identification and resolution
- Higher degrees of goal achievement
- Reduced personnel turnover

Since empowered employees have greater opportunities to express their capabilities in creative ways and are entrusted with greater authority to make decisions, it stands to reason that their organizations also enjoy:

- Faster time to market for new products
- Greater adaptability to changes in their external environment, such as regulations and market conditions
- More responsiveness to internal dynamics, such as changes in workload, shifts in the priority of activities, and changes in project requirements

The financial implications of an empowered organization are significant and affect a wide variety of the enterprise's activities, including:

- A flatter organization with reduced compensation expenses
- Production of higher-quality products and services, leading to reduced costs and higher revenues
- Faster time to market for new products and services, leading to higher market share and greater revenues
- Quicker problem resolution, which reduces production costs
- Lower personnel turnover, which reduces costs

## CULTURAL CHARACTERISTICS
## RELATED TO EMPOWERMENT

Enterprises with high performance on the Empowerment cultural characteristic and coincidental, complementary strengths on their Goals and Objectives, Coordination and Integration, and Organizational Learning characteristics can be real competitive powerhouses. The Empowerment and Goals and Objectives characteristics work together to create a work environment that communicates clearly defined outcomes to people who have the motivation, the responsibility, and the related rewards to make certain the outcomes are achieved as efficiently and effectively as possible.

High performance on both Coordination and Integration and Empowerment makes certain that all levels of the organization work together and contribute to the achievement of the enterprise's vision, mission, strategies, and desired outcomes for its stakeholders. These strengths work particularly well together when people from different work groups are brought together on ad hoc committees and matrix organization projects, since such people are accustomed to working as team members in collaborative group efforts.

Organizational Learning is at the core of an enterprise's ability to evolve by being in touch with its external dynamics, such as:

- Market innovations
- Changes in regulations
- Industry variables that affect suppliers, customers, lenders, and competitors
- Economic trends that affect supply and demand

Organizational Learning provides the knowledge that enables empowered people to achieve the goals that have been delegated to them.

## M&A IMPLICATIONS OF THE EMPOWERMENT CHARACTERISTIC

### Strong Acquirer, Strong Acquired

Business combinations between enterprises that are both strong on the Empowerment characteristics are very likely to outperform those in which either or both of the enterprises are weak in the trait because empowerment significantly improves the processing and performance of work. The operational changes typical of new ownership, such as vision, mission, strategies, and goals, if communicated well and properly supported by required resources, should have few negative implications for the performance of individuals, teams, and groups.

As a result of the shared Empowerment strengths, the delegation and achievement of early-stage M&A activities, such as the due diligence and negotiation phases, should proceed on or ahead of schedule. The later stages of the process—integration and postintegration—should similarly go more smoothly and more quickly as a result of the empowerment of people on both sides of the deal.

## Strong Acquirer, Weak Acquired

A business that has capitalized on the integrity, creativity, adaptability, and innovation of its people will find frustration throughout the M&A process and the subsequent operations when it partners with a business with a weak Empowerment culture. The acquiring organization will be unaccustomed to the dependence of the acquired organization's top-down, command-and-control management system. Several important steps of the merger and acquisition process are likely to be more difficult and time-consuming:

- Data gathering for due diligence will take longer.
- Negotiations and closing may be extended as people scramble to make decisions and move forward.
- Integration and postintegration will suffer from the inability to decide who has responsibility for decisions and actions.
- The upward and downward cascade of information through in-baskets will delay decisions, actions, and outcomes.

The financial implications of this type of cultural mismatch can be significant, including an extended time before payback is realized; diminished market share, revenue, and income as the organizations struggle to come together; and higher costs of operations as both the acquirer and the acquired enterprise learn ways to integrate their organizations for decision making, problem resolution, and coordination of production efforts.

The use of Quantitative Organization Culture Analyses during the prospect selection and due diligence process can be an extremely effective way to identify this cultural dichotomy and take steps to mitigate problems during or preferably even before the integration phase. Compared to resolving such cultural differences as those associated with the Core Values and Creating Change characteristics, building empowerment within the acquired organization is relatively easy to accomplish. With clear goals, training, support, resources, and patience from the acquiring company, the people of the acquired business may be eager to play a more empowered role in the combined organization.

## Weak Acquirer, Strong Acquired

It is not necessarily a disaster when a highly empowered organization is acquired by a business that is weaker in this cultural characteristic if the acquirer is aware of the difference in the way the businesses are managed and reacts accordingly. Once again the timely use of QUOCA during the prospect selection and due diligence process can be an extremely effective way to identify the differences in cultural and management styles. If the acquirer is wise, it will recognize the value of empowerment and take the steps needed to develop its own empowerment prior to the integration of the businesses.

A less effective but also disaster-avoiding approach would be to allow the organizations to operate as independently as possible.

However, buyer hubris often raises its ugly head during acquisitions. The acquirer, since it can be perceived as the victor in a competitive business environment, can fall into the trap of perceiving itself as being universally superior to the vanquished. The imposition of a less empowered or, worse, command-and-control management system on an empowered workforce will, in fact, tempt disaster. People who have been entrusted with the goals of the organization, given the authority to make decisions, and given the autonomy to perform tasks in their own way and receive rewards based on their success, will feel trampled upon, distrusted, impotent, and unnecessarily dependent on others for their success.

The functional benefits of the acquired business's empowered culture, higher quality and greater employee satisfaction, are very likely to disappear, along with the best and the brightest people. Consequently, the envisioned financial rewards of the deal, as measured in profits, market share, and return on investment, are likely to vanish as well.

### Weak Acquirer, Weak Acquired

Command-and-control systems of management have been effective for a very long period of time. The fact is, however, that the business environment has changed to the point where command and control is no longer the optimum approach in most industries. And the fact is that the majority of businesses have yet to fully embrace empowerment. So the combination of two enterprises with a weak Empowerment characteristic is the norm rather than the exception. As a result, the likelihood of success for these deals is only about a miserable one in seven.

## SUMMARY

Empowerment is power sharing, the delegation of power or authority to subordinates in the organization. It means giving the power to others in the organization so they can act more freely to accomplish their jobs.[21]

Empowerment is not the greatest business innovation since the personal computer, but it is a very effective way to respond to the significant changes that are taking place in the business environment. Perhaps the greatest change in the workplace is the shift of knowledge and power from a few at the top to the fingertips of everyone. Empowerment effectively drives decisions, methods, innovativeness, and proactivity to the people who know the work the best. With all of this clout, people expect to be treated professionally, with intellectual respect.

The financial rewards for empowerment of the workforce are significant—a flatter organization chart with fewer administrative and management people, higher quality of products and services, and greater employee satisfaction. Ripple effects can also be quite profound—quicker problem solving, greater innovation, and faster response to external environmental dynamics.

# 18

# TEAM ORIENTATION

There are, of course, many ways to develop a vision, and what works best depends on individual company situations. But whatever the circumstances, the most important element is to involve as many people, both managers and rank-and-file, as is possible with efficiency. Team-based processes seem to work best in reaching this kind of buy-in and acceptance of a vision.[1]

THE OBJECTIVES OF THIS CHAPTER are for the reader to become familiar with the contribution that the Team Orientation cultural attribute makes to the operational and financial performance of an enterprise; to understand the leaders' and employees' responsibilities in Team Orientation efforts within the organization; and to understand how quantitative organization culture assessments can improve the performance of combinations involving organizations with a weak Team Orientation characteristic.

## TEAM ORIENTATION—ACCOMPLISHING ORGANIZATIONAL GOALS THROUGH THE COLLABORATION OF INDIVIDUALS

The key element of effective teamwork is a commitment to a common purpose. The best teams are the ones that have been given an important performance challenge by management and then have come to a common understanding and appreciation of their purpose. Without such understanding and commitment, a group will be just a bunch of individuals.[2]

High-performing organizations place and receive tremendous value on working cooperatively and collaboratively to achieve common goals. These enterprises rely on team efforts to:

- Define client/customer needs and determine how best to fulfill them
- Set organizational goals and objectives
- Develop strategies and plans for the future to meet the defined goals
- Solve problems and eliminate barriers to meeting goals
- Develop standards for measuring and adjusting performance
- Determine resources needed and their requirements
- Get work done

People often have several different roles to perform within their employing organization—one as an individual contributor and many others as members of a work team. The Team Orientation cultural characteristic is concerned with the organization's ability to get people to cooperate and collaborate with one another to meet the needs of the organization while functioning as members of their several teams.

For an organization to develop effective teams, its culture must acknowledge and encourage the appropriate individual attitudes, values, opinions, and behaviors that encourage and enable people to function as productive team members. The performance of a team is largely dependent upon the ability of the members of the team to individually and collectively form a strong, effective miniculture for the team. Team cultures require a critical mass of interactions in order for people to make the transition from a group of talented individuals to an effective team. As with overall organizational cultures, people must have a number of somewhat varied interactions in order for the beliefs and assumptions that guide members' attitudes, values, opinions, and behaviors to form. Some experts use a rhyming series to identify the interactions that occur in the transition process from a group of individuals to an effective team:

- *Forming*. Group members attempt to lay the ground rules for the types of behaviors that are acceptable.
- *Storming*. Hostilities and conflicts arise and people jockey for positions of power and status.
- *Norming*. Group members agree on their shared goals, and norms and closer relationships develop.

- *Performing.* The group channels its energies into performing its tasks and becomes a team.

To a large extent the culture of the overall organization will influence the behaviors of team members and contribute to the beliefs and assumptions of the teams' cultures. Organizations with strong cultures are likely to have traits and characteristics that contribute to the faster, easier, and more productive formation and functionality of teams than organizations with weak cultures.

Ongoing team functionality is important to an organization's long-term success. Once successfully formed, however, even the most effective teams inevitably face conflicts and must decide how to manage them. The objective should be to make conflict productive—that is, for those involved to believe that they have benefited rather than lost from the conflict. It has been shown that people believe that they have benefited from a conflict when:

- A solution is implemented, and as a result the problem is solved and is unlikely to emerge again.
- Work relationships have been strengthened.
- People believe they can work together productively in the future.[3]

Team success is often dependent on the quality of the information that is available for analysis and decisions. A critical competency of a highly functional team is the ability to individually and collectively gather, share, learn, and use objective information. According to organizational development expert Peter Senge:

> It cannot be stressed too much that team learning is a team skill. A group of talented individual learners will not necessarily produce a learning team, any more than a group of talented athletes will produce a great sports team. Learning teams learn how to learn together.[4]

In other words, the culture of the team must embrace:

- The recognition and acceptance of mistakes
- The awareness of internal and external dynamics
- The desire to make the best-informed decisions possible in order to optimize the team's effectiveness

A powerful and effective way to expose new employees to the culture of their new employer is to assign them to teams that will function as a microcosm of the overall organization's culture. The new employee can quickly be engaged in situations that reflect the enterprise's culture by observing and participating on teams. Virtually every team activity involves and reflects the cultural beliefs and assumptions of the overall organization through the words, thoughts, and actions that members express and exhibit, such as:

- Current goals, objectives, and desired outcomes for the organization's various stakeholders
- Core values and behaviors that are acceptable and unacceptable
- Methods for achieving coordination and integration of activities
- Propensity and mechanisms for adaptability and continuous learning
- Degree of organizational delegation to and empowerment of individuals and teams

Including new employees on teams also exposes the incumbents to the knowledge, skills, and perspectives of the new employee and the ways and means of his or her prior organizations. The fresh ideas, viewpoints, and examples of newly hired people can provide a boost for the standing team's creativity and effectiveness.

## THE ROLES OF TEAM ORIENTATION IN STRENGTHENING THE PERFORMANCE OF THE ORGANIZATION

One of the most important properties of a work team is cohesiveness. Cohesiveness refers to how attractive the team is to its members, how motivated the members are to remain in the team, and the degree to which team members influence one another.[5]

People often develop tremendous pride in and loyalty to their work teams because of the sense of empowerment, importance, and contribution that are evoked through their contributions to the team's and the organization's successes. Productive teams improve the overall effectiveness of the organization by facilitating goal achievement through focused deployment of the enterprise's greatest resource—its human intellect. High-performing cultures are able to use teams to:

- Improve the coordination and integration of disparate organizations' goals and methods
- Define and effectively remove the root causes of problems rather than simply dealing with the problems' symptoms and effects

- Prevent or mitigate the effects of emerging problems and challenges
- Confront and resolve conflicts that involve two or more suborganizations
- Analyze changes in the external environment that threaten the overall success of the enterprise
- Develop the confidence and ability that will enable the organization to prosper and succeed in the face of its challenges

It is important to have objective criteria that can be used to measure team effectiveness, since the success of the overall business is so dependent on the functionality of its teams. Team effectiveness can be measured by three criteria:

- Whether the team's outputs meet the needs of its stakeholders
- Whether the team is able to develop enthusiasm, pride, and satisfaction in its efforts
- Whether the team members can maintain their level of energy and enthusiasm, remain viable, and have good prospects for repeated success

Many organizations recognize the importance of highly functioning teams by including some type of team training as part of the new employee indoctrination program. This, too, serves to give the newly hired employee an early look at the beliefs, assumptions, and norms of the business, and can accelerate the employee's orientation and jumpstart her or his effectiveness within the company.

## THE LEADERS' ROLE IN THE TEAM ORIENTATION CHARACTERISTIC

Having a healthy sense of independence, self-reliance, and self-responsibility is the mark of a good team.[6]

Two types of leaders are involved in the success of the Team Orientation characteristic: the official foremen, supervisors, managers, and executives of the functional organizations and the leaders of the teams. Both have important roles in the success of the organization's teams.

Functional leaders (e.g., supervisors) contribute to the overall success of the organization, in part, through their subordinates' effective participation in teams. In that context, leaders can aid the success of their team members and the organization by:

- Being appropriate examples of an effective team member
- Investing the time, money, and opportunity costs in team training for their people
- Factoring the time and effort required for team membership activities such as meetings, research, networking, and so on into workload calculations and assignments for the team members
- Maintaining a running dialogue about the team activities with members as a means of awareness, feedback, and management

Team leaders also have responsibilities for the effectiveness of their teams and the management of team members, including:

- Indoctrinating team members into the team's purpose, expectations, goals, limits, and projected time frame
- Tracking and providing feedback on the team's achievements and progress
- Anticipating, responding to, and communicating changes in the scheduling of team activities and any problems and conflicts that result
- Assisting in the development and contribution of team members
- Communicating with functional leaders about the team's decisions, problems, activities, and progress, including such things as the members' performance, workloads, conflicts, and so on
- Communicating with the larger organization about the team's activities, accomplishments, and needs
- Removing barriers to the team's success
- Helping with and setting the example for managing conflicts
- Handling the logistics from the room to the doughnuts, including appropriate visual aids and supplies[7]

## THE INDIVIDUAL'S ROLE IN THE TEAM ORIENTATION CHARACTERISTIC

One of the things that can help a team to work well is the feeling on the part of the members that they are an integral, connected part of the group. On a task-oriented team, this means that their contributions are welcomed and valued, that they are as important as any other member of the team to the final product. After all, why waste scarce organizational time to feel irrelevant?

Just as there are two leaders in the life of the team member (the leader of the functional organization and the leader of the team), individuals who are members of teams have two roles. The first is to remain a viable, productive member of her or his functional organization through open communication with her or his boss and by effectively accomplishing her or his assigned tasks.[8]

The second role of the individual is to be a responsible member of the team. This role can be accomplished by:

- Staying focused on the purpose and goals of the team
- Concentrating on the success of the team instead of personal success
- Contributing to the functioning of the team by treating teammates with sincere trust and respect and by valuing different perspectives
- Using the ears and mouth in the same ratio in which God provided them by listening more than talking
- Communicating openly, honestly, and clearly
- Participating fully
- Making and keeping realistic commitments[9]

Behaviors that benefit both the individuals and the organizations of a business are contagious. When people achieve results through their collaborative and integrated activities, their colleagues notice and emulate the behaviors. Organizations in which individuals are effective team members have a tremendous ally and vehicle for creating the changes necessary for adaptability, survival, and prosperity.

## OPERATIONAL IMPLICATIONS OF THE TEAM ORIENTATION CHARACTERISTIC

Organizations that are strong on the Team Orientation cultural characteristic have the advantage over weaker competitors in that they are able to more effectively draw on their collective intellect and experience to overcome internal problems and external challenges.

If you have been a member of an effective team, you can understand the link between being able to rise to the occasion and the Team Orientation attribute. My first exposure to a truly effective team was very enlightening, invigorating, and satisfying. After the accident at Three Mile Island, the leaders of the utilities with operating, under construction, and/or planned nuclear power plants realized that they had a very clear industry mission and public mandate to make certain that another significant accident would never occur.

With 7 years of active Navy duty under my belt, some of it working and sailing on nuclear submarines, and another 7 years maintaining and teaching commercial nuclear power systems, I had been an early recruit and employee of the Institute of Nuclear Power Operations (INPO), a consortium formed and funded by the domestic utilities to develop "benchmarks of excellence" for nuclear power plant operations, perform periodic inspections of the plants, publish the inspection findings, and share good practices that we had observed. Our mission was quite different from the mandated government oversight function of the Nuclear Regulatory Commission. Its role was to develop and enforce standards of operations and maintenance that served, basically, as the minimum that people and their organizations had to do in order to comply with the law. Investigations of the accident at TMI yielded indications that it was active, although unintentional, human performance that had allowed a relatively simple equipment malfunction to become a disaster, with significant implications for the operators, the Middletown residents, the nuclear power industry, and the American energy strategy. In other words, compliance did not preclude or play a mitigating role in the accident. Clearly, the nuclear industry had to self-manage a change in its approach to plant operations from compliance to continuous improvement.

Since human performance was at the heart of the problems at TMI, INPO's Training & Education Division played an important role in defining excellence in the human and organizational performance of nuclear power plant operations, maintenance, and administration. To that end, INPO assembled an oversight committee to establish the goals, provide direction, and give feedback on the benchmarks of excellence that we developed for the subsequent evaluations and reports.

The Training & Education Division Oversight Committee was made up of some of the most impressive people I had ever met. INPO's founding chairman and president was retired Admiral Dennis Wilkinson, the first skipper of the USS *Nautilus* and the man who enthusiastically first stated, "We are underway on nuclear power!" Other members of the committee from the successful Navy nuclear program were Joe Colvin (now head of the Nuclear Energy Institute), Bill Quigley, Ken Strahn, Fred Tollison, and Zack Pate, who eventually succeeded Admiral Wilkinson as the head of INPO. Notable nuclear power executives were Bill Lee, chairman of the highly respected Duke Energy; his training expert, Red Thomas; and Vin Poeppelmeyer from the Electric Power

Research Institute. Ad hoc members included notable academicians, scientists, and executives from utilities and consulting firms.

The common denominator of the members was their ability to respond to the immediate need for rebuilding the confidence of the American and international public in a technology that, at that time, produced some 20 percent of the nation's energy. To put the situation in perspective, think about the economic and lifestyle impacts when crude oil prices jump. There would have been tremendous ramifications if public and government pressure had mounted to the point where all of the nuclear plants had been shut down. The NRC clearly was not in a position to move beyond its licensing and compliance role, and so the burden fell on the industry to muster its best efforts to salvage the image and operations of a significant infrastructure technology.

As a relatively young man in the presence of industry notables, I was deeply impressed by the lack of ego that the team members exhibited. On the heels of one disaster and in the face of another, they approached their duties with humility, insight, humor, and collaboration. Within a matter of 6 months, they had:

- Defined the objectives, criteria, and style for human and organizational performance standards
- Delegated the development of performance standards to a hand-selected team of training and organizational development experts with Navy and civilian nuclear power plant expertise
- Critiqued and eventually approved the performance standards for nine professional disciplines as well as evaluation procedures for site inspections
- Overseen and critiqued two pilot evaluations at commercial power plants
- Approved the final versions of evaluation criteria and procedures and a schedule for the entire domestic commercial nuclear power industry

As impressed as I was with the effectiveness of the members of this team in accomplishing a very challenging task in a very short period, I was even more impressed as a member of the team carrying out the pilot and regularly scheduled evaluations. Utility executives, technical professionals, and plant people could have perceived us as outsiders, troublemakers, and boat rockers when we conducted our 2-week in-plant evaluations. But our team proved to be as expert outside of the meetings as it was inside. The team members effectively communicated the necessity for and importance of the evaluations for the public perception of the industry and its long-term viability. They assured the utility executives and plant people that the evaluators were solid in their expertise and objective in their conduct.

Clearly, INPO had a valuable impact on the public's perception of the nuclear power option. Of course, some plants were shut down, and others that had been planned were never built. But nearly a quarter of a century after the accident at Three Mile Island, we still generate about 20 percent of our electric power from nuclear steam supply systems. And just recently, in the face of escalating problems in the Middle East and their threat on our energy security, came the announcement of the first commercial nuclear power plant to be built in this country in this millennium. Were it not for the effectiveness of the INPO teams, the history and the future of our energy program might have been quite different.

Most teams don't carry the burden of an industry's viability on their shoulders. However, the success of a business does depend on the effectiveness of the sum of its actions, particularly those that set the direction and affect the success of several suborganizations. Thus, the ability of a business to successfully form teams and enable them to function can be a significant facilitator or barrier to its overall well-being.

## FINANCIAL IMPLICATIONS OF THE TEAM ORIENTATION CHARACTERISTIC

Businesses with high performance on their Team Orientation cultural characteristic outperform weaker cultures on two significant measures: quality of products and services and employee satisfaction. Businesses with high-performing teams are better at defining, resolving, and promulgating solutions to problems that affect quality. Higher quality of products and services leads to greater profitability and market advantages as a result of:

- Less scrap and rework
- Higher production efficiencies from better use of resources
- Reduced inventories
- Improved company reputation
- Higher market share and sales volume

Cultures that are strong on Team Orientation also have higher employee satisfaction, which improves productivity and reduces personnel turnover. In a sense, great teamwork is a gift that keeps on giving by contributing to a self-perpetuating chain of employee involvement in problem solving, leading to greater tangible and intangible rewards, leading to more empowerment, greater job satisfaction, and better problem-solving skills. Fewer production, operational, and administrative problems and better planning and execution contribute to higher net profits. High employee satisfaction reduces personnel turnover and the cost of hiring and training replacement people, while maintaining the organization's strong Team Orientation.

## CULTURAL CHARACTERISTICS RELATED TO TEAM ORIENTATION

Businesses with cultural strengths on both the Coordination and Integration and the Team Orientation characteristics are better able to implement team decisions and actions than their weaker competitors because they enable groups of people from disparate organizations to collaborate more effectively. As a result, plans are put into place sooner, problems are resolved more quickly, and people are more adept at embracing change. The organizational impact is faster time to market for new products and services, which can lead to higher revenues and market share, as well as faster, more effective problem resolution, which reduces inefficiencies and opportunity costs.

Cultural strength on both the Strategic Direction and Intent and the Team Orientation attributes improves performance through greater collaboration across vertical and horizontal organizational boundaries. By enjoying an understanding between the groups' productivity and the organization's overall strategy, interactive organizations with strong teams are able to more quickly and effectively resolve their differences for the sake of the greater good. The ability to respond by making changes in strategies or techniques in order to meet, mitigate, or prevent problems has faster, greater acceptance and engages creative thinking and greater teamwork throughout the organization.

Organizations that have strengths on the Creating Change and Team Orientation culture characteristics are better able to implement the recommended team actions than those organizations that are weaker on either or both of these attributes. This is due to the group's better understanding of the need for and methods of change, which is complemented by the existence of effective change agents—the teams. As a result, the business is more nimble and more adaptable to new ways of doing things. The teams that analyze, discuss, and respond to both internal and external challenges to the success and well-being of the organization have a faster, wider, and deeper impact on company activities because of the company's propensity to accept and implement team decisions and directions.

## M&A IMPLICATIONS OF THE TEAM ORIENTATION CHARACTERISTIC

### Strong Acquirer, Strong Acquired

Combining businesses that are strong on the Team Orientation cultural attribute should be able to collaborate effectively, using these strengths to effectively resolve the inevitable problems that come up throughout the merger and acquisition process. The benefit from the similar cultures can be significant to the short- and long-range success of the deal. The due diligence and negotiation steps will benefit from effective team skills. Perhaps even greater benefit will occur during the integration and postintegration activities, when planning, problem solving, and collaboration are so critical to the success of the combined businesses.

Meeting the financial forecasts of payback period, return on investment, capture of market share, and so on for the deal should be enhanced by the shared Team Orientation appreciation and capabilities.

### Strong Acquirer, Weak Acquired

An acquiring business that recognizes and capitalizes on its superior Team Orientation capabilities should be able to smooth and shorten the challenging interactions between the merging parties. As with the indoctrination of a new employee, the acquiring team can use its effective team skills to set an example and develop the collaboration skills, creativity, and determination of "greater good" outcomes of their counterparts in the acquired business.

The differences in the cultures of the two organizations will quickly become evident during the steps of the combination process. However, damage to relationships and mutual regard may already have occurred. When Quantitative Organization Culture Analyses are used to assess the culture during the due diligence process, the knowledge of this particular difference in the strengths of the respective cultures can be used to capitalize on the acquirer's Team Orientation capabilities during the remaining steps of the combination.

The impact on the success of the deal of using QUOCA should be faster, smoother, and easier negotiation, closing, integration, and postintegration collaborative efforts. The financial rewards should be a less protracted return on investment and payback period and greater market capture.

## Weak Acquirer, Strong Acquired

Problems in the combination process are frequent when the acquired business's culture is stronger than the acquiring company's culture on one or more characteristics. It can be somewhat bewildering to the acquired organization when the acquirer lacks its strength on certain enabling cultural attributes, such as Team Orientation. Imagine being part of an organization that has used teams to effectively guide and facilitate the organization's success to the point where it becomes attractive to another, perhaps better known or more admired, company. Certainly the usual concerns will be shared by the people in the acquired organization, but excitement and anticipation will abound, with the promise of higher price and liquidity of equity, greater resources for investment in the future, and more potential for personal growth.

The excitement will be quickly tested and diminish the first time people who are accustomed to having a strong team orientation attempt to resolve a problem or plan an activity with people who have no clue about team processes. Problems will be compounded and resolutions protracted. Each step of the deal will take longer and cost more than anticipated. Soon animosity and frustration will begin to mount, and working relationships between the organizations will become acrimonious. Poor working relationships become a significant barrier to success, and the deal begins to sour. The payback for the deal, if it ever happens, is delayed well past the projected dates. Meanwhile, the team orientation of the acquired business has been diluted by the departure of key team players. The downward spiral continues to gain momentum until the acquirer either accepts a total loss on the deal or attempts to sell the gutted operation it had once been so excited about buying.

In this type of deal, where the acquired business is stronger on the Team Orientation characteristic than the acquiring business, QUOCA can be used to recognize the cultural dissimilarities and mitigate their effects. An understanding of the importance of teamwork in the acquired business may lead the acquirer to develop its own team skills, perhaps even involving the acquired enterprise's organizational development people in the development process.

## Weak Acquirer, Weak Acquired

Weak Team Orientation on both sides of the deal will present significant obstacles to all phases of the combination process, including the internal activities of each of the parties. The deal will take longer to set up, close, and integrate because no vehicles will exist to effectively and quickly bring people together in collaborative efforts. Again, QUOCA can cost-effectively identify and avoid these problems well before they have an opportunity to sidetrack and destroy a potentially profitable relationship by shortening the time and effort required to execute the deal and realize its anticipated benefits.

## SUMMARY

High-performing organizations place tremendous value on collaboratively working to achieve common goals, and receive tremendous value from this in return. Productive teams improve the overall effectiveness of the organization by facilitating goal achievement through focused deployment of the enterprise's greatest resource—its human intellect. Strength on the Team Orientation cultural characteristic is an important enabling asset during the phases of the combination process and for the long-term success of the combined organization.

# 19

C  H  A  P  T  E  R

# Capability Development

The value created by a firm resides in the accumulated knowledge of the people within it, expressed in the form of products and services sold. A firm succeeds by building the capabilities of its people first. Only then do the capabilities translate into efficient operations, more satisfied customers, and higher levels of financial performance.[1]

THE OBJECTIVES OF THIS CHAPTER are for the reader to understand the importance and value for the organization's long-term success of investing in employees' capabilities; define what leaders and employees must do in order to make employee capability development work in an organization; and understand how quantitative organization culture assessments can improve the performance of combinations involving organizations with weak Capability Development characteristics.

## CAPABILITY DEVELOPMENT—ENABLING CONTINUOUS IMPROVEMENT AND SUSTAINED SUCCESS

Continuous improvement is the key to excellence. Companies and individuals striving for world-class excellence must improve constantly. . . . In an environment of continuous improvement, everyone engages in exploration, discovery, and action, continually learns what is effective and what is not, and adjusts and improves accordingly.[2]

High-performing organizations continually invest in the knowledge, skills, and abilities of their employees. The return on this investment has

245

been demonstrated to be higher-quality products and services, greater employee satisfaction, and powerful ripple effects that include faster time to market for new products, greater bench strength during high-demand business cycles, and greater adaptability to internal and external dynamics.

There are several key indicators of the organization's propensity to develop its human capital, including:

1. Widespread delegation of responsibilities and empowerment to make job-quality decisions
2. The overt perception that its people are a strategic competitive advantage in the marketplace
3. Depth and breadth of technical capabilities so that employees can cover for and supplement one another during heavy workloads
4. Infrequent productivity and quality problems caused by human capital shortages
5. A willing, significant, ongoing investment in the knowledge, skills, and capabilities of employees, regardless of their rank and responsibility in the organization

## APPLICATIONS OF EMPLOYEE DEVELOPMENT ACTIVITIES

By promoting individual learning, the corporation recognizes the individual's responsibility for his or her own personal and professional development, while accepting its responsibility for creating an environment of opportunity in which all can thrive. As greater numbers of individuals with high self-esteem unleash their creativity, they reshape the contours of the firm. The corporation comes alive as employees continuously adapt and improve the way they do their work, and constantly redefine their roles and interactions.[3]

The company's education and training process should have clear objectives, such as creating a highly competent and empowered workforce, enhancing problem-solving abilities, and equipping people with the communication skills necessary for close customer contact and group interaction. Employee development programs and processes are deployed for three very specific reasons:

- To prepare for, anticipate, or react to technology changes in the external environment

- As a component of the individual's planned personal development program
- To mitigate performance problems

High-performing organizations are constantly on the alert for threats to their capabilities imposed by such external factors as new technologies, innovative products and services developed by competitors, changes in regulations, the fickleness of consumer demands, supplier developments and dynamics, the availability and cost of resources, and so on. Strength on the Capability Development cultural characteristic and also on the Organizational Learning and Customer Focus characteristics is a powerful combination that enables high-performing businesses to stay abreast of changes in customer demands and external market factors so that employees have both the insight and the technical awareness to identify and pursue their specific development needs.

Training and development programs take time to prepare, schedule, and put on. Companies that are proactive are more likely to maintain state-of-the-art capabilities by developing their own training programs or being early participants in vendor programs. It is common in high-performing cultures for trained employees to inform their colleagues of the content and direction of the programs they have completed. Cross-training is an important part of the group's effort to broaden and deepen its bench strength.

> What makes a company attractive (to an employee) is its ability to provide learning opportunities—chances to grow in skills, to prove and improve one's capability—that enhance the person's ability to keep employable.[4]

We have discussed how today's workforce differs from any workforce in the past by being committed to having work that intellectually challenges them and by being much less concerned about job security than past generations. As a result, they are highly mobile. In order to attract and retain the best employees (those with the strongest technical skills, greatest creativity, most energy and drive), companies must serve the development desires of their people.

The current generation of upwardly mobile people tend to be very specific in defining their capability development, often seeking the support and approval of their bosses for setting learning objectives in their formal goal-setting discussions. In response to these development interests, high-performing companies recognize that such an investment of time and money in current employees can be far cheaper than the loss of production as well as recruitment and training costs incurred when a lost competent employee must be replaced.

Another major motivation for ongoing employee development programs is the inescapable nature of change in the work environment, which leads to obsolescence of employee capabilities. There are four major causes of competence obsolescence:

1. Technological change is inescapable and leaves professionals behind.
2. Technological change is often accompanied by social and cultural change.
3. The economic worth of knowledge changes, with an accompanying decline in the human asset.
4. Sometimes the individual declines in personal abilities, energy, or health.[5]

Consider the technological changes that have affected the workforce over the past 20 years—cell phones, personal computers, PDAs, widespread use of the Internet. We haven't magically absorbed the skills necessary to accept, embrace, and use these technologies—we've had to make a concerted effort to master them and to integrate their use into our daily routine. More than ever, competency is a very transient thing. Consider also that this relentless storm of information and communication developments has had a significant impact on our social customs and cultural norms. Cell phone conversations while dining out were considered rude a few years ago; now they are accepted as inevitable. Nearly every executive I know uses the commute to and from work to catch up on voicemails. Emails and instant messages have significantly reduced employee-boss face time. As all of these professional, social, and cultural developments infiltrate the work environment and routines, they affect the competency of employees.  Therefore, the dynamics of technology are a constant threat to the competency of employees and the competitiveness of businesses.

In most jobs, something less than 20 percent of an employee's intellect and abilities is required to perform the tasks competently. Yet an employee's competence can significantly erode over time as a result of boredom, overfamiliarity with the tasks, subtle changes in the job, and aging-related loss of energy and focus. Greater empowerment of employees often helps to offset some of these competence-diminishing factors, and some companies rotate people through various task-intensive positions to achieve the same purpose. Training, retraining, and par-

ticipation in industry seminars and trade shows can also provide a
needed boost to maintain continued high performance.

> Think of change as skill building and concentrate on training as
> part of the change process. Even if people understand and accept
> a change, they often don't have the required skills and ability to
> carry out the new plan. This is a major impediment to successful
> change.[6]

Businesses can easily render their workforce incompetent through
their efforts to adapt their strategies, goals, objectives, and work
processes; their organization; and their modes of communication in
response to market changes. Each of these changes poses an obstacle to
the continued success of employees and therefore to the survival of the
enterprise. High-performing businesses analyze and prepare for the
direct and indirect effects of change on their people's ability to meet the
new goals, schedules, and quality requirements. Capability development
is considered an important, foreseen, and necessary component of the
enterprise's quest for survival and prosperity.

## THE INDIVIDUAL'S ROLE IN CAPABILITY DEVELOPMENT

Employee development—continuing education, continually honing and
expanding the mind—is vital mental renewal. Sometimes that involves the
external discipline of the classroom or of systematized study programs;
more often, it does not. Proactive people can figure out many, many ways
to educate themselves. Continuous capability development is an important
part of the employee/employer partnership. Employer and employee
share the common goal of making certain that people are fully equipped for
the dynamic knowledge, skill, and ability challenges of their current and
evolving responsibilities. The onus is on both parties to be aware of changes
that are transpiring that reduce the effectiveness of employees. The role of
the company is to invest the time and money necessary for capability development, just as the role of the individual is to learn and apply as much as
possible when opportunities for development are presented. This partnership is a powerful competitive edge in high-performing organizations with
strong Capability Development cultural characteristics.

Organizations with cultures that are high on the Team Orientation,
Coordination and Integration, and Capability Development culture characteristics are likely to spread the knowledge developed in one person
across the team and throughout the organization. Teaching others via
brown-bag seminars, formal presentations, and distribution of course

material strengthens personal relationships, cross-functional communications, and the overall organization's aggregated skill base, resulting in a more savvy and proficient enterprise.

## THE LEADER'S ROLE IN CAPABILITY DEVELOPMENT

> Leaders can energize learning behavior by rewarding it when it happens. Teaching is a way of showing people how they are connected—to their peers, their products, and their customers.[7]

Leaders have several important roles to play in the continuous capability development of their people. First, they must be vigilant and ready to respond when additional training and development is the appropriate remedial vehicle for performance shortfalls. Second, they must collaborate with their people to define and implement continuous improvement processes as part of their periodic goal-setting and evaluation process and in response to employee requests. Third, they must be aware of changes in the organization's goals, strategies, and desired outcomes; translate those changes into requisite human competency needs; and provide development accordingly. Fourth, they must be great coaches and example demonstrators for their people.

## THE EXECUTIVE'S ROLE IN CAPABILITY DEVELOPMENT

It is a sad fact that many businesses regard training and other capability development activities as an expense rather than an investment. In times of financial difficulty, training is often one of the first activities to be cut. The investment in people often has subtle returns that pop up in ways that seldom appear to be directly connected to the development activity. A problem avoided, a new market pursued, the ascent of an employee to a more influential position can all take place without someone attributing the activity to a mentor, a seminar, or a training program—yet these investments of time and money yield those returns as surely as invested cash principal yields cash interest payments.

Executives have an important responsibility to demonstrate how much they appreciate and value the organization's human capital and the confidence they place in it by continually supporting Capability Development throughout downturns in the business cycle and demands to cut expenses. Wise leaders who are able to keep the Vision of the enterprise alive in the face of difficulty know that the critical resources for slowly, gradually, and methodically turning that vision into reality are the people working in the business and the capabilities they bring to it. To stop investing in intellectual capital is tantamount to putting the dream on hold. Once that star has dimmed, it may be quite difficult to relight.

Key corporate people also have the responsibility to "walk the talk" in terms of their own continuous capability development. I have known several senior businesspeople who have proclaimed that their businesses were on the leading edge of technology, but who couldn't use a personal computer themselves. People in the rank and file can sense insincerity. Executives demonstrate their ongoing quest for knowledge and personal growth through the wisdom of their decisions, their emotional intelligence in times of trial, and their comfort in surrounding themselves with people who are competent and intelligent.

## THE FINANCIAL IMPLICATIONS OF A STRONG CAPABILITY DEVELOPMENT CULTURE

The value of a firm consists first and foremost of the knowledge possessed by the individuals that comprise it.[8]

As with the other two Involvement trait characteristics, Empowerment and Team Orientation, cultural strength in Capability Development is a powerful force for both higher product and service quality and higher employee satisfaction. Businesses report that, when they total all of the benefits gained from investment in employees, the financial return on their Capability Development dollars can be as high as 30 to 1.

It is clearly understandable that an organization that encourages and supports the ongoing capability development of its people will be better prepared to recognize, confront, and successfully deal with situations that affect product and service quality. Higher quality of products and services, in turn, improves profitability through reduced scrap and rework, higher production efficiencies from better use of resources, and reduced inventories. Company reputation, market share, and sales volume are often favorably affected by higher quality as well. Finally, state-of-the-art technical and market knowledge can be a powerful force for new product development and for reducing the time to market for new products and services. Strength on Capability Development can be a powerful competitive force, a source of a differentiating market advantage, greater and more diversified revenues, and higher profits.

Cultures that are strong on Capability Development also have higher employee satisfaction, which improves productivity and reduces personnel turnover. An individual's improved productivity as a result of having a powerful command of the technical, administrative, and market-related aspects of her or his work leads to:

1. Faster problem solving
2. Greater ability to recognize and mitigate problems
3. More innovation
4. Lower production costs
5. Higher net profits

Low personnel turnover, in turn, reduces the cost of hiring and training replacement people, as well as avoiding the decrease in productivity that is usually incurred as a result of the absence of the departed experienced people.

## CULTURAL CHARACTERISTICS RELATED TO CAPABILITY DEVELOPMENT

To recap, enterprises with cultures that are high on the Team Orientation, Coordination and Integration, and Capability Development culture measures are likely to spread the knowledge developed in one person across the team and throughout the organization by virtue of their common, coordinated interactions and their reliance on collaboration for widespread success.

Organizations that have high performance on the Capability Development cultural characteristic and coincidental, complementary strength on the Creating Change and Organizational Learning characteristics are more adept at translating the expanded knowledge, skills, and abilities of individuals into team, work group, department, and companywide learning and adaptation.

## M&A IMPLICATIONS OF THE CAPABILITY DEVELOPMENT CHARACTERISTIC

### Strong Acquirer, Strong Acquired

When two organizations that are combining are both strong in their desire and ability to develop their people, this clears the path of many obstacles to the success of the merger or acquisition. New ways of doing things, a different breadth and depth of knowledge, and unique capabilities are likely to be easily translated and transferred between the organizations because the cultures and their people have a desire and propensity for accepting new information.

The real benefit of these shared strengths should be seen in the integration and postintegration phases of the deal, when the hierarchies of the respective businesses begin to develop relationships. The combining businesses can leverage their technology, production, systems, and capability differences by encouraging tours of the facilities, the sharing of descriptive literature, and cross-training sessions. In summary, the ability to integrate and incorporate the knowledge, skill, and ability differences into a single, strong, aggregated human resource should provide a powerful technological market advantage.

## Strong Acquirer, Weak Acquired

An organization that is not accustomed to investing in the capabilities of its workforce may look favorably upon acquisition by a business that is strong on the Capability Development cultural characteristic. And the buyer will be in a position to spread the return on investment for training across its new acquisition in order to extend the benefits of highly capable people. The obstacle to success in such a deal can be overcoming the inertia of the status quo—getting supervisors, managers, and executives in the acquired business to embrace the concept of setting aside time and resources to develop the employees.

The financial implications of this type of merger or acquisition are not daunting, but they should be acknowledged and anticipated when working through the projections and the steps of the transaction. Executives and managers of the acquiring business may take for granted or assume that the people in the acquired business have the same exposure to, interest in, and benefit from capability development as their own people. In fact, the acquired business may not be reaping the benefits of high product and service quality and high employee satisfaction, as well as their ripple effects, which are typical of organizations with strength on the Capability Development culture characteristic. Consequently, the integration and postintegration phases of the combination may be extended, causing a lower than projected return on the investment, a longer payback period, delayed capture of market share, and a longer time to market for products and services.

Quantitative Organization Culture Analyses performed during the due diligence process can be quite effective in assessing the impact of integrating a "non-continuous improvement" group of people into the business. Fortunately, part of the cost-benefit of the QUOCA process is to enable the integration team to seize opportunities for smoothing the way to long-term good relationships between the combining organizations. Investing in people through training is a powerful way to convince the people in the acquired company that things have the potential to improve in the new organization.

## Weak Acquirer, Strong Acquired

As frequently noted in the descriptions of other cultural characteristics, when a cultural characteristic is stronger in the acquired business than in the acquirer, this creates a sense among the people of the acquired business that they are being overrun by heathens. This is especially true when the cultural aspect has such personal impact as Capability Development, in which the value of the individual to the organization is so effectively expressed. If the buyer has no awareness or appreciation of the degree of importance of capability development within its new acquisition, it may:

- Blindly cut training budgets to improve financial results
- Erroneously assume that it has superior human capital simply because it is the firm that was able to buy the other
- Treat the people of the acquired organization as inferior to its own people

The financial implications of this type of cultural dichotomy for an acquisition can be significant. Cuts in budget that result in the curtailment of capability development and attitudes of superiority can quickly eliminate what may have been at the core of the attractiveness of the deal in the first place—high-quality products and services from highly motivated and qualified people. The effect of the cultural difference on the financial performance of the combination can manifest itself as longer payback period, lower return on investment, and less than optimum capture of markets.

When QUOCA is used in the selection and due diligence phases of the acquisition, it will quickly point out this and other cultural differences so that they can be dealt with during the remaining steps of the deal. Recognition of the dichotomy may lead the acquiring enterprise to:

1. Rethink the value of the acquired enterprise's prospective contribution to the long-term success of the overall organization
2. Take a more hands-off approach to the management and operations of its new business unit
3. Emulate the Capability Development practices of the acquired organization

## Weak Acquirer, Weak Acquired

In some rare cases, shared weakness in a cultural characteristic may be better than a situation in which the acquirer organization is weaker than the acquired business. When both parties are weak in Capability Development, they literally don't know what they don't know. The financial outcome of a deal such as this is likely to be what is projected by the experts but far from the optimum because of the organization's underdeveloped human resources.

When both organizations involved in a combination are weak in a cultural characteristic and are not aware of it, they are missing an opportunity to use the change process that is inherent in the integration phase to implement needed cultural and organizational improvements. QUOCA is a powerful, cost-effective resource for enabling organizations to recognize their shared cultural weakness and take steps to improve Capability Development as an investment in the long-term success of the deal.

## SUMMARY

Enlightened personal development benefits both the employee and the company.[9]

Capability Development is a cultural attribute with implications that go well beyond current financial results. Organizations that are weak on this characteristic are short-changing themselves and their stakeholders, particularly their employees, by not optimizing their true differential advantage—the unique interests and capabilities of their people. The direct and indirect consequences of weak Capability Development are extensive: poorer quality of products and services and lower employee satisfaction, with accompanying reduced responsiveness to both internal and external business developments and dynamics.

On the other hand, enterprises with strong Capability Development characteristics have invested in their future by enabling employees to expand their expertise. These organizations will very likely be more proactive in dealing with both internal and external variables that affect the business. People in such organizations are also likely to feel better able to succeed at their jobs, be more satisfied with their efforts, and receive greater satisfaction from their work. The organization, in turn, is often rewarded by reduced employee turnover, greater productivity, higher quality, and increased nimbleness and creativity in dealing with challenges. Businesses report financial return on their Capability Development of as high as 30 to 1, making training and development of employees one of the best investments a business can make.

C  H  A  P  T  E  R

# THE ADAPTABILITY TRAIT

If an organization is to meet the challenges of a changing world, it must be prepared to change everything about itself except (its basic) beliefs as it moves through corporate life. . . . The only sacred cow in an organization should be its basic philosophy of doing business.[1]

THE OBJECTIVES OF THIS CHAPTER are for the reader to understand the cultural purview and characteristics of the Adaptability trait; the external perspective of the Adaptability trait and its bearing on the flexibility of the organization; and how quantitative organization culture assessments can improve the performance of combinations involving organizations with weak Adaptability trait characteristics.

## EVOLUTION AND THE BUSINESS ENVIRONMENT

Charles Darwin may have inadvertently been talking about the survival and prosperity of business as well as species when he stated that there are only three fates for beings in a changing environment: Adapt appropriately to the environmental changes, move to a location where the species's state of evolution is suitable for the environment, or perish. If you don't think adaptability is important, take a good look around you next time you drive down Main Street or walk through the mall. One store is gone, another is expanding, and soon to come is the next hopeful entrepreneurial merchant. The earlier section of this book describing the history of mergers and acquisitions barely scratches the surface of change agents within the business environment. Facilitated by viral marketing and the Internet, a little technology change in Finland or Japan can springboard your business into unexpected and unprepared-for growth or antiquate your products and services in a heartbeat.

I was once part of the marketing squad of a start-up company with a great idea, technically strong and dedicated people, and virtually no budget. The first round of our start-up and operating capital came from friends, families, and business associates of the founding officers and board members for the purpose of developing a business model and creating the basic infrastructure for the business. The next two rounds of money we raised were dedicated to developing quality product and service capabilities. The line item in the budget for marketing was blank—we made guerilla marketing look like a perk.

We peddled our services to anyone who would listen—individuals, small businesses, big corporations, even a couple of multinationals. Each pitch we made was met with enthusiasm, and, like all start-ups, we were delighted to talk about our production, quality, and innovation all in the same breath. Suddenly something both wonderful and terrible happened: We got a huge corporate client. The good news was that we were going to have more orders than we could ever have imagined. The bad news was that we were going to have more orders than we had ever imagined. We were about to find out whether adaptability was in our repertoire of cultural characteristics.

> It might be far more satisfactory to look at well-adapted vision-ary companies not primarily as the result of brilliant foresight and strategic planning, but largely as consequences of a basic process—namely, try a lot of experiments, seize opportunities, keep those that work well (consistent with the core ideology) and fix or discard those that don't.[2]

## THE ADAPTABILITY CULTURAL TRAIT

The Adaptability trait of organization cultures concerns and measures the group's ability to sense the dynamics of its external environment and translate those dynamics into appropriate organizational and operational changes that perpetuate the organization's well-being and success. Organizations can muddle along for quite some time with a poor sense of Mission, a low degree of employee Involvement, and a serious lack of Consistency, but a deficiency in Adaptability puts the death of the organization on the fast track.

Adaptability serves as the scout for the organization, enabling it to sense and make sense of the world outside the organization's walls. The sensory elements of adaptability include an understanding of which environmental variables are important and which are trivial; knowledge of the most effective way to monitor the important variables, their rate and amount of change; and a sense of benchmarks against which the changes are measured. Good scouts know what they don't know, and their curiosity goes well beyond simply gathering information to fully understanding the environmental elements that pose danger and/or opportunity. They constantly gather and assess information regarding law and regulatory changes, new competitors, old competitors with new products, changes in the dynamic world of customers, the supply chain and its variables, and so on. Unfortunately, not all companies' organizations are strong in their ability to monitor and respond to changes in the environment. Those that are weak are at a competitive disadvantage to their more Adaptable counterparts and so are more likely to flounder or fail in the market.

> In most companies that fail, there is abundant evidence in advance that the firm is in trouble. This evidence goes unheeded, however, even when individual managers are aware of it. The organization as a whole cannot recognize impending threats, understand the implications of those threats or come up with alternatives.[3]

Adaptability is the critically important link between the flexibility of the organization and its external focus. It is the involvement of everyone in the organization in being aware of, communicating, and embracing the changes that are needed to perpetuate the success of the enterprise. As stated so well in the opening quotation of this chapter, groups that prosper are adept at appropriately changing everything except their fundamental purpose.

I once worked for an extraordinary reinsurance company that constantly challenged its assumptions and fervently studied its business environment in an effort to distinguish itself in a market in which most of the key players regarded their products and services as being rather boring commodities. Our leaders rethought our purpose of "risk management" and decided that our emphasis on understanding and serving the "risk" aspect of our business was, in fact, limited in opportunity. Instead, we began to focus on the "management" element and created a host of value-added services that not only yielded very nice profits but also differentiated us from our competitors. In a succession of brilliant strategic moves, we bought ourselves from our parent, went public, and eventually were purchased at a very high premium because of our ability to innovate and evolve in what had traditionally been a pretty stodgy industry.

> If organizations are to be continually changing, then the employees must be continually learning and growing. Individually, most people do not grow on a linear basis; they do not learn in predetermined, syllabus sequence. Rather, they seek learning experiences, as they need them, acquiring the knowledge and skill to solve a particular problem or understand an issue. Consequently, executives in flexible organizations have learned that the employee development must be broad enough to allow individuals to explore and grow, while maintaining a focus on the organization purpose.[4]

High-performing organizations regard change as being inevitable and therefore something that must be reckoned with. They often have a sixth sense, an ability to anticipate important changes, and they have a predisposition to react quickly and appropriately when threats and opportunities arise. Dynamics are appreciated as fundamental elements in the challenging journey toward prosperous growth. In organizations with a high degree of adaptability, everyone is a scout and "continuous improvement" is the mantra. People have and share deep personal feelings about their work, products, and companies. As Stephen Covey[5] would say, they are expert at "sharpening the saw"—that is, dedicating the time, effort, and resources required to respond to the next challenge. People in highly adaptive groups are proud of their products and continually aware of threats and opportunities. Often their adaptability is aided and supported by high degrees of Coordination and Integration, Core Values, Team Orientation, and Empowerment.

> Change is constant. The history of mankind is about change. History is a chronology of change. One set of beliefs is pushed aside by a new set. The old order is swept away by the new. If people become attached to the old order, they see their best interest in defending it. They become the losers. They become the old order and in turn are vulnerable. People who belong to the new order are the winners.[6]

Adaptability involves three closely related components: Creating Change, Organizational Learning, and Customer Focus. Creating Change involves the group's ability to redirect its efforts, thinking, structure, resources, and processes to meet the dynamics of its environment. As stated in an earlier quotation, change is inevitable. High-performing enterprises adopt a mindset that sees their ability to accept, respond to, and anticipate change as an important element in their competitive edge. Tom Peters emphatically makes this point in his best-selling *Thriving on Chaos* when he states, "Today, loving change, tumult, even chaos is a prerequisite for survival, let alone success."[7]

> The most intriguing leadership role in culture management is the one in which the leader attempts to develop a learning organization that will be able to make its own perpetual diagnosis and self-manage whatever transformations are needed as the environment changes.[8]

Organizational Learning involves the ability of the group to accept, translate, and employ information concerning the dynamics of its environment. It addresses the group's beliefs and assumptions regarding innovation, its ability to coordinate its activities with those of other groups for the overall success of the organization, and its ability to properly respond to failures, errors, and mistakes. As in all elements of organizational culture, there is no "silver bullet" that will ensure successful and effective efforts toward continuous improvement, and the process that embraces and facilitates organizational learning is itself dynamic. Peter Senge states in the introduction to the paperback edition of *The Fifth Discipline* "The cultural changes that take place when people begin operating in a true learning orientation vary from company to company, but by and large they represent deep universal changes in the traditional culture of western management."[9] Organizations that embrace a continuous improvement mindset coincidentally embrace the vehicle that enables successful evolution in their dynamic environment—a critical attribute for their survival and prosperity.

> The winning companies spend enormous amounts of energy and money to find out what the customer wants. . . . Knowing the customer is not considered marketing, or worse yet, market research's job alone. Everyone gets involved, from the president downward. . . . These firms make certain that every department participates in learning about the customer.[10]

Customer Focus involves the group's beliefs and assumptions concerning their relationship with the recipients of their work. The ultimate customer is the person who pays the bills by purchasing the products and/or services that the enterprise creates. With the exception of the sales and customer service people, few members of the typical organization interact with the ultimate user. Yet everyone involved in the organization's efforts, in some respect, contributes to the purpose of the organization and its need to add value for its external customers. An individual or work group's link in the chain may be to serve an internal customer, but somehow, in some way, the efforts of all the people in the organization affect the ultimate customer—otherwise, they wouldn't have a job. In high-performing organizations, everyone is facing in the same direction—toward the client.

The degree of variation in Customer Focus is well illustrated by the story of the three masons building a church. The culture is strong when everyone knows what his or her role is in "building God's waiting room."

As with Organizational Learning and Creating Change, the group's beliefs and assumptions regarding its Customer Focus reflect its aptitude for and attitude toward Adaptability to the dynamics of its environment and, ultimately, the long-term viability and success of the organization. Fisher's research[11] demonstrated the close relationship between an organization's ability to adapt to its dynamic environment and its financial performance on three important measures: sales/revenue growth, market share, and product development/innovation.

Customer Focus transcends simply meeting the physical requirements and expectations of the recipient of the work. Customer Focus acknowledges that there is an interdependent relationship between the supplier and the user. As Harvey Mackay, the very successful envelope salesman, commercial real estate developer, and author of the best selling *Swim with the Sharks*, says:

> Knowing your customer means knowing what your customer really wants. Maybe its your product, but maybe there's something else, too; recognition, respect, reliability, concern, service, a feeling of self-importance, friendship, help—things all of us care more about than we care about malls or envelopes.[12]

Each individual within each of the groups that make up a high-performing organization is committed to the success of each link in the chain that connects him or her to the genuine needs of the ultimate customer. Market share and the growth of sales and, consequently, revenue and profits are intuitively related to the organization's ability to define the real needs of its ultimate customers as well as its ability to create appropriate internal change based on the dynamics of its external environment. Thus, high performance on the Adaptability trait, and particularly on the Customer Focus and Creating Change indices, is useful in predicting an enterprise's ability to survive and prosper through profitable operations.

Innovation and new product development appear to be subjective terms until we look at how truly creative businesses set objective goals for their creativity. 3M is generally regarded as being one of the most innovative companies in the world. Its customer commitment is to provide "innovative and reliable products and services from a company you can trust." 3M's strong financial performance is tied directly to its ability to dream up new markets for old products (four-color graphics on the O-Cello sponges were a recent hit), new products (especially adhesives and abrasives), and new ways of operating its business (a self-directed factory with universal people empowerment). People are encouraged to spend up to a fourth of their work hours on projects that they want to work on, and 30 percent of each year's revenue projections are expected to come from new products or other innovations. And while these are lofty goals, the 3M reality of profitability, revenue growth, and global recognition demonstrates that a culture that is strong in its ability to adapt has the capability to achieve long-term success and prosperity.

## FINANCIAL AND OPERATIONAL IMPLICATIONS OF THE ADAPTABILITY TRAIT

The Adaptability trait should be considered the bellwether for the enterprise's ability to survive and prosper in the face of inevitable changes in its external environment. Customer Focus is the measure of how well the organization is able to monitor and respond to the needs of both its external and its internal customers. Organizational Learning assesses the extent to which adaptability is accepted and facilitated. Creating Change reflects the enterprise's ability to overcome inertia and stimulate adaptation in its beliefs and behaviors to ensure the prosperity and survival of the organization. Consequently, organizations that enjoy an overall strength on the Adaptability trait typically are high-performing in product development and innovation that translates into higher market share and sales/revenue growth.[13]

Conversely, an organization that is weak in Adaptability will suffer from declining results because of its ignorance of external dynamics or its inability to integrate such dynamics into new ways of doing things. Weak Adaptability often leads to:

- Lower sales/revenue growth
- Reduced market share
- Extended time to market of new products as a result of retarded product development and innovation[14]

In most cases, astute leaders will discover the poor results and respond to them by initiating change processes. The dilemma with challenges in adaptability is that the organization is not adept at initiating change and corrective actions. It must first learn how to learn before it can learn what to do differently. If Customer Focus is weak, those change processes are unlikely to be effective because of the disconnect between the enterprise and its market. If Creating Change is weak, adaptation will be a long and painful process, if it happens at all, because the lack of wherewithal for change *is* the problem. And if Organization Learning is weak, the enterprise will always find itself catching up with and reacting to its environment rather than anticipating or even influencing it.

One very effective way to objectively and emphatically illustrate a group's Adaptability challenges is to share the Quantitative Organization Culture Analyses results with the group's constituents in such a way that they discover and diagnose their own problem from their own culture survey input. This self-discovery is a very powerful experience—an "Aha!" kind of moment that awakens perception of the undeniable existence of the situation and motivates changing behaviors to overcome it. With awareness and motivation, the Adaptability of the organization can begin to improve.

## ADAPTABILITY TRAIT IMPLICATIONS FOR MERGERS AND ACQUISITIONS

### Strong Acquirer, Strong Acquired

Coincidental strengths on the Adaptability trait in combining organizations should facilitate quick integration of the organizations' best abilities, systems, and resources. Their ability to adapt will certainly be an aid during one of the greatest challenges to any organization: the changes of leadership, mission, responsibilities, expectations, and culture that are inherent in mergers and acquisitions. Cultures that are strong on their Customer Focus, Organizational Learning, and Creating Change characteristics have the built-in capability to quickly and effectively integrate dynamic market objectives, processes and techniques, and other organizational changes into their day-to-day activities. As a result, the combination of enterprises that share strength on the Adaptability trait and its characteristics should enjoy a shorter integration period and more efficient, effective combined operations.

QUOCA is a powerful tool for optimizing the quick integration of two organizations that are strong on Adaptability by illustrating to the constituents that their virtues are recognized and reassuring them that their coincidental strengths will complement one another for continued and expanded success. Should either the acquirer or the acquired prove to be more adaptable than its counterpart, wise leadership will capitalize on the strength during the integration process in order to retain the trait and spread it throughout the combined organization.

### Strong Acquirer, Weak Acquired
When an organization that is strong on its ability to adapt to its external environment acquires an enterprise that is weak on this cultural trait, the acquirer has a clear opportunity and responsibility to use its strengths to set the stage for a successful combination. With that said, however, the acquiring business must acknowledge the fact that the timing and degree of success for the deal is dependent upon the combined organization *in toto* being able to retain its Customer Focus in order to define and meet its market needs; its Organizational Learning in order to adapt to changes in the organization and its way of doing things; and its Creating Change capabilities in order to view changes as being inevitable, positive, and rewarding. Early recognition of the cultural differences through QUOCA should enable the acquiring team to adjust the price and performance expectations for the deal and to anticipate the need to develop the adaptability of the acquired company during the integration process.

### Weak Acquirer, Strong Acquired
The following three chapters will provide an in-depth discussion of each of the Adaptability trait characteristics and help to make it clear why this trait, above the others, is so important to the success of mergers and acquisitions. The worst possible M&A scenario for differences in organizational cultures is when the acquired organization is stronger in its ability to sense and meet its customers' needs and/or create change in response to its dynamic environment and/or actively learn from mistakes and changes in the work requirements.

If the acquirer is blissfully ignorant of the cultural characteristics of an adaptable organization and attempts to impose its ways of doing things upon the acquired organization, then both will quickly lose an asset that, although probably unbeknown to the acquiring company, made the acquired company attractive in the first place. Coincidentally, the acquired company will lose an opportunity to incorporate what might well be a strategic advantage into its culture and operations. The most likely result will be a significant loss of key people in the acquired enterprise, with extensive ripple effects such as reduced quality, market share, and profitability of the combined organization, due primarily to a rapid drop-off in the performance of the acquired business.

### Weak Acquirer, Weak Acquired

Coincidental weakness in Adaptability will be tantamount to two blind people lost in a new city—lots of fear, loathing, and acrimony as they stumble around, not knowing where they are going or how they are going to get there. An opportunity for tremendous return on the investment of time, effort, and money occurs when QUOCA identifies two prospective combining organizations that both have weakness on the Adaptability trait. Not knowing what they don't know, unable to learn, and married to their inertia, two such companies attempting to combine would be like the last dodo bird mating with the last carrier pigeon in a desperate attempt to have their genes survive. In such a situation, QUOCA can save all the stakeholders from a doomed, misguided, and fruitless relationship.

## SUMMARY

Adaptability is the invaluable cup of water that enables you to prime the pump and tap into the well. It is the critical organizational trait for coping with and succeeding during significant business upheavals, such as a merger or an acquisition. Strength on this trait and its characteristics will facilitate the ability to evolve quickly—and correctly—for the safety, survival, and prosperity of the organizations and their constituents. Weakness on this trait or any of its characteristics could be the fatal flaw that leads to the combination underperforming or ultimately failing.

# 21

# CUSTOMER FOCUS

> Most human beings have a higher purpose than mere survival. They have a "reason for being" that drives them to do what they do. . . . Winning companies establish customer satisfaction as an overarching goal . . . as their reason for being.[1]

THE OBJECTIVES OF THIS CHAPTER are for the reader to be able to identify the key characteristics and strategic advantages of customer-focused organizations; view Customer Focus as a critical element for the organization's survival and long-term success; and understand how quantitative organization culture assessments can improve the performance of combinations involving organizations with weak Customer Focus characteristics.

## THE NATURE OF A CUSTOMER-FOCUSED ORGANIZATION

The winning companies spend enormous amounts of energy and money to find out what the customer wants. They do this because they want to know what their customers want today, expect tomorrow and are likely to ask for the day after. They really want to "get inside their customers' skins" as it were, they want to know their customers' needs better than the customers themselves. This enables them to anticipate these needs in designing their products and services. It also allows them to create and control the expectations customers may have about their performance.[2]

The Adaptability trait measures and expresses the organization's ability to monitor its external environment and to appropriately adjust its internal operations in order to assure its survival and prosperity. The other two Adaptability characteristics, Creating Change and Organizational Learning, combine to address the challenges of adapting the organization to its dynamics and adapting its individual and collective capabilities to meet its challenges, respectively. Customer Focus is concerned with the organization's ability to be aware of and respond to the changing needs and desires of its customers.

High-performing organizations have a very broad definition of *customer*, embracing the concept that a customer is anyone whose decisions and actions determine whether the enterprise will prosper. This sense of continuity from the front-line employee through production through delivery to intermediates and, finally, to acquisition and employment by the end user acknowledges that any failure along the way will eventually affect the ultimate customer and impair the enterprise's competitive position. Every employee serves the interests of each and every person downstream of his or her outbox. Effective organizations create in employees a sense of responsibility for understanding and meeting the needs of their succession of customers. And effective enterprises provide the wherewithal to enable their people to adjust their activities as needed in order to assure that the overall process is an efficient and effective collaborative effort to satisfy end-user needs.

> The only right way to run a company—and the most profitable way—is to saturate your company with the customers' voice. Follow this practice and most customers won't end up dissatisfied. You'll hear the voices of both those who are happy and those who are not, and you'll use the information to give an even better experience to your customers.[3]

It is the active use of the wherewithal—the collection of awareness, interest, and resources—that differentiates organizations that have effective Customer Focus from those that don't. Candid feedback, whether favorable or unflattering, is broadly shared in the organization and is used to commend excellence or to stimulate troubleshooting. High-performing organizations consider their people to be allies in quality improvement rather than culprits when failure occurs and so engage them in pinpointing the root causes of problems and eliminating them. Recognition of problems, the definition of their root causes, and descriptions of corrective actions are widely shared as part of the continuous improvement process.

> You never persuade clients of anything. Clients persuade themselves. Your function is to understand the issues that matter to your clients. You have to feel their problems just the way they feel them. You have to sit on their side of the table and look at issues from their point of view.[4]

Often the source of customer input is employees who engage their clients rather than simply getting them to buy. Customer Focus begins with a sales mentality that seeks to define and meet the customer's situation and needs. Both parties clearly benefit from a trusting, personal, candid customer-supplier relationship.

For example, my friend and dentist, Kirk Huckel, has built his very successful practice around the simple concept that teeth, with proper care, were built to last a lifetime. He could stay busy day in and day out filling cavities and treating gum disease, but he prefers to involve his clients in their own prophylactic dental care habits. From the moment you meet him or anyone on his staff, it is very clear that everyone there considers tooth and gum remediation to be a preventable disappointment. Of course, Kirk has the latest in orthodontic equipment and stays on the leading edge of his field. But following the necessary repair or during a check-up or after a cleaning, he and his staff spend extra time to discuss the latest techniques and materials for improved hygiene and preventive tooth care. They give personal feedback on things that each customer could do better, ask for questions, and hand out a new toothbrush and enough floss to last until the next appointment. They don't just hope for a happy customer, they ensure it.

In high-performing organizations, inputs from customers and prospective customers are major factors in decision making. Some truly gifted companies have a knack for sensing what is missing in their customers' lives and filling the void. I certainly didn't know that I needed a Sony Walkman until I saw one. Of course this so-called knack is probably based on extensive market analysis, focus group input, and test marketing—these efforts, too, are part of the Customer Focus mentality.

> If you really listen to your customers, they're never happy—they'll let you know what you're doing wrong—and it just forces you to get better. Fat headedness is what bothers me the most. I think we get so much press about our service and all this stuff and we start believing it and then we think we're better than the customer. And then we're dead right there.[5]

A couple of years ago I worked with a major financial services company that had invested a huge amount of time and money in developing its first interactive web site. As a market leader, this company wanted to be the first to enable a variety of online services for existing customers and to attract web-savvy noncustomers to become clients. The manager, a brilliant man who ably provided both technical and project management expertise, had assembled teams of very bright, dedicated people to create and integrate the various components of the project. However, he was being pulled in a number of different directions by senior executives, who had clear visions of what the web site would do *for the company*.

Once the site was up and running, the project manager asked me to assist the teams in making the transition from 70-hour-a-week development activities to 40- or 50-hour a week normal operations. I had done some team building, leadership development, and one-on-one coaching with many of the people on the project team, and so I enjoyed close relationships and a lot of understanding of the issues confronting the team members as they developed the project. In the course of my interactions, the project people had expressed an unusually high amount of frustration as they tried to develop a site that met the senior executives' moving targets for requirements, image, and functionality. It became very clear that the people were relieved that the development phase was over but were very concerned about top management's judgment of the web site.

The project executive and I defined a need to assess the overall culture and the project development team culture as a vehicle to identify their strengths and weaknesses. The results would be used for input into the overall reorganization of the group in response to the change of mission from development to operations. Every employee who had worked on the project completed a survey, and the data were cut several different ways to reflect the assumptions and beliefs of the people on the various teams and across the levels of hierarchy. As we had expected, the data reflected very high scores on the Consistency and Involvement traits, the Vision characteristic in the Mission trait, and both Creating Change and Organizational Learning in the Adaptability trait.

The data revealed mid-range scores on Strategic Direction and Intent and Goals and Objectives, reflecting the internal confusion about the nature of the web site. However, the most telling information came from the scores on Customer Focus: They were in the tenth percentile or lower. The team had spent so much of its time and effort trying to understand and meet the requirements of senior management that the customer was left out of the development process.

I ran into my friend a while back. He said that 2 years after the web site was launched, the company acknowledged failure and pulled the plug. The site had been universally panned by professional critics, had never caught on with existing clients, and had never attracted the new business executives had envisioned. The company wrote off the entire project—some hundreds of millions of dollars and untold opportunity costs—and started over from scratch. The moral of the story is obvious: Customers need executive brainstorms like a fish needs a bicycle. Products and services must be developed to meet the needs of the end user, not to meet the fancy of the visionaries who created them. To avoid disasters like this, the Edsel, and New Coke, high-performing organizations communicate externally with customers and prospects to define their needs and internally with people throughout the organization to make certain that the customers' needs are met. As Thomas Wallace espouses in *Customer Driven Strategy*, "This means frequent communication, teamwork, trust, mutual respect—and providing superior customer service."[6]

## THE INDIVIDUAL'S ROLE IN CUSTOMER FOCUS

> Most employees want to serve their customers well. One of our surveys showed, surprisingly, that the factor most strongly correlated to employees' remaining in a company was simply whether employees think that the organization was providing good service to customers. If they think so, then turnover was low.[7]

Effective organizations recognize and relish the joy of making the customer happy. In fact, the overriding reason that I do what I do is the sense of satisfaction I get from people expressing their gratitude to me for a job well done. The fact is that I could probably get more financial compensation if I worked for a large consulting firm. But the rewards I receive from personal contact in rooting out my clients' situation and needs, personally developing and presenting services to meet those needs, and then directly observing the performance improvements more than compensates for a lower income. In high-performing enterprises, whether it's your favorite restaurant, dentist, car mechanic, or bank, the employees sincerely express their desire to meet your needs—the joy of customer satisfaction is an important part of their reward system.

> In short, today companies have to do right by the customer every time.[8]

High-performing organizations effectively communicate customer input—whether adverse or complimentary—as the means to keep doing what the customer wants and to develop alternatives for what the customer doesn't want. Negative feedback, as the submarine skipper once said, provides "another opportunity to excel." Formal and informal communication processes focus everyone's attention on the ultimate values of their efforts—customer satisfaction, profitability, and the resultant survival and prosperity of the enterprise.

A key element in the effective communication of customer needs throughout the organization is a broad definition of "customer." Whitley tells us:

> Your customers include everyone whose decisions determine whether your organization will prosper. That may be a complex, multi-layered group, but you've got to know and serve them all to guarantee prosperity.[9]

In other words, customers include the salesperson who develops the opportunity and processes the order, your boss who provides you with task requirements, the Accounts Receivable employee who processes the invoices that pay for your work, and the Shipping Department person who sends your output to the client. The organization with strong Customer Focus knows that its survival and prosperity are dependent upon each step in the link from customer to customer functioning effectively. The high-performing organization works very candidly, honestly, sincerely, and tirelessly to satisfy the customer.

## THE LEADER'S ROLE IN CUSTOMER FOCUS

> The leader's job is to put his or her customers first. He or she does that by determining what each of them wants or demands in terms of great performance from the leader, and then by working assiduously to deliver great performance. The leader encourages others by setting the example to follow and adopt the same methodology.[10]

The leader's role in customer focus is threefold. First, the leader must determine and communicate the organization's customers' needs. Second, the leader must create an environment that strives for continuous improvement in accomplishing its responsibilities. Third, the leader is to set an example of the first and second behaviors. These are not easy tasks for today's administratively burdened managers, as Davidow and

Uttal state in *Total Customer Service*:[11] "The most important reason for the gap between managerial awareness of the service crisis and managerial performance in dealing with the problem, we believe, is tunnel vision. The majority of managers tend to take a narrow view of service and hence a narrow view of how to produce it." It is the overall culture of the organization that develops and rewards the broad view of customer service as being both a critical external function and, just as important, an interdependent internal process that requires participation by all hands.

> The leader leads by providing directions and focus on what the customers really buy [12]

Each element of the manager's words and actions and the aggregate of those words and actions must communicate the need for customer satisfaction. Managers must show employees that the company's number-one job is to serve customers—and that they, the employees, are the key to the entire system.[13]

## RELATED CULTURAL CHARACTERISTICS

### Customer Focus + Goals and Objectives + Coordination and Integration + Empowerment = Prosperity

> Not only does the total company have customers, so does each element of the work force. These are the internal customers: the next department, the next work team, the next production unit— the group or groups within the company that receive "our output." The same principles apply to the inside relationships: close to their customers via customer partnerships.[14]

A strong Coordination and Integration characteristic complements strength on Customer Focus in high-performing organizations by providing an alignment of goals through collaborative efforts. As a shared desired outcome for the overall enterprise, Customer Focus serves as a uniting force to optimize the sense of community and shared purpose across organizational boundaries. High-performing organizations efficiently and effectively coordinate their activities toward the integrated goal of satisfying customers.

> The creation of close working relationships with customers must be the centerpiece of the company's operational strategy. This goal needs to be clearly articulated and widely communicated

throughout the company, and then the company leaders must reinforce the message. Live by it. Walk the talk. Make certain it happens.[15]

Organizations that enjoy strength on both Goals and Objectives and Customer Focus are better able to translate the customer's needs into specific outcomes related to the individual and collective efforts. Well-articulated and mutually agreed-upon goals and objectives serve a dual purpose in high-performing enterprises. By breaking the end result, customer satisfaction, into bite-sized chunks, leaders are able to provide unambiguous goals for their people. Additionally, unachieved outcomes initiate collaborative troubleshooting efforts that mitigate the flow of problems through to the client.

> This and this alone is the key to the winner's success. They get all their employees in every department or function closely involved in the effort to provide superior customer satisfaction. It's as simple—and as complex—as that. Everything else they do—being obsessive about knowing the customer, setting extremely high standards, designing products that maximize customer satisfaction—is aimed at achieving this one overriding goal.[16]

Empowerment is also a strong ally for organizations that have excellent Customer Focus. Pride and ownership in the work blossom when people understand the desired end result and are entrusted with the wherewithal to perform their tasks in the most effective manner. In the story of the empowered mason, each brick was an incremental success in the process of building a cathedral. Individual contributions aggregate to ongoing organizational success when Empowerment is coupled with a sincere commitment to understanding and fulfilling the needs of the customer, thus leading to the expanded success of the organization and eventually providing greater personal security and prosperity.

## THE IMPACT OF CUSTOMER FOCUS ON FINANCIAL PERFORMANCE

Strength on Customer Focus in and of itself is no assurance of success—it must be complemented by strengths on other traits such as Goals and Objectives and Coordination and Integration in order to optimize its influence on the success and survival of the enterprise. However, strengths on all traits but Customer Focus put the organization on a very slippery slope. Coca-Cola was very good at producing and distributing as much New Coke as the public could consume—the public just didn't want to consume it.

Poor Customer Focus is a double-edged sword that cuts the bottom line by producing a high inventory of stuff no one wants and cuts revenue by not producing what the customers do want. A short-term loss of focus on the customer is often seen in:

- Longer sales cycles from more difficult sales closings
- Higher inventory of low-demand products and supplies
- Higher Accounts Receivable from dissatisfied customers
- Increased returns of products
- Spikes in overtime as production tries to catch up with real demand

Outsourcing much of the initial information gathering can minimize a major expense for organizations that are trying to improve Customer Focus. However, the true cost of developing a customer-oriented enterprise is the time and effort required to bring the focus of people's eyes, hearts, and minds onto the ultimate boss: the customer. Getting salespeople to stop throwing a sales pitch and start listening is a challenge. Directing the organization's attention to customer need–based goals and objectives requires discipline and commitment. Coordinating and integrating activities that are consistently dedicated to meeting the ultimate boss's needs rather than being diverted by the crisis of the moment takes true grit and resolve. Empowering people to err on the side of the customer requires trust. Clearly, making the transition to an effectively Customer Focused organization is a significant investment in the long-term success of the enterprise, but the alternative is a tacit acceptance of an inevitable death sentence.

## M&A IMPLICATIONS OF THE CUSTOMER FOCUS CHARACTERISTIC

### Strong Acquirer, Strong Acquired

Combining two organizations with a strong Customer Focus characteristic has great symbiotic potential. While each enterprise will have its own particular methods for sensing and responding to its customers' needs, the real value is the awareness of the *need* for customer focus. Each organization should have a wealth of information on its customers and their needs, market factors, and competitors—perhaps even objective information on its counterpart in the deal. With a combined focus on collective customers, redundancies can be eliminated and voids can be filled, resulting in greater revenue and profitability, a reduced integration effort, and a shorter payback period.

## Strong Acquirer, Weak Acquired

An acquiring organization with a strong Customer Focus will be confounded by the inexplicable absence of the end user as a driving force in the acquired business. In fact, a significant dichotomy in the scores for Customer Focus (with strength in the acquiring organization) can predict a very difficult integration process. Alert acquirers will adjust the purchase price, their expectations for the payback period, and their assumptions concerning the scope, costs, and duration of the integration process according to the degree of difference between the organizations' scores on the Customer Focus characteristic.

The use of Quantitative Organization Culture Analyses early in the combination process will give the acquirer an opportunity to factor the prospect's weakness on the Customer Focus characteristic and ripple effects from that weakness into the go/no-go decision, the price calculations, and, if the deal goes through, the integration process. The buyer should be aware that the prospective partner may have products and services that are not up-to-date, a passé inventory, and a cultural inability to translate customer needs into viable products.

## Weak Acquirer, Strong Acquired

It is difficult for me to imagine how the initiating company in a business combination can underappreciate an acquisition candidate with a strong Customer Focus characteristic if it performs a reasonably good due diligence. The acquisition's relatively high market share and lower than average cost of sales, inventories, and accounts receivable should awaken the buyer to the fact that it may have something to learn from its prospective asset.

If the acquirer is blind to the acquired organization's Customer Focus or doesn't attempt to integrate it into the newly combined enterprise, adverse consequences are inevitable. Recall that strong Customer Focus translates into employee satisfaction and retention, which can flip to dissatisfaction and high turnover should the new culture deemphasize the employee-customer connection. The list of potential consequences of a combination of organizations with a Customer Focus imbalance is extensive, but is sure to include:

- Longer payback and integration periods
- Longer time to market for new products

- Decreased customer loyalty, sales, and revenues

It is unfortunate that the cultural characteristics of the acquirer often dominate in combined organizations. In the case of Customer Focus, like that of other cultural aspects, the acquirer has the opportunity to gain far more than a business when it acquires a higher-performing organization. But like a blind man buying a beautiful house, the acquiring company will fail to appreciate what it has bought, and the majesty soon fades, leaving everyone poorer. Once again, QUOCA can cost-effectively illustrate the mismatch and prompt the acquirer to build a nurturing bond with its new partner and learn from an organization that appreciates the customer as a strategic partner.

**Weak Acquirer, Weak Acquired**
Combinations of organizations that are both weak on the Customer Focus characteristic may be prompted by a last-ditch effort on the part of the acquiring company to acquire market share. Although strength on Customer Focus on only one side or the other is not a favorable situation, the combined organization may be able to buy enough time to recognize and remedy the situation. However, the unforgiving nature of business is such that it will not tolerate a big weak player any better than it will tolerate two little weak players. The winds of change in this circumstance are the sucking of money from pockets and life from the businesses.

There are two very good reasons for such dire consequences. First, and most obvious, the blind will be leading the blind into the battles for customer attention and favor. Second, enterprises that are disconnected from their end users are often internally disconnected as well. A larger organization made up of people who don't look beyond their own in-basket is even less effective than two independent collections of self-centered people going nowhere together. QUOCA provides an invaluable opportunity to avoid the inevitable disaster of combining two businesses that haven't a clue as to what their customers want.

## SUMMARY

Having poor Customer Focus is like having a kidney stone—it's not an immediate threat to life, but it's so distractingly painful that death doesn't seem like such a bad thing. Sales are difficult, inventory is piling up, customers are unbillable, cash has stopped flowing, and people are lethargic, unhappy, and disengaged. Unless the situation is remedied, secondary infections may arise, and then life is not only uncomfortable but in jeopardy.

In competitive markets, there are winners and losers—those who succeed in the contest for the favorable attention and dollars of the customer and those who go home empty-handed. Organizations that enjoy strength on the Customer Focus characteristic truly enjoy it for many reasons. Employees of such an organization have a personal sense of being connected to and serving the needs of the customer. There is a strong shared commitment with team members and fellow employees to do what it takes to attract and keep clients. And there is the knowledge that by serving customers well, the organization will generate the revenues it needs in order to survive and prosper, thereby safeguarding the well-being of the employees. It's good to be a winner.

C H A P T E R

# CREATING CHANGE

We live in a world of change, yet we act on the basis of continuity. Change is unfamiliar; it disturbs us. We ignore it, we avoid it; often we try to resist it. Continuity, on the other hand, is familiar; it provides safety and security. Thus, when we plan for the future, we prefer to assume present conditions will continue. But they rarely do. As a result, we experience unnecessary losses and miss unseen opportunities. If we could learn to anticipate change and to prepare for it, we could make it work for us, not against us.[1]

THE OBJECTIVES OF THIS CHAPTER are for the reader to accept changes in the business environment as being inevitable; to view change that has been anticipated and prepared for as an ally in the future survival and prosperity of the enterprise; to identify other organization culture characteristics that enable or retard change; and to understand how quantitative organization culture assessments can improve the performance of combinations involving organizations with weak Creating Change characteristics.

## THE ONLY THING THAT DOESN'T CHANGE IS CHANGE

Lord, give me the serenity to accept the things I cannot change; the courage to change the things I can; and the wisdom to know the difference.[2]

We all accept the fact that change is inevitable in virtually every facet of our lives. We consciously recognize change without thinking about the fact that change is merely the dynamic for moving from what we had accepted as being static to something different. Change requires a point of reference. Change is from something to something different. For example, when we recognize a change in a market dynamic—say, the number of sales of a particular product—it is a change from one number that represented market demand to a new number that reflects the new demand. The degree of change is the difference between the two numbers that represent demand; the rate of change is expressed by putting the change in a temporal context, such as "a 20 percent drop in the last quarter."

Even strong organizations have an Achilles heel when dealing with the dynamics of their world. When the reference point for how an enterprise is to function is no longer valid, then the enterprise's goals, objectives, decisions, and actions are no longer appropriate—it is as simple as that. If organizations are to survive and prosper, they must continually confirm that their definition of the world accurately reflects the world as it is now—and now. Because in the time it took you to read "and now," the world has become subtly but profoundly different. To ignore this fact is to invite extinction.

Change has a life of its own—an idea here turns into an opportunity there that becomes a new product that has a positive impact on our lifestyle but poses a tremendous threat to our source of income. If change and its intended and unintended consequences were easy to anticipate, we could just cut to the chase and create the future now. But, as they say in sports, "That's why they play the game." So, we are left to our own resources to anticipate and influence change whenever possible and to simply be nimble enough to react appropriately to change in most cases.

As a species, mankind is pretty well equipped to assess and respond to environmental changes. In part, we depend on our cultural colleagues to be our scouts while we are sleeping or are otherwise inattentive to our environment. Our culture has developed and is continuously modified as a means for us to survive and prosper. Humans are well equipped to survive, with our physical senses of sight, hearing, touch, taste, and smell and our unique intellectual abilities. We use our abilities to sense dangers and respond to opportunities. We measure our environment using our senses, and we use our intelligence to make decisions that are intended to preserve and protect our well-being. Our sensory skills and abilities are greatly complemented by our vast array of communication mechanisms, from whispers to CNN to cell phones that can connect with virtually anyone, anywhere.

The process of combined measurement, interpretation, and decision making is analysis. Some of our analyses are purely subjective, that is, based strictly upon our opinion, such as whether a movie is good or bad. Some analyses are objective in that they are measured against some benchmark, such as how our sense of right and wrong is based on our values. Other analyses are objectively comparative, such as when we conclude that one person is taller than another or that we can get across the street before the oncoming car hits us. And some of our measurements and decisions are standardized in that they use a proven measurement instrument and the results are compared to an established norm, such as when we use a thermometer to determine whether someone has a fever. There are situations in which each type of analysis is appropriate and others in which an analysis with a higher degree of sophistication would be of more value. For example, we have all learned how inaccurate the back of the hand is when trying to determine whether someone has a fever—the thermometer is a much more accurate and, therefore, more useful measurement tool for deciding if a loved one's well-being is in danger.

In the aggregate of an organization's culture are the beliefs and assumptions that support people's ability to sense and respond to the changes occurring in their business environment. This ability to sense, and even anticipate, the dynamics taking place in their field of enterprise and translate the knowledge into appropriate actions is critical to the survival and prosperity of the organization.

## EMBRACING CHANGE

> By encouraging innovation and entrepreneurship at all levels, by building an environment in which more people feel included, involved and empowered to take initiative, companies as well as individuals can be the masters of change instead of its victims.[3]

Embracing the nature and pace of organizational change is the responsibility of leaders and the accountability of all the constituents within the culture. Leaders must continually be aware of the external forces that necessitate change. They must be equally aware of the internal inertia that prefers to maintain the status quo. Successful leaders enjoy their success in part because of their ability to respond appropriately to environmental dynamics with well-planned, communicated, accepted, and embraced changes in organizational behaviors. Organizations that are adept at anticipating appropriate change are regarded as proactive; those that respond to change inappropriately by misreading the signs and making incorrect changes and those that respond appropriately but too late to optimize outcomes are regarded as being reactive. Reactive companies are very seldom the change leaders in their fields. However, in markets where there are lots of participants, it can be very rewarding to be a discriminating, nimble number two player who doesn't bear the penalties and risks of being a market leader.

## THE NATURE OF CHANGE

> Not to respond to change is to be out of step, to fall behind, to be at a growing disadvantage, and thus to do less well: and because structural changes are permanent and irreversible our responses to them also must be permanent and irreversible. The discovery of new knowledge and the creation of new techniques and new equipment make the old obsolete.[4]

Leon Martel, in his remarkable book *Mastering Change: The Key to Business Success,*[5] describes two types of change that affect business organizations—*structural changes* and *cyclical changes. Structural changes* involve a significant, permanent, irreversible transformation of an activity or an institution from a relatively stable state. The invention of fire, boats, gunpowder, electricity, penicillin, the airplane, the automobile, and the computer were all structural changes, and all of them had widespread impacts on the lives of virtually everyone. Within structural changes lie qualitative and quantitative changes that provide incremental variations and sophistications of the altered structure, such as the communications succession from telegraph to telephone to radio to wireless telephones or the succession from the creation of a microchip prototype to the production of thousands in a single batch to the production of microchips to very specific performance standards.

Some structural changes come out of the blue and promptly challenge the validity of the enterprise's mission, the functionality of its systems, the well-being of its clients, and the viability of its suppliers. Structural changes require organizational nimbleness, flexibility, and innovation. Imagine the scenario in which a neighbor comes home with the first gas-powered lawn mower and everyone rushes to the source of this new noise. Within seconds, everyone thinks about how hard it is to push that old reel mower and says, "I've got to have one of those!" Suddenly the hardware store has to dedicate shelf space to one-gallon gasoline cans, the gas station has to stock two-stroke motor oil, and the seed store has to hire somebody full time to assemble lawn mowers. And the "Old Reliable Reel Mower Company" sees the bottom drop out of its market. As the saying goes, the bell has been rung and can't be unrung. Once people shift to the new two-stroke mowers with an 18-inch cut, they may buy a newer four-stroke grass cutter with a mulching blade (qualitative changes) and wider cut (quantitative change), but they will never, ever buy another push mower. The gas station will sell less two-stroke oil, sales of gas cans will slow down, and the guy at the seed store will have to learn new assembly skills, but these will be relatively minor changes in their operations. The reality is that the Old Reliable Reel Mower Company will either adapt itself to the new market realities or perish—structural changes are irreversible and permanent until the next structural change makes them as antiquated as they made their predecessor.

On the other hand, *cyclical changes* are repeating patterns of change with relatively regular scope and duration. Like the endless cycle of the seasons, they follow an inevitable trend toward a gradual but complete reversal of conditions and then, just as subtly, return to conditions similar to today's. Business cycles, consumer tastes, labor markets, and supply and demand variations are all examples of the bewildering number of cyclical changes that affect and influence an enterprise's well-being.

Because of the nature of cyclical changes, they require change-creating skills different from those required by structural change. However, these skills are equally important to the long-term survival of the enterprise. Cyclical changes require vigilant attention to trends and recognition of changing environmental patterns. Coincidental strengths on Organizational Learning and Coordination and Integration provide strong complements to Creating Change capabilities to deal with cyclical changes. Organizational Learning functions as a reference for what did and did not work during the last cycle of a similar nature, while Coordination and Integration facilitates uniform implementation of the response plan.

High-performing organizations complement their strength on Creating Change in response to structural change with coincidental strengths on their Strategic Direction and Intent and Agreement characteristics. The combined strengths on Creating Change and Strategic Direction and Intent enable bidirectional coordination of the long-term purpose of the organization and its relevance to the enterprise's external dynamics. The result is the tight-loose relationship between where the organization wants to go and how it is best going to get there.

Strengths on both Agreement and Creating Change in the face of structural dynamics facilitate support and collaboration for the organization's people in their accepting of the redirection of their goals and efforts in response to major changes in the external landscape.

Organizationwide agreement regarding the *why* and *what* of change is greatly enabled by the Creating Change strength in *how* to change.

## THE ROLE OF LEADERSHIP IN CREATING CHANGE

> Pride-in-company, coupled with knowing that innovation is mainstream rather than counter-cultural, provides an incentive for initiative. A feeling that people inside the company are competent leaders—that the company has been successful because of its people—supports this. . . . But opinion leaders are innovative only if their organization's norms favor change; this is why the values of leaders are so important.[6]

It is almost impossible to overstate the importance of leaders' sincere and overt involvement in embracing the needed changes and demonstrating them in their own behaviors if they want the organization as a whole to change. In 1985 I was working for a company that had been a leader in the energy services market. We had been a groundbreaking engineering services provider for the siting, engineering, and operation of nuclear power plants. The accident at Three Mile Island had suddenly changed the public's perception of nuclear power and utilities' appetites for new nuclear power plants. The leaders of our company had to take bold steps if the business was to survive. We looked externally for market trends and emerging opportunities. Laws demanding proper management of hazardous materials and the cleanup of abandoned hazardous waste sites had recently been implemented. We looked internally at our core capabilities. Our engineers were expert at the handling of hazardous materials. Our experienced, world-class geologists, soils engineers, and hydrologists could easily adapt to new applications of their skills.

The company's recognition of and reaction to the nexus of our opportunity and ability enabled us to successfully pursue major government contracts. Our leaders were open and realistic in describing the circumstances on which our change was predicated; they acknowledged that succeeding with a new mission and making the requisite changes would be difficult, and they offered support and encouragement to the staff throughout the change process. We were able to adapt our organization from being at the forefront in one field to being at the forefront in another field within a year.

But it was a whole different story a year or so later when our president jumped on the Quality Improvement bandwagon without engaging the support of his department heads. While the president quoted statistics about cost savings and improved competitiveness, second-tier leaders openly regarded the process as a waste of time and effort. The company incurred huge external and internal training costs trying to change peoples' attitudes from blame and incrimination for errors to acknowledgment and resolution of error causes; from sweeping problems under the rug to recognizing the cost of errors versus the cost of solutions and the price of diminished reputation; and from surprise and reaction when problems occur to an investment of up-front time and effort to prevent surprises. This organization, which only a year before had had the capability to adapt to a new market, failed to embrace the quality improvement process. Our president was disgraced and replaced, the word *quality* was forever corrupted, and the company began a downward spiral that led to a name change and takeover by our corporate parent.

> Ultimately, a process of organization change cannot succeed without the direct and personal support of the top person in the hierarchy.[7]

Without a unified voice and a consistent, enthusiastic embrace of change by leaders within the organization, planned and intended change will not occur. People will adopt new attitudes, values, opinions, and behaviors only when they are adequately assured that the odds on their survival will increase and that the quality of their lives will be improved. Many people's reluctance to change can be summarized as, "The devil you know is preferable to the angel that's a stranger." The root cause of many organizations' failure to accept and employ change is the unwillingness of their leaders to accept the change themselves and to demonstrate the safety and benefit of doing things the new way. As Peter Senge said in *The Fifth Discipline*:

> In most companies that fail, there is an abundance of evidence in advance that the firm is in trouble. This evidence goes unheeded, however, even when individual managers are aware of it. The organization as a whole cannot recognize impending threats, understand the implications of those threats, or come up with alternatives.[8]

Clearly, then, organizations that develop and engage their leaders in creating change have better odds for survival and prosperity for their stakeholders than those that don't. In fact, Kotter and Heskett, in a major study of the characteristic differences between high-, mid-, and poor-performing organizations, observed:

Within the constraints of this methodology, the message from the data is clear. In firms with more adaptive cultures, the cultural ideal is that managers throughout the hierarchy should provide leadership to initiate change in strategies and tactics whenever necessary to satisfy the legitimate interests of not just stockholders, or customers, or employees, but all three.[9]

Of the three elements of organization cultures—heroes, myths, and artifacts—nowhere do the actions of an organization's leaders have greater impact on the culture, and therefore on the attitudes, values, opinions, and behaviors of the organization's people, than in how they personally regard and react to change.

I am reminded of the attitude of the commanding officer of a submarine I sailed on while I was in the Navy. The boat had been in dry dock and then alongside the tender for an extended period of time. The crew was anxious to get out on patrol and perform its mission in support of the war in Vietnam. There had been a change of command while the sub was undergoing its planned maintenance, and, while the old skipper had been very highly regarded, the new captain had an undeniable charisma. Each additional day of extended stay in port as a result of unanticipated problems could have led to increased strife and lower morale—a problem in any organization, but particularly significant in the confines of a submarine. But our new skipper refused to allow the sudden change of unexpected setbacks to distract us from his vision.

In his acceptance speech at the change of command, the old man had said, "Your job is to do everything with pride and excellence. My job is to enable you to do your job the very best you can." He expected openness and candor in identifying problems, and every setback was regarded as "another opportunity to excel." When at last the boat was ready to undergo sea trials, we left port with confidence that our vessel, our home, was safe and able to do its job. Our pride, preparation, and professionalism paid off by shortening the shakedown cruise, and the boat went out on patrol right on schedule.

## CREATING CHANGE AND THE ORGANIZATION'S SENSE OF TIME

Timing is the essence of a successful life.[10]

The "sense of time" aspect of organization cultures further complicates this situation. The "sense of time" variable deals with what the group perceives as its time horizon and the pace of change between the present and the point in time where planning and anticipation cease to be practical because of the number and scope of the environmental dynamics. For makers of microprocessor chips, Internet businesses, and software companies, the time horizon is measured in weeks and the pace of decision making and process changes reflects a very brief sense of time. Groups with a fast sense of time must be organized in such a way that information is effectively, efficiently, quickly, and broadly shared; decisions are accepted as being imperfect; and people are accustomed to quick changes in direction.

## THE INCREASING SCOPE AND PACE OF CHANGE

> I think that we've overestimated the ability of enterprises, individuals, and organizations to absorb change, and we've seriously underestimated the amount of discipline it may take to do that well.[11]

One of the astounding statistics I recently learned is that the historical midpoint of human knowledge is the middle of the twentieth century. That is, mankind has learned as much about our universe in the past 50 years as we did in all of the time prior to then. This knowledge is the source and basis for our understanding of our world and its dynamics, and we must incorporate this knowledge into our efforts to survive and prosper. The tremendous rate of change in the volume of our knowledge naturally translates into a tremendous pace and scope of change in all aspects of our lives.

Humans' natural instinct and gifts for sensing our environment and responding to its changes have been very important elements in our civilization, survival, and prosperity. The sheer volume of new information, when combined with the near impossibility of avoiding its relentless deluge from seemingly unlimited sources, makes analysis and discrimination of information extremely important. The lack of proper discrimination can lead to sheer bewilderment and "caught in the headlights" inaction. Excessive discrimination can result in poor decisions and improper actions. Uncontrolled bouncing between the two extremes is pure chaos for everyone. With so many changes and so much information, it is virtually impossible to maintain an ongoing equilibrium concerning what to leave in and what to leave out for the sake of making decisions and perpetuating the well-being of the organization and its constituents. Thus, the bottom line for the long-term success of enterprises is the ability to create and implement appropriate changes in their Creating Change processes.

## THE IMPACT OF THE CREATING CHANGE CHARACTERISTIC ON THE ORGANIZATION'S FINANCIAL PERFORMANCE

The truly objective measure of business success or failure is dollars earned or lost. The ability or inability of an enterprise to Create Change has significant implications for that enterprise's financial performance. An organization that is highly effective in determining and implementing appropriate changes realizes the benefit in:

- Shorter time to market for new products
- Proper levels of inventory
- Higher product quality
- Lower cost of goods sold
- Reduced variable costs
- Greater employee satisfaction
- Lower personnel turnover[12]

Of course, weakness on the Creating Change cultural characteristic will have the opposite impacts on the enterprise's financial and competitive performance, beginning with poorer quality and lower employee satisfaction and moving through all the negative ripple effects.

## CULTURAL CHARACTERISTICS RELATED TO THE CREATING CHANGE CHARACTERISTIC

In addition to the Creating Change cultural characteristic, complementary strengths on the Organizational Learning, Coordination and Integration, and Empowerment characteristics are vitally important for the long-term success and survival of enterprises with a fast sense of time, such as those in the computer hardware and software industries, telecommunications, and other technology-dependent sectors.

On the other hand, enterprises in more stable, traditional organizational sectors such as transportation, heavy manufacturing, agriculture, and government have a much more distant time horizon and a slower sense of time. Their pace of decisions, decision-making processes, and means to create change can afford to be more thorough. Enterprises with a slow sense of time typically have many-tiered organization charts, bureaucratic decision-making processes, and a strong resistance to whimsical changes in the way things are done. Strength on the Creating Change characteristic may not be as critical for organizations with a slow sense of time. However, in order to assure their success and survival, weakness on Creating Change must be offset by strengths on Strategic Direction and Intent, Agreement, and Team Orientation.

## M&A IMPLICATIONS OF THE CREATING CHANGE CULTURE CHARACTERISTIC

### Strong Acquirer, Strong Acquired

Strength on the Creating Change characteristic in both combining organizations is a tremendous enabling asset for the future success of the combined organization, as measured by high return on investment and a reduced payback period, and should be reflected in the purchase price and integration planning. However, the leaders of the respective organizations should be candid as to how they monitor and manage change information and the communication processes that drive awareness and empower the people within the respective organizations to determine and implement appropriate responses to their environmental dynamics.

### Strong Acquirer, Weak Acquired

Often the acquiring company is stronger on the Creating Change cultural characteristic than the acquired enterprise, as demonstrated by its initiative in seeking a complementary organization. In some cases, the root cause of a company's becoming an acquisition target is its inability to climb to the top of its market and thereby be a diner rather than dinner. Moderate to low scores on Creating Change are indicative of an organization that is not predisposed to accept and adeptly incorporate the significant changes innate in the new ownership, leadership, policies, and procedures, and so on that are common in combinations. In fact, the best and brightest people in the acquired organization, who frequently are also adept at creating change, are also the most desirable in the employment market and so are often the first to leave.

Quantitative Organization Culture Analyses results can be effectively used in the selection of potential combining businesses, the go/no-go decision, and the calculation of the purchase price to factor in the impact of the acquired business's weakness. Should the deal go ahead, QUOCA results can be used to improve the scope and duration of the integration process through initiatives that develop the adaptation capabilities of the new organization.

## Weak Acquirer, Strong Acquired

In some cases an enterprise will recognize that its best change mechanism is to be acquired. This is a common exit strategy for technology and other highly innovative start-up companies once they feel that they have added as much value to their product as possible and decide that it is time to cash in on their creativity. It can be an extreme shock to an innovative organization to be acquired and overseen by a company that is less dynamic and less responsive to change. Unless employment agreements capture the creative people, they are often driven by the thrill of innovation and newfound riches to fund their next idea. The loss of this innovative talent can delay or destroy the newly acquired organization's ability to replicate its previous success at creating and producing new products. Longer time to market and increased cost of goods sold can extend payback periods and reduce return on investment for combinations between slow-to-change acquirers and innovative acquired enterprises.

QUOCA can identify the mismatch in the strengths on this cultural trait and preempt the effects. Of course, in this case, the acquirer must be willing to acknowledge its shortcomings and commit to overcoming them. But the objective results of QUOCA can be very effective in convincing management of the cost-benefit of becoming proactive.

## Weak Acquirer, Weak Acquired

Unless both organizations are in a market where structural changes have not taken place or can be easily anticipated and cyclical changes are minimal, coincidental weakness on the Creating Change characteristic in the combining organizations is a recipe for disaster. There is no greater challenge to an enterprise's adaptability than suddenly having new bosses or subordinates; imposing or responding to new policies and procedures; knowing who and what are likely to be a problem, who and what can be a solution for problems, and on and on and on. The shock of the combination of coincidentally low-performing Creating Change organizations will stifle the integration process, thereby reducing the odds for any payback from the deal. Such combinations are nightmares for virtually every stakeholder and often lead to shutdown or divestment of the acquisition.

Circumstances such as these make the investment of time, money, and effort to perform QUOCA during the due diligence extremely beneficial. Early awareness of the shared weakness and its financial and competitive implications should stimulate a beefing up of the enterprises' abilities to adapt through training and development programs prior to or as part of the integration of the businesses.

## SUMMARY

> If a new order is to take root (in American enterprise), revolutionary restructuring of our business firms and institutions will be required. They . . . stand at a turning point: Either they allow inertia and momentum to carry them blindly in the downward path to mediocrity and oblivion, or they confront outcomes, mobilize attention, brainstorm solutions, and implement changes that enhance their effectiveness.[13]

Highly effective organizations perceive change as an opportunity to maintain their competitive edge, renew their capabilities, and demonstrate their creativity. Enterprises that fear and ignore change are preoccupied by its danger, immobilized by threats of inadequacy, and frozen in time by the comfort of the known. The ends of the effectiveness continuum are survival and prosperity for those that create change and a downward spiral toward death for organizations that ignore the need to appropriately respond to their dynamic environment.

.

# 23

# ORGANIZATIONAL
# LEARNING

The critical question asked by a visionary company is not "How well are we doing?" or "How can we do well?" or "How well do we have to perform in order to meet the competition?" For these companies, the critical question is "How do we do better tomorrow than we did today?" They institutionalize this question as a way of life—a habit of mind and action. Superb execution and performance naturally come to the visionary companies not so much as an end-goal, but as the residual result of a never-ending cycle of self-stimulated improvement and investment for the future.[1]

THE OBJECTIVES OF THIS CHAPTER are for the reader to be able to identify the key strategic advantages of learning organizations; to view organizational learning and continuous improvement as the means for developing effective organization cultures; and to understand how quantitative organization culture assessments can improve the performance of combinations involving organizations with weak Organizational Learning characteristics.

## KNOWING WHAT YOU DON'T KNOW

It is no accident that most organizations learn poorly. The way they are designed and managed, the way people's jobs are defined, and most importantly, the way we have all been taught to think and interact (not only in organizations but more broadly) create fundamental learning disabilities. These disabilities operate despite the best efforts of bright, committed people. Often the harder they try to solve problems, the worse the results. What learning does occur takes place despite these learning disabilities—for they pervade all organizations to some degree.[2]

Darwin's theory, referred to earlier, concerning an entity's three options in a changing environment—evolve, move, or perish—is manifest in the organization's cultural attitudes, values, opinions, and behaviors concerning its awareness of and response to its external dynamics and internal challenges. Organizational Learning is at the core of an enterprise's ability to evolve through being in touch with such external dynamics as market innovations; changes in regulations; the business variables that affect suppliers, customers, lenders, and competitors; and economic trends that affect supply and demand.

> Organization Learning is the process by which an organization obtains and uses new knowledge, tools, behaviors, and values. It happens at all levels in the organization—among individuals and groups as well as system wide. Individuals learn as part of their daily activities, particularly as they interact with each other and the outside world. Groups learn as their members cooperate to accomplish common goals. The entire system learns as it obtains feedback from the environment and anticipates future changes. At all levels, newly learned knowledge is translated into new goals, procedures, expectations, role structures and measures of success.[3]

The Organizational Learning characteristic of the Adaptability trait measures and reflects the organization's ability to receive, translate, and act upon both information concerning changes in its external environment and its self-assessment of its operational performance. Organizations that excel in appropriately reacting to their external dynamics and employ objectivity in assessing their effectiveness are often referred to as "learning organizations" or as embracing "continuous improvement" efforts.

> The processes involved in continuous improvement generate a creative discontent with the status quo. This makes it unacceptable for the company to rest on its laurels and forces it to improve.[4]

Organizational Learning plays the dual role of sensing and assessing the organization's external dynamics and facilitating the organization's need to be flexible in responding to those dynamics. Therefore, Organizational Learning is not a periodic activity or someone's adjunct responsibility—it is a process that, to one degree or another, involves everyone. According to management experts Bateman and Snell,[5] the recipe for high-performing learning organization requires several important ingredients:

*Critical thinking.* Organizational constituents must engage in disciplined thinking and tend to details, making objective decisions based upon data and evidence rather than guesswork and assumptions.

*Professional curiosity.* People search constantly for new knowledge, looking for expanding horizons and opportunities rather than quick fixes.

*Objective self-evaluation.* Members carefully review both successes and failures, looking for lessons and deeper understanding.

*Benchmarking.* Learning organizations benchmark—people identify and implement the best business practices of other organizations, stealing ideas shamelessly.

*Sharing information.* Thoughts, ideas, feedback, and criticisms are shared throughout the organization via reports, information systems, informal discussions, site visits, education, and training.

## CRITICAL THINKING

Experience is not what happens to you but what you make of what happens to you.[6]

Organizational Learning requires a realistic view of the organization's universe. Making effective, knowledgeable decisions based on objective information is the hallmark of high-performing enterprises. Implicit in this capability is the awareness of where and how relevant information can be gathered, the ability to discern the potential impact of the information on the organization, the identification of the individuals within the organization who would benefit from the information, and the distribution of the information to those individuals. Jim Collins, in *Good to Great*, states that high-performing organizations have a culture of discipline that "is not just about action. It is about getting disciplined *people* (who are committed to the continuous improvement of the organization) who engage in disciplined *thought* and who *then* take disciplined action."[7] Critical thinking requires shared cultural beliefs that the success and well-being of the organization is the impersonal, primary goal of everyone. Scrutiny, critique, and criticism are regarded not as a personal attack but as a mechanism to make work life easier and more successful. Thus, people engage in critical thinking concerning their work processes and activities with enlightened self-interest, just as a dedicated athlete seeks advice from a coach.

## PROFESSIONAL CURIOSITY

> If organizations are to be continually changing, then the employees must be continually learning and growing. Individually, most people do not grow on a linear basis; they do not learn in predetermined, syllabus sequence. Rather, they seek learning experiences, as they need them, acquiring the knowledge and skill to solve a particular problem or understand an issue. Consequently, executives in flexible organizations have learned that the employee development must be broad enough to allow individuals to explore and grow, while maintaining a focus on the organization purpose.[8]

I love attending industry trade shows. I have been to many such events as a vendor or a speaker, or simply as one of the interested attendees. The programs feature informative presentations and panels with representatives from leading-edge organizations who share their expertise with the audience. The exhibition hall is crowded with booths peddling the latest products and services. There is always a buzz of excitement that seems to say that for this industry, this event is the center of the universe and all of the people there are at the forefront of the industry. I find that the people at trade shows display a great sense of wonder and curiosity. And it is not surprising to me that, regardless of the industry, the leading organizations have the largest number of attendees—not just as speakers and peddlers, but as *learners*.

Recall from the description of the Adaptability trait that it is the nexus of the organization's assumptions and beliefs regarding its external focus and its flexibility. Learning organizations—like Willie Sutton, who robbed banks "because that's where the money is"—participate in trade shows, read trade magazines, and surf the Internet because they know that's where the latest knowledge can be found. They recognize that no one knows everything about their dynamic industry, and they embrace a humble sense of professional curiosity as a means to stay on top of the game.

## OBJECTIVE SELF-EVALUATION

> A learning culture must contain a . . . shared assumption that the appropriate way for humans to behave is to be proactive problem solvers and learners.[9]

High-performing organizations are brutally honest in their self-assessment of their performance. Members carefully review both successes and failures, looking for lessons and deeper understanding. The objective of their assessment is not to find culprits, idiots, or saboteurs. Learning organizations assume that their people suffer from problems rather than cause them. And, if the cause of the problem is determined to be human error, learning organizations view it as training or job fit failure and invest their resources in addressing the true root cause of the problem rather than having a public crucifixion. High-performing organizations know that if they are to learn the truth about the root causes of barriers to their success, they need to engage the involvement and intellect of their people. In order to do that, the culture must reflect the assumption that people want to succeed and do well in their work.

> Learning organizations are possible because not only is it our nature to learn but we love to learn. Most of us at one time or another have been part of a great "team," a group of people who functioned in an extraordinary way—who trusted one another, who complimented each others' strengths and compensated for each others' limitations, who had common goals that were larger than individual goals, and who produced extraordinary results.[10]

Further, high-performing organizations regard failure and problems as being net-sum positive challenges where everyone benefits from the resolution. Many organizations tend to polarize problems and pit the involved people against one another rather than engaging them in dealing with the real issue—the root cause of the problem. The win-lose approach is a cultural impediment to openness, sharing, intellectual curiosity, personal growth and esteem, and, in the long run, the process of continuous improvement. Winners align their resources against the problem and spread the solution and its benefits across the organization.

## BENCHMARKING

> Knowledge of results is a vital and motivating influence upon
> the behavior of people at work. Yet the results themselves are
> meaningful only if there are clear objectives to begin with. . . .
> Take away knowledge of results from human activity and you
> rob people of motivation and either create zombies or foment a
> rebellion.[11]

An important element of *objective self-evaluation* is the use of standards
against which performance can be objectively measured. Learning
organizations set both internal and external benchmarks to gauge trends
in their ongoing performance.  A benchmark can be any credible reference—industry reports, input from focus groups, financial statements—
that creates awareness of the organization's performance in such a way
that it reinforces activities that improve operations and identifies unde-
sirable outcomes that lead to objective self-evaluation and improvement.

Benchmarks must be regarded as being dynamic and, therefore,
require constant vigilance and effective internal communication of
changes in the external environment. Some enterprises use external consultants such as the Gallup Organization and independent testing organizations such as Underwriters' Laboratories to develop benchmarks and
gather objective information. Many firms use internal independent quality
control professionals to benchmark the conformance of products to internal or industry standards. Learning organizations supplement these traditional methods of assuring the quality of production output with more
up-the-pipe benchmarks in order to reduce and prevent inefficiencies.

Finally, enterprises that are dedicated to continuous improvement
create personal awareness of individual performance standards for their
activities and ongoing comparison of their results to their own personal
benchmarks. Thus, objective self-evaluation according to meaningful
standards, and early recognition and resolution of problems, are as much
a part of the culture as the woodwork is part of the structure.

## SHARING INFORMATION

I firmly believe that poor communication is the heart of all evil. We are so
desperate to effectively send and receive information that as soon as a
technological advancement comes along, such as voicemail, paging, cell
phones, email, and instant messaging, it becomes swamped. Part of the
challenge of continuous improvement is the objective analysis of infor-

mation-sharing systems and proactive solution of the problems that are found. And this proactivity transcends the organization chart and the walls of the enterprise itself to include the suppliers, customers, and other stakeholders, who are interdependent for the success of the organization.

In high-performing organizations, problems are often solved or avoided through informing task suppliers and customers of the challenges and involving them in those challenges. One of the great successes of Total Quality Management programs was the recognition of the interdependency of the people involved in the discrete steps in work processes. As with a chain, no matter how good all of the other links are, a single weak link puts the success of the unit in jeopardy. You can understand how important each crew member's competency and success is on a submarine. When something goes wrong, it is ludicrous to say, "Your end of the boat is sinking." It's all *our* boat. To be able to relax when you are off watch or to sleep when it is your turn requires confidence in your shipmates and communication of detailed operational information. Anything less than a learning organization puts the ship, its crew, and its mission in jeopardy. You better believe that submariners are excellent practitioners of organizational learning through effective communication

Failure is our most important product.[12]

Sooner or later, most organizations recognize errors of commission—the mistakes people make when they do the wrong thing. Even enterprises that rely on last quarter's results to establish next quarter's priorities are eventually aware of their shortcomings. However, errors of omission are a completely different story. Lost opportunities, unrecognized problems, and failure to prevent problems are far more difficult to recognize and reckon with than mistakes. But organizations that insist on dealing with the real world are just as observant and candid about what they should have done as they are about what they did wrong, and, when oversights occur, they readjust their vigilance and focus. As Jim Collins, in *Good to Great*, says of high-performing organizations, "The good to great companies did not focus principally on what to *do* to become great; they focus equally on what *not* to do and what to *stop* doing."[13] Thus, in high-performing organizations, introspection, candor, and feedback include the same degree of conscious thought regarding errors of omission as regarding failures, errors, and mistakes.

These five elements—critical thinking, shared curiosity, objective self-evaluation, benchmarking, and sharing information—are the mechanics of an effective learning organization. While strength in these skills is important for continuous improvement, they alone do not ensure that the culture of the organization is optimum for the organization's long-term survival and success.

## RELATED CULTURAL CHARACTERISTICS

Strength on Organizational Learning is a great asset, but it doesn't by itself assure the ongoing success of the organization. Enterprises with extremely dynamic markets must complement their strengths on Organizational Learning with similar strengths on Customer Focus, Creating Change, Capability Development, Agreement, Vision, and Goals and Objectives in order to optimize their responsiveness to the dynamics of their market and to maintain their viability in that market.

The rationale for needed complementary strengths on the Customer Focus and Creating Change characteristics is to optimize the understanding of the client's continuously shifting desires and needs. Analyses of sales data as a vehicle for staying in touch with client needs are like driving by looking in the rear-view mirror. Proactive, responsive, high-performing organizations breathe the same air as their customers. When clients develop an itch, the high-performing companies know where to scratch.

A friend of mine works in the aftermarket auto accessory business. His company puts sunroofs, stereo systems, VCRs, and TVs in cars, vans, and SUVs. A year or so ago, I asked Mike what was going on with these souped-up coupes that kids were driving, with big spoilers on the back, very cool see-through taillights, and throaty exhausts. He said that such modifications were the rage for kids getting their first car to distinguish their ride from the consumer vehicles their parents and un-cool kids drove. Mike said that the demand was unbelievable and that adults were beginning to emulate the kids. It didn't take long for proactive, market-leading auto manufacturers to catch on. Look at the new Nissan Altima— spoiler on the back, throaty sound, and oh-so-cool taillights. It is no surprise that the dealers cannot keep the new Altima in stock and that they tack on a premium for orders. Nissan did the same with its Xterra 2 years ago, and I bet Nissan has people scouting the school parking lots for the next trend, too. Somewhere down the road, innovation followers such as GM will jump on the bandwagon as the trend begins to fade.

> The most intriguing leadership role in culture management is one in which the leader attempts to develop a learning organization that will be able to make its own perpetual diagnosis and self-manage whatever transformations are needed as the environment changes.[14]

Hand in hand with Organizational Learning in high-performing organizations is the ability to transform fast-changing information into appropriate organization infrastructure responses. Complementary high capability on Creating Change enables the learning organization to quickly and expertly spread its new knowledge and capabilities throughout the organization.

An enterprise's inability to be aware of its external dynamics and to translate such intelligence into organizational changes can be devastating. Some organizations become so convinced that they have a "silver bullet" that is able to prevail in any market conditions that they ignore all information to the contrary. And simply having what is, in reality, a superior product doesn't mean that that product will be a winner in the market. For example, in the early 1980s, when videocassette recorders were on the verge of becoming the next consumer have-to-have, Sony and JVC developed different, competing formats. Sony called its system BetaMax. It had higher sound and picture quality, used less tape, and had a smaller cassette and so was cheaper to build and buy than the competing VHS format. Sony had a great reputation for innovative, quality products. By all rights we should have libraries of Beta-format movies in our homes and on the shelves of the local video rental shop. But we don't—we have VHS. JVC knew that its product wasn't as good as Sony's, but that didn't stop JVC from seizing the market through aggressive marketing to capture film title rights and licensing its technology to any company that could produce consumer electronics. The burgeoning video rental chains opted for the VHS format because there were more VHS movies to sell and rent. Consumers enjoyed the price wars between the burgeoning numbers of VCR manufacturers using the VHS technology. Within a very short time, the format battle was over.

But Sony didn't grasp the realities of its environment. The people at Sony knew that they had a better product and continued to pour money into product development and marketing. Sony amended its thinking about being the sole Beta manufacturer and attempted to license its technology. However, the major players had already committed to VHS, and their production was already maxed-out. In spite of overwhelming evidence in the marketplace, Sony continued to promote and refine Beta.

The market information was certainly there for Sony to receive, interpret, and use. By ignoring the market dynamics, Sony suffered significant and long-term penalties. The damage to the bottom line from wasted production and R&D dollars was huge. But perhaps more damaging were the opportunity costs of devoting its R&D to a dead product rather than developing new ones and its loss of reputation as a relevant technology innovator.

High-performing organizations complement their strength on the Organizational Learning characteristic with a strong sense of Vision and mutually agreed upon Goals and Objectives. These coincidental strong characteristics reflect the enterprise's sense of the importance of its external focus and of effective systems dedicated to accomplishing its defined purpose. A well-defined, well-articulated, and uniformly understood and accepted vision is the standard by which a learning organization compares its knowledge of external dynamics to its operating assumptions, recognizes the gap, and translates the information into appropriate actions.

Through a network connection, I was introduced to someone who was hailed as being the next Bill Gates. A Princeton graduate, he had successfully envisioned and launched two highly regarded high-tech firms, had been the local Chamber of Commerce Entrepreneur of the Year, and had been written up in *Fast Company* magazine, the leading-edge business chronicle. I was engaged to critique a business plan he had developed for a new company. The concept was brilliant, but since no one had seen or used the product, it was hard to guess whether it would be a boom, like the hula-hoop, or a bust in the market. My comments on the plan were eagerly accepted and incorporated. After a little more due diligence, I decided to invest and subsequently was asked to join the company as the vice president of market development, which I did. Once inside the organization, I became aware of the founder's love of the next new variation on the technology theme. Each day he would arrive at work with a new application, a new end user, a new bell or whistle to be added to the product. At first, I was encouraged by the seemingly endless uses for the product. But as the vice president for business development I had real difficulty pinpointing what it was I was to define and create a market for. It became apparent to me that the vision and purpose of the organization were as fluid as the creativity of our founder. After several false starts, I became exasperated and said to my boss, "Look, we have fifty great ideas and no money in the bank for anything but a guerrilla marketing campaign. I don't care what product you decide to sell—they are all great ideas—but pick something, anything, that I can concentrate on developing."

After 2 years, the business continues to attract modest batches of start-up capital from people who are intrigued by the founder's next great idea. The core business is surviving thanks to a very capable vice president of operations who learned long ago to ignore the hype and stick to running the original, well-conceived core business. But the company is far from prosperous. Competitors eventually used our business's creativity as their R&D operation by monitoring our ever-changing features, picking the best ones, and concentrating on making them work. The consequences of an uncertain vision and the inability to use it as a standard for Organizational Learning are, if you don't know where you are going, then any road will take you there. To paraphrase, without a fixed, universally understood and accepted vision, the knowledge, skills, and abilities and the propensity to adapt them to market dynamics are useless.

Strength on the Goals and Objectives characteristic complements similar strength in Organizational Learning by translating knowledge of external dynamics and the ability to learn from them into desired outcomes for the organization. It's nice to know that Competitor X is folding its tent, thereby leaving Y amount of market share unserved. But translating that knowledge into sales plans, goals, and production schedules; developing the capabilities of additional human resources; and so on is a whole different ballgame. High-performing organizations know that people are motivated by the opportunity to perform to expected levels. Without goals and objectives to measure performance, there is no standard of success to celebrate or failure from which to learn. Why do you think coaches keep score and record statistics from meaningless preseason games? The numbers mean nothing in and of themselves. The coaches keep track because this is a rich source of information for identifying changes in performance and for continually measuring and thereby improving the contribution of individuals and their squads to the overall success of the team.

> In the learning organization, employees are given the opportunity to know what's going on, think constructively about the important issues, look for opportunities to learn new things, and seek creative solutions to problems. Learning organizations are committed to openness to new ideas, to generating new knowledge, and to spreading information and knowledge. Learning organizations seek high levels of collaboration among people from different business disciplines. Learning organizations are more successful at continuous improvement.[15]

High capability on the Organizational Learning characteristic is also complemented by strength on the Agreement trait in high-performing enterprises. Agreement is the mutual understanding, on the part of both the people who determine the objectives and everyone who is responsible for the various activities that contribute to achieving those objectives, of the organization's desired outcomes and the way they are to be achieved. As you might guess from the example of the high-tech start-up company, Agreement is the "how" bridge between the Vision "what" and the Organizational Learning "why." Enterprises with strengths on any two of these three characteristics will suffer from the frustration of an ongoing succession of failures. It's not hard to imagine (and perhaps you have experienced) how exasperating it can be for an intelligent, hardworking person to be in a situation where you know what you want to do, but not why or how, or where you know what you are doing and how to do it, but are ignorant of the purpose of your efforts. Organizations that suffer from a lack of continuity between Vision and Organizational Learning are incapable of sustained prosperity or survival.

> By promoting individual learning, the corporation recognizes the individual's responsibility for his or her own personal and professional development, while accepting the responsibility to create an environment of opportunity in which all can thrive. As great numbers of high self-esteem individuals unleash their creativity, they reshape the contours of the firm. The corporation comes alive as employees continuously adapt and improve the way they do their work, and constantly redefine their roles and interactions. Rather than dealing with a machine-like firm, leaders become conductors of the bio-corporate symphony, orchestrating the organic growth of the firm as cells and organs of the corporate body adapt, change and reproduce.[16]

High-performing organizations invest in the Capability Development of their people because they know that continuous improvement of outcomes requires continuous improvement of organizational and individual capabilities. Often knowledge gained via an enterprise's strength in Organizational Learning translates into development needs for the knowledge, skills, and abilities of teams and individuals. It is probably no surprise that Collins and Porras stated, "The visionary companies also invested much more aggressively in human capital via extensive recruiting, employee training and professional development programs. Merck, 3M, Motorola, GE, Disney, Marriott and IBM all made significant investments in their 'universities' and 'education centers' for intensive training and development programs."[17]

A strong Team Orientation also complements Organizational Learning in high-performing organizations. While formalized training and development programs are critical to the success of an organization, they alone do not ensure that employees are fully competent for their on-the-job challenges. Effective Organizational Learning also incorporates effective methods for sharing information, particularly knowledge about the occurrence, causes, and remedies of mistakes and problems with colleagues, suppliers, and end users.

> Within organizations, team learning has three critical dimensions. First, there is a need to think insightfully about complex issues. Here, teams must learn how to tap the potential of many minds to be more intelligent than one mind. . . . Second, there is a need for innovative, coordinated action. The championship sports teams and great jazz ensembles provide metaphors for acting in spontaneous yet coordinated ways. . . . Third, there is the role of team members on other teams . . . a learning team continually fosters other learning teams through inculcating the practices and skills of team learning more broadly.[18]

Effective Organizational Learning involves the entire organization—not just the individuals involved in a particular operation and their colleagues. On many occasions, I've seen well-intended changes in one operation have tremendous unintended consequences in subsequent steps in vertical processes. Continuous improvement recognizes the continuity of production processes. A change in one person's operations is likely to have an effect on the people she or he shakes hands with—the suppliers and customers for her or his work. Thus, high-performing organizations utilize both formal and informal communication systems to ensure the capture and sharing of operational knowledge and experiences among interdependent individuals and groups.

## THE ROLE OF LEADERSHIP IN CONTINUOUS IMPROVEMENT

> Learning leaders must have faith in people and must believe that ultimately human nature is basically good and in any case mutable.[19]

Managers do things right; leaders do the right things. Part of the leader's doing the right thing is setting the example and being the role model for his or her people. As we discussed, one of the three key elements in shaping organizational cultures is the heroes who set precedent and contribute to the folklore that sets the norms of behavior for the group. How leaders react to problems, learn from mistakes, emphasize problem prevention, deal candidly with adversity, coach their team members, and so on, is very powerful in shaping the expectations and serving as examples for their colleagues, peers, and subordinates. Leaders who truly believe in a learning organization and are successful in having such an organization are themselves the best students and practitioners of personal growth. Their willingness to deal realistically with their own need to learn from their mistakes, practice problem prevention, maintain awareness of the environmental dynamics, and so on, creates a benchmark by which their subordinates will measure themselves. Conversely, leaders who are themselves unwilling to evolve cannot realistically hope to establish and maintain a learning organization.

## THE IMPACT OF ORGANIZATIONAL LEARNING ON FINANCIAL PERFORMANCE

The strength or weakness of an enterprise's Organizational Learning characteristic has significant implications for financial performance. An organization that is highly effective in monitoring its external environmental dynamics and implementing appropriate internal responses will enjoy positive impacts on the top, middle, and bottom lines of the income statement as follows:

1. Higher revenues:
   - More timely development and faster time to market of market-demanded products and services
   - Premium pricing to reflect higher quality
2. Reduced expenses:
   - Proper levels of inventory
   - Higher product quality
   - Reduced fixed and variable costs
   - Greater effectiveness of its human resources
   - Higher employee satisfaction, lower turnover, and associated cost savings and efficiencies
3. Net income:
   - Obviously, since net income is the difference between revenues and expenses, any increase in the top line or decrease in the middle line will lead to more profitable results.

On the opposite side of the coin are enterprises with weakness on their Organizational Learning cultural characteristic, which, of course, has the opposite impacts on the enterprise's financial and competitive performance, beginning with poorer quality and lower employee satisfaction and including all of the negative ripple effects.

The critical difference between learning organizations and their weaker counterparts is the recognition of each individual's role in continuous improvement; empowerment of every individual to seize every opportunity to learn and improve; and ongoing efforts to communicate, coordinate, and integrate individual learning for the collective success and benefit of all the enterprise's constituents. The qualitative list of financial rewards for a culture that is dedicated to continuous improvement is nearly impossible to assemble, as are the overall quantitative results. But those who have experienced both the joy of being part of a learning organization and the frustration of participating in a nonlearning organization will tell you that, in addition to the effects on the bottom line, the rewards of the learning organization are priceless.

## M&A IMPLICATIONS OF THE ORGANIZATIONAL LEARNING CULTURE CHARACTERISTIC

### Strong Acquirer, Strong Acquired
Coincidental strength on the Organizational Learning characteristic on the part of both the combining organizations is a tremendous enabling asset for the future success of the combined organization as measured by a higher return on investment and a reduced payback period and should be reflected in the purchase price and integration planning of the deal. However, differences in how the respective organizations create external awareness and implement internal changes should be anticipated and recognized. Appropriate use of the organization's respective Organizational Learning strengths can be an opportunity for an early win-win in the integration process.

### Strong Acquirer, Weak Acquired
Perhaps the acquiring company's relative strength on the Organizational Learning cultural characteristic is what prompted it to initiate the deal in the first place. However, there is significant peril for a company that does not recognize the implicit rewards of its own continuous improvement mentality and blindly assumes that such a characteristic prevails in the culture of its acquisition. Moderate to low scores on Organizational Learning for the acquired enterprise are indicative of an organization

that is not accustomed to dealing with external dynamics and readily adapting its capabilities for the sake of improved results and higher work satisfaction. In fact, low scores on the Organizational Learning characteristic may be a harbinger of a long and difficult integration process.

Quantitative Organization Culture Analyses can provide objective input to enable the acquirer to more realistically determine the purchase price, expectations for the payback period, and assumptions concerning the scope, costs, and duration of the integration process based on the degree of difference in the relative scores of the buying and selling enterprises on the Organizational Learning characteristics.

## Weak Acquirer, Strong Acquired

If ever the buyer has something to learn from its new asset, it is when a strong learning organization is acquired by an enterprise that is weak in its own continuous learning capabilities. Unfortunately, such a situation is a little like the tail wagging the dog. In most deals, the fact that the acquirer is not a learning organization blinds it to this superior trait in an organization that it, by some virtue, was able to acquire. This arrogance can be extremely costly in that much of what made the acquired organization attractive in the first place may stem from its ability to adapt to its environment. In some cases, an enterprise will recognize that its best change mechanism is to be acquired. As noted in the discussion of Creating Change, it can be a tremendous shock to an adaptive enterprise to be acquired and overseen by a less adaptive organization.

In such acquisitions, the predeal projections of payback periods and return on investment will very likely not be met. Typical of these deals is an acquiring company that perceives itself as the victor and its new acquisition as the vanquished.

Like a pirate that has no sensitivity to the history or value of its prize, acquirers that are weak on Organizational Learning are ignorant of the elegance of the true assets of their new possession and are amazed when it doesn't provide them with the same value and rewards that it provided to its former owners.

Quantitative Organization Culture Analyses can provide the acquirers with objective evidence that their own organization may be a liability to the success of the deal. The QUOCA should provide the buyer with the motivation and opportunity to strengthen its culture prior to integration.

## Weak Acquirer, Weak Acquired

As with coincidental weaknesses on Creating Change, when both organizations are weak on the Organizational Learning characteristic, a disaster may be in the works. The acquiring company will enjoy the blissful ignorance of not knowing what it doesn't know. There will be no vehicle by which the combining organizations can adapt to each other or to the external environment. Ever-increasing command-and-control systems, bureaucracy, and policies and procedures will be imposed to assure the coordination and integration of activities, stifling the sense of ownership and the creativity of the work processes. Odds are that the combined weaknesses will also include unawareness of external dynamics, and the long-term viability of the combined organization will be in jeopardy.

If the acquirer even bothers to develop an integration plan to instruct and develop people on how to adapt to the new ownership scheme, it will probably underestimate the time, attention, effort, and resources that will be required if the new organization is to function effectively.

The use of QUOCA to identify this shared cultural weakness should stimulate the integration team to develop the Organizational Learning characteristic in both organizations during the integration process.

## SUMMARY

Long ago, when I was in the Navy, I had the good fortune to work for a grizzled old machinist mate who had served on diesel submarines during the Korean War and was now serving on what, at that time, was the latest in nuclear propulsion and nuclear warhead delivery submarines. He was showing me how to operate a milling machine, and he asked me if I knew what was unique about the device. When I answered that I didn't know, he said, "A mill is the only machine that can be used to remake itself. A pretty amazing irony, isn't it?"

The same amazing thing is true of the Organizational Learning characteristic of organizational cultures. With it, the organization can reproduce and evolve itself to enable its long-term viability. Without it, there is no lever to take advantage of knowledge, experience, intellectual growth, mistakes, or successes. If one cultural attribute can make the difference between prosperity and perishing, it is Organizational Learning. Beware of organizations that don't know what they don't know.

# GLOSSARY OF TERMS

A N IMPORTANT FACTOR IN GETTING the most out of this book is under-standing the terminology used by two distinct professions: financial services and organization development. It is the author's hope that members of each of these professional groups will be interested in the subject matter, including the terminology used by their counterparts. Therefore, it is necessary to define terms that may be unfamiliar but that must be understood in order to derive value from the research.

## FINANCIAL TERMS

*Acquisition*—A formal business relationship in which the acquirer, in consideration of assets such as stock from the acquiring company, cash, or other financial instruments, purchases and assumes control of the assets of another business entity, such as a company or a company suborganization.

*Capital gain or loss*—The amount by which the selling price of an asset exceeds or falls short of the initial purchase price.

*Cash flow*—The difference between the company's cash receipts and its cash payments in a given period.

*Combination*—An inclusive term that refers to mergers, acquisitions, and other formal business relationships, such as strategic alliances and joint ventures.

*Cost of capital*—The required rate of return for various types of financing.

*Divestiture*—A formal business relationship in which the seller, in consideration of assets such as stock from the acquiring company, cash, or other financial instruments, sells all or some of the assets of his or her business entity, such as a company or a company suborganization.

*Due diligence*—The process of investigating a potential combination company for the purpose of gathering and analyzing information that will affect the decision to complete the combination and the financial success of the relationship.

*Earnings per share*—The company's net income divided by the number of outstanding common shares.

*Equity*—Claims against or rights in the assets of a business in the forms of liabilities to the business' creditors and claims of ownership of the assets by its proprietors, partners, or stockholders.

*Income/investment ratio*—A ratio computed by dividing income by total investment, including long-term debt, preferred stock, minority interest, and common equity. A powerful measure of the company's ability to increase income through internal investment.

*Income/sales ratio*—A ratio computed by dividing income by net sales. An excellent indication of the efficiency of a company's operations, showing the return on each dollar of sales. Also a particularly valuable tool for comparing firms within the same industry.

*Market capitalization*—The total value at market prices of a company's securities, determined by multiplying the number of shares times the market price per share.

*Merger*—The coming together of two companies to become one business entity.

*Net income, earnings, or profit*—A company's financial income after all expenses and taxes have been deducted.

*Stock price*—The market value that a share of stock commands on the stock exchange.

## ORGANIZATION DEVELOPMENT TERMS

*Artifacts*—The tactile, substantial attributes of an organization's culture, such as attire, plaques, photographs, icons, and so on.

*Assumptions*—Premises or suppositions that something is true.

*Attitudes*—Relatively stable and enduring predispositions to behave or react in certain ways toward persons, objects, institutions, or issues.

*Beliefs*—Convictions or opinions.

*Culture*—The integrated pattern of human behavior that includes thought, speech, action, and artifacts and depends on the human capacity for learning and transmitting knowledge to future generations.

*Heroes*—Persons recognized for their notable achievements; role models.

*Myths*—Traditional beliefs without historical verification.

*Opinions*—Beliefs, particularly those that are tentative and remain open to modification.

*Organization culture*—The underlying values, beliefs, and principles that serve as the foundation for an organization's management system, along with the set of management practices and behaviors that both exemplify and reinforce those basic principles.

*Organization development*—A planned change process, managed from the top, that takes into account both the technical and the human sides of the organization and uses inside or outside consultants in the planning and implementation of changes to be made.

*Principles*—Working hypotheses or maxims for conduct.

*Traits*—Relatively persistent and consistent behavior patterns manifested in a wide range of circumstances.

*Values*—Social ends or goals that are considered desirable of achievement.

# A CASE STUDY OF BUSINESS ACQUISITION USING QUANTITATIVE ORGANIZATION CULTURE ANALYSES (QUOCA)

*The Overall Clothing Corporation Acquires the Three Band Garment Company*

## INTRODUCTION

The Overall Clothing Corporation, a publicly traded, 40-year-old work clothing manufacturer with 51 employees is considering the purchase of the Three Band Garment Company, a 35-year-old privately held company being divested by its founder and owner, Sam Blackett.

## THE THREE BAND GARMENT COMPANY

Sam began his career as a trade school–trained welder. During his fledgling apprentice period, he became tired of having to replace work clothes because of spark burns. Three Band Clothing (TBG) began in Sam's basement in Aiken, South Carolina, where Sam made heavy denim spark-proof aprons by hand, first for himself, then for colleagues, and finally, with help from a catalog welding supplier, for virtually every welder in North America. Sam's gritty drive and unwavering quality and work standards provided legendary examples of "tough people making tough stuff." Sam's workforce came from family members, friends, and neighbors. Each employee enjoyed a personal relationship with Sam, and Sam openly shared his vision and plans for the business, and his profits from it.

Over the years, the product line and the production process changed very little. The products—capes, jackets, chaps, and gloves—were made in quarterly batch modes. The production system required people to master several different jobs and work closely with a variety of people. TBG enjoyed high productivity, very nice profits, great worker satisfaction, and very low personnel turnover.

In spite of TBG's growth to a business with $6 million a year in revenue, Sam handled all of the marketing and external relationships with customers and suppliers himself. He kept the books himself and handled virtually all administrative functions. Everything was fine until increasingly serious illnesses eventually convinced Sam of his mortality and he had to confront the fact that the business was in decline because of the diversion of his attention and time. Quality and inventory problems were becoming serious. The former organizational strengths of teamwork and following Sam's lead were causing a downward spiral as people enthusiastically did what they thought Sam would have directed with an understandable degree of inaccuracy. When the doctor eventually advised Sam to retire, he decided to sell the business and contacted a highly recommended broker.

## THE OVERALL CLOTHING CORPORATION

The Overall Clothing Corporation was founded in 1960 by Jim Quigley, a retired career Navy officer who had spent nearly 25 years on submarines. Jim realized that the Navy would be needing special work clothing for its rapidly expanding nuclear submarine fleet, and he also knew that, as a retired military man, he would have specified bidding advantages over nonveterans. Jim pulled together a team of retired officers and enlisted men to organize the business and advise him on the ideal products for several military uses and the features they should have, especially the one-piece nylon "poopy-suit" that nuclear submariners wore. The jointly developed products were jobbed out for production, and OCC made a competitive bid to the Navy. OCC won the contract and quickly purchased and modified a small garment factory in Charleston, South Carolina, that had been left idle when production of the polo shirts that had formerly been made there moved offshore. Charleston had a small Navy shipyard, and Quigley staffed the plant with retired servicemen and many Navy and Marine wives. The workforce was OCC's greatest asset, with only the fairly frequent reassignment of spouses causing turnover and, therefore, challenging coordination and integration of operations.

OCC's quality and professionalism almost assured it of continued contracts, and eventually the company expanded its product lines into Navy, Marine, Army, and Air Force flight suits. Quigley and his fellow founders took the company public in 1982, and management continued to be a succession of retired military people who were groomed for promotion through training and education. Revenues have grown roughly 25 percent per year, reaching $15 million last year with $2 million in EBIT. OCC has prospered and was recently approached by a suitor who wanted to purchase the company's assets and absorb them. After conferring with his board and direct reports, David Claghorn, the current CEO, decided that OCC's best move would be to grow via acquisition. The marketing and finance departments created a matrix team to study OCC's opportunities and decided on the tactic of buying a company that had a proven civilian product line to smooth any market fluctuations as well as new products that could be marketed to the military. A third criterion was that the target company serve civilian markets where demand for OCC's garment products could be created. A broker was hired to find a target company that met OCC's requirements.

## OCC BUYS TBG

The brokers ultimately matched the two companies, and OCC began the process of acquiring TBG. Recognizing this as their first foray into buying a company, the disciplined OCC management team knew what it didn't know (the due diligence process), and so they hired the consulting arm of an accounting company to assist them. An internal M&A team with representatives from executive management, operations, marketing, sales, purchasing, and human resources was also formed. In addition, OCC's outside accounting and legal firms participated on the combination team on behalf of the company. OCC executives were asked to delegate their normal responsibilities so that the company would continue to operate smoothly during the combination process. The following people assumed these important due diligence functions:

- David Claghorn, along with the firm's accountant and the firm's attorney—Corporate matters such as TBG's financial and legal documents, records, meeting minutes, licenses, regulatory records, ownership documents, employment agreements, litigation and claims, consulting agreements, supplier and customer contracts, and so on.
- Bob Stevenson (the VP of human resources), along with the firm's attorney—Employment contracts, EEOC and OSHA records, employee benefit plans, safety records, policies and procedures, and the names and phone numbers of present and past TBG officers.
- Jim Smith (the VP of purchasing), along with the firm's accountant and the firm's attorney—TBG's material contracts, insurance policies and records, service contracts, waste material disposal records, operating licenses, permits, and so on.
- Bill Newhall (the VP of marketing), along with the VP of sales, and the VP of operations—TBG's business plan, its marketing plan, marketing literature, sales records for the past 5 years, product samples, production/quality records, equipment inventory and maintenance records, research on TBG's competitors, tour of production, storage and warehousing facilities, and so on.

Sam Blackett was not accustomed to people sticking their nose into his business, and a couple of times he questioned whether he really did want to sell TBG. But as he led the OCC due diligence team members through the TBG information and operations, he began to see his business from their perspective, and he realized how far removed he had been from the company and what a toll this had taken on its operations. As the founder and sole owner, and, for 35 years, the CEO of TBG, Sam recognized that he no longer had the desire or the ability to operate the business, yet he felt a strong obligation to the people who had made TBG what it was. He consulted with his accountant and his attorney to devise a way to assure their continued employment and to reward them for their past efforts.

OCC's interaction with TBG was mostly positive. Sam was a bit of a curmudgeon, and his people were not as well trained or as sophisticated as their OCC counterparts. But they were forthcoming with the requested information and cooperative considering the potential impact of a combination. The OCC team's due diligence concluded that there were no "deal killers" in TBG's past, present, or future. TBG's plant and equipment were modern and well–maintained, and its administrative systems were all in good shape. With that established, the team of the CEO, the accountant, and the attorney, along with the consultants, set about determining the financial terms of the deal including the price to be offered and the form of payment. Research on both TBG and similar acquisitions within the professional apparel industry led the OCC team to a price between 3 and 4 times earnings before interest and taxes (EBIT). In its latest fiscal year, TBG's EBIT had been approximately $1 million. OCC tentatively decided that an offer of $3 million in cash and $1 million in OCC common stock would be a rational and fair offer for TBG.

As the combination process moved along, Claghorn assembled a team consisting of himself, the VP of human resources, the VP of operations, and the VP of purchasing, along with an organizational development consultant, to investigate the potential operational challenges of combining companies. The consultant, Mark Iorio, suggested performing quantitative organization culture surveys of the two businesses as a vehicle to adjust the valuation/compensation for any significant cultural differences as well as to incorporate such data into the payback period calculations for the deal. The VP of human resources concurred and expressed his interest in investigating the culture traits of the organizations in order to identify any potential operational problems and to develop a communications strategy for the integration.

The consultant described the purpose and conducted a Quantitative Organization Culture Analysis (QUOCA) using the Denison Culture Survey for all OCC and TBG employees. The culture survey results are presented on the circumplexes in Figures B-1 and B-2, respectively. Mark analyzed the QUOCA data for each of the companies and then the implications of the integrated traits of the combined organizations.

## OVERALL CLOTHING CORPORATION QUOCA RESULTS

OCC has more isolated problems to solve than a need for a complete overhaul. The stimulus of the combination may cause the somewhat complacent OCC organization to either raise or lower its general third-quartile characteristics. OCC's 40 years of successful but noncompetitive marketing and production have lowered its Customer Focus to very low levels. In open markets, companies with low CF suffer from poor sales/revenue growth, market share, and product innovation. The com-

**Figure B-1**   *The Overall Clothing Corporation Culture Survey Results*

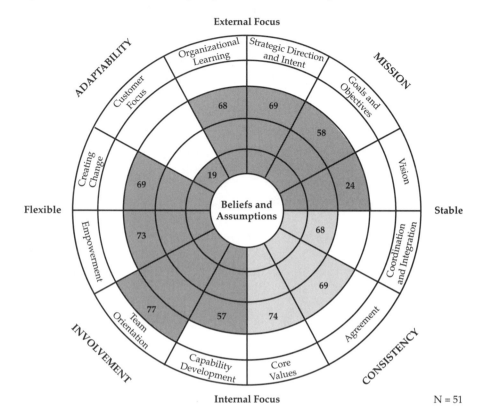

pany will have difficulty taking on TBG's unfamiliar products and markets as well as moving the OCC products into TBG's market.

The lack of diversity of OCC's production and the somewhat top-down military management style have affected the Coordination and Integration aspect of its operations. Companies with low C&I traits often have problems with product quality and employee satisfaction. Bringing in new people and products will be a management challenge for the OCC team. Other observations include the following:

- Higher scores on Vision and Strategic Direction and Intent than on Goals and Objectives are symptomatic of organization leaders who can't convert their corporate Vision into action. This characteristic affects future market share, revenue, and earnings.

- Higher Team Orientation than either Empowerment or Capability Development is indicative of low substance to the organization's teams—they are more "teams for teams sake" than the result of a real commitment to or ownership of the organization's goals. This characteristic manifests itself in lower product quality and employee satisfaction and eventually affects market share, revenues, and earnings.

- Lower Customer Focus than either Creating Change or Organizational Learning is indicative of organizations that are good at recognizing best industry practices but poor at implementing these practices in their products. This characteristic also manifests itself in lower product quality and employee satisfaction and eventually affects market share, revenues, and earnings.

- Higher Agreement and Core Values than Coordination and Integration indicates an organization that is good at developing buy-in but poor at implementation. This characteristic affects production efficiencies and product quality, thereby decreasing market share, revenues, and earnings.

- Higher external than internal focus is typical of an organization that may be resting on its reputation in the market and experiencing some internal personnel competition for management attention and growth opportunities. Such cultural traits affect personnel turnover, product quality, and innovation, and have both short-term and long-term earnings implications.

- OCC has balanced flexibility and stability, but the company could be stronger on both sides to improve productivity and innovation and therefore short- and long-term earnings.

- OCC can use its strength on Team Orientation, Empowerment, Core Values, and Vision as change agents to (1) develop greater leadership for Coordination and Integration of operations and (2) develop bridges to customers and their needs.

## THE THREE BAND GARMENT COMPANY QUOCA RESULTS

The TBG organization culture reflects the extended loss of Sam's involvement and leadership. It is a floundering company that is looking for direction. Of the twelve organization indices, TBG scores at or below average on seven and in the first quartile on two—Coordination and Integration (22 percent) and Customer Focus (7 percent). Companies with similar traits have or tend to develop poor productivity and declining quality. The high scores on Team Orientation, Empowerment, and Core Values indicate that Sam's residual influence is carrying the company. Other observations include the following:

**Figure B-2**   *Three Band Garment Company Culture Survey Results*

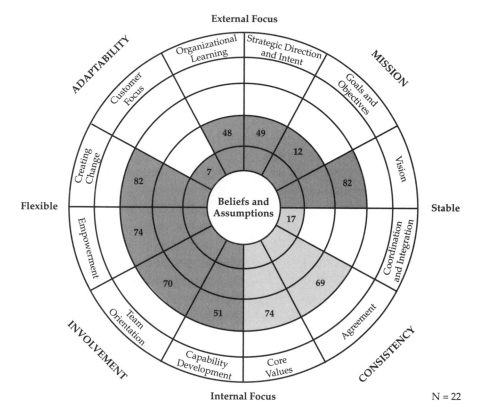

- Low Goals and Objectives and Strategic Direction and Intent combined with modest Vision is symptomatic of an organization whose strategy and mission are poorly understood. This characteristic will affect current operational efficiencies, quality, and employee satisfaction and also future market share, revenue, and earnings.

- Higher scores on Team Orientation and Empowerment than on Capability Development are indicative of organizations in which people may be making decisions that they are not capable of making well. Without complementary leadership or capability development, poor choices will be made and implemented. Additionally, the operations may not have the bench strength to react appropriately to internal and/or external environmental changes such as those imposed by the acquisition. This characteristic manifests itself in employee satisfaction and may significantly affect present and future quality, market share, revenues, and earnings.

- A lower score on Customer Focus than on either Creating Change or Organizational Learning is indicative of organizations that are good at recognizing best industry practices but poor at implementing those practices in their products. The extremely low score on Customer Focus is symptomatic of a company that may be producing products for which there will be little demand. Overall low to mediocre Adaptability scores are indicative of a company that is in a product/production rut and may have difficulty coordinating the demands of the OCC combination. Such characteristics may lead to integration problems and an extended payback period for the acquisition.

- Higher scores on Agreement and Core Values than on Coordination and Integration indicate an organization that is good at developing buy-in but poor at implementation. This characteristic affects production efficiencies and product quality, thereby decreasing market share, revenues, and earnings. Of greater impact will be the very low Coordination and Integration score, which has immediate and ongoing effects on employee satisfaction, quality, and production efficiencies, and consequently on market share, revenues, and earnings.

- Higher internal than external focus is typical of an organization that is searching for direction, with employees competing with one another rather than with the market. The company may be protecting what it has rather than trying to develop its future. Such cultural traits affect employee satisfaction, personnel turnover, product quality, and innovation with both short-term and long-term earnings implications.

- Low, balanced flexibility and stability is indicative of a lot of nice people going nowhere together. Strengthening is needed on both sides to improve productivity and innovation and, therefore, short- and long-term earnings.

- TBG's overall weakness in Mission will have a negative impact on profitability/ROA, sales/revenue growth, market share, quality, and employee satisfaction.

- The overall low Adaptability scores will have a negative impact on sales/revenue growth, market share, product development, and innovation.

- OCC can capitalize on TBG's strength on Team Orientation, Empowerment, Core Values, and Agreement to make significant changes that will counteract TBG's weaknesses on Adaptability and Mission.

## THE COMBINED OCC AND TBG ORGANIZATION CULTURE IMPLICATIONS

The unified organization will benefit from OCC's and TBG's coincidental strengths on the Team Orientation, Empowerment, and Creating Change characteristics. The shared strength in Core Values may be an asset or a liability depending upon how similar or different the core values are. (See Table B-1.)

The combined organization will suffer from the coincidental weaknesses on Customer Focus, Coordination and Integration, and Organizational Learning. The collateral weakness in Customer Focus should be factored into both the valuation and the long-term financial projections. OCC must bolster its own Coordination and Integration prior to closing so that it can capitalize on TBG's C&I weakness and thereby have an immediate positive impact on the combined organization. Coincidental weakness on Organizational Learning means that there is little talent to draw upon in the event of personnel losses, thereby making a successful integration even more critical to the long-term success of the expanded OCC.

OCC does enjoy superiority and capability on the Strategic Direction and Intent, Goals and Objectives, and Organizational Learning cultural aspects. These are important and powerful resources for effecting a successful integration and thereby will affect the success of the deal. Unfortunately, TBG has no superior cultural traits to lend to the combined OCC organization.

On two cultural characteristics, Strategic Direction and Intent and Organizational Learning, OCC is much stronger than TBG and can use the integration process to bolster TBG's knowledge of the combined strategic direction. Organizational Learning can be a very interactive topic to develop through a mentored training program, which should coincidentally serve to create goodwill and good working relationships early in the integration process.

## PRICE AND PAYBACK PERIOD ADJUSTMENTS DUE TO CULTURAL WEAKNESSES AND DIFFERENCES OF THE COMBINING COMPANIES

The financial experts involved in the OCC/TBG deal must realize that OCC contributes its own weaknesses to the ideal outcome of the combined organizations. However, OCC is the initiating party and is purchasing a business with cultural characteristics that will have a negative

**Table B-1** *Significant Cultural Differences between OCC and TBG, Their Potential Impact, and Suggested Action*

| Culture Characteristic | TBG Score | OCC Score | Potential Impact | Suggested Action |
|---|---|---|---|---|
| Customer Focus | 7 | 10 | *Reduced product development/innovation:* Leads to slower time to market for new products, loss of market share, higher inventory of passé products<br><br>*Lower market share:* Leads to lower revenues and profits, with the associated direct and indirect effects; lower profit margins and less ability to negotiate prices with customers; higher physical inventory and inventory costs; lower production efficiencies from underutilized resources; and reduced buying power/loss of volume discounts<br><br>*Lower sales/revenue growth:* Leads to decreased stock price and company valuation; lower availability and higher cost of capital; and reduced profitability, along with its associated direct and indirect effects | 1. Hire a consulting firm to perform an in-depth market analysis to identify depth, breadth, dynamics, and buyer motivations.<br>2. Create new marketing positions requiring strong background in market and customer knowledge.<br>3. Develop strong, interactive relationship between new marketing group and production.<br>4. Use follow-up QUOCA results to measure progress. |
| Coordination and Integration | 42 | 22 | *Poorer quality:* Leads to reduced sales, lower revenue, reduced market share, higher inventory costs, and higher production costs for scrap and rework<br><br>*Lower employee satisfaction:* Leads to higher rates of injury, absenteeism, and grievances; higher turnover; and reduced productivity, efficiency, and effectiveness | 1. Investigate to determine root causes and to develop a strategy to determine what good coordination and integration looks like for us by time of closing.<br>2. Develop and implement a training program for all OCC and TBG employees, to be presented within 2 weeks of closing on the deal.<br>3. Use follow-up QUOCA results to measure progress. |

*(continued on next page)*

**Table B-1**  *Significant Cultural Differences between OCC and TBG, Their Potential Impact, and Suggested Action (continued)*

| Culture Characteristic | TBG Score | OCC Score | Potential Impact | Suggested Action |
|---|---|---|---|---|
| Goals and Objectives | 42 | 55 | *Reduced profitability:* Leads to lower cash on hand to compensate stakeholders in the form of dividends, bonuses, and salary increases; lower earnings per share, which decrease the stock price and the organization's ability to borrow money at optimum rates; reduced revenues and borrowing ability, which impede the investment in capital improvements that maintain or increase the company's competitive position in the marketplace. Continued low revenues and a high cost of capital can lead to cutbacks in spending for such things as maintenance, marketing, and training, which eventually further affect profitability through unexpected breakdowns, lower market share, and lower employee effectiveness<br><br>*Poorer quality:* Leads to reduced sales, lower revenue, reduced market share, higher inventory costs, and higher production costs for scrap and rework | 1. Use the combined business planning aspect of the acquisition integration plan to develop specific goals and objectives in support of the Strategic Direction and Intent for both companies' line and staff organizations.<br>2. Clearly communicate each organization's goals and objectives to responsible leaders for the purpose of them developing measurable benchmarks, communicating goals and benchmarks to their constituents and to develop and implement goal achievement plans. Benchmarks should include profitability and quality measures.<br>3. Implement biweekly goal progress communiqués within departments, divisions, and businesses.<br>4. Investigate and mitigate root causes for goal shortfalls. |

*(continued on next page)*

**Table B-1** *Significant Cultural Differences between OCC and TBG, Their Potential Impact, and Suggested Action (continued)*

| Culture Characteristic | TBG Score | OCC Score | Potential Impact | Suggested Action |
|---|---|---|---|---|
| Strategic Direction and Intent | 69 | 44 | *Reduced profitability:* Leads to lower cash on hand to compensate stakeholders in the form of dividends, bonuses, and salary increases; lower earnings per share, which decrease the stock price and the organization's ability to borrow money at optimum rates; reduced revenues and borrowing ability, which impede the investment in capital improvements that maintain or increase the company's competitive position in the marketplace. Continued low revenues and a high cost of capital can lead to cutbacks in spending for such things as maintenance, marketing, and training, which eventually further affect profitability through unexpected breakdowns, lower market share, and lower employee effectiveness | 1. Convene key OCC people to determine our combined SD&I. <br> 2. Determine, develop, and implement a program that clearly establishes our SD&I for our employees, customers, suppliers, and all other stakeholders of both OCC and TBG. <br> 3. Use QUOCA follow-up to measure progress. |
| Organizational Learning | 68 | 44 | See Customer Focus | 1. Need to use our strength to overcome TBG's weakness. <br> 2. Figure out what works for us and see if we can develop a training program or other development vehicle to make sure TBG's OL gets up to speed. <br> 3. Use QUOCA follow-up to measure progress. |

impact on the optimum combination results. Clearly, OCC would use full valuation figures in its pricing calculations if TBG scored in the fourth quartile in each of the cultural traits, just as we would expect to pay close to blue book price for a nearly perfect used car. Each flaw should lead to an equitable deduction in price, since it will cause OCC to make additional investments in TBG in order to optimize its current functionality.

The impact on the price of the cultural characteristics is based on the snapshot of the current organizational weaknesses and differences, but the future impacts of the cultural dynamics must be considered as well. The price offered should reflect the organizational impacts on the future performance of the combined organization.

## FINANCIAL IMPLICATIONS OF THE OCC AND TBG QUOCA INFORMATION

The acquisition team sat down with Iorio, the QUOCA expert, to factor in the cultural implications along with other pricing factors such as up-to-date market trends and cost of capital. After extensive discussions, during which Iorio explained how the cultural differences would affect the financial and competitive measures of the deal, the team agreed to make adjustments to their earlier pricing strategy. The impact of the individual and collective cultural weaknesses and differences between the combining organizations will have the following financial implications on the deal:

*Short-Term.* Profitability and return on investment should be adjusted downward by 15 to 20 percent to reflect the operational impacts of the combined cultural weaknesses. Thus, if industry price is between 3 and 4 times EBIT, OCC may want to set its multiple at 3.5 to reflect TBG's mediocre cultural characteristics. A 10 to 20 percent additional downward adjustment may be warranted as a result of TBG's weaknesses on Customer Focus and Coordination and Integration, yielding a multiple of 3.05 to 2.8 times EBIT.

*Long-Term.* Sales/revenue growth projections should be adjusted downward 20 to 30 percent because of the extended implications of TBG's cultural characteristics that affect product quality through likely personnel turnover, poor leadership, and low bench strength. Long-term prospects for sales/revenue growth are also poor because of the lack of innovation and product development resulting from TBG's very poor Customer Focus and Organizational Learning characteristics.

Mark briefed the CEO, the VP of human resources, the VP of operations, and the VP of purchasing on his findings. David Claghorn asked Mark to work with the finance team to factor the QUOCA results into the acquisition pricing sensitivity analyses. The adjustments considered not just TBG's challenges but those within OCC as well. The recalculated price reflected both the true value of the TBG operational environment and the cultural implications that would affect the integration period and the profitability of the integration.

Armed with the QUOCA results, the buying team was able to articulate TBG's cultural flaws and their pricing and profitability implications to Sam Blackett. Sam knew that his illness and his absence from the business would affect the value of TBG, but the QUOCA data unequivocally illustrated the nature and scope of the impact. Sam accepted the adjusted price, and the closing of the deal was organized and scheduled.

An integration team consisting of the CEO, the VP of human resources, the VP of operations, and Mark, the consultant, put together a plan to bring the two organizations together as quickly as possible while minimizing the impact on their individual and collective operations. Based on TBG's QUOCA results, the transition team set the following goals:

1. Strategically, it was determined that the TBG brand had a good reputation and brand name recognition. Based on that fact, plus the cash flow advantage of leaving the TBG operations where they were and the disparity between the organizational cultures, the team decided to keep the OCC and TBG operations separate. OCC would keep David Claghorn as CEO and would appoint a president for both TBG and OCC who would report to him.

2. Hal Turner, a senior OCC executive, was named president of TBG. He and Sam Blackett scheduled a meeting with the TBG employees the week before closing. Sam introduced Hal very cordially and explained that he was sorry that he was selling TBG, but that his health demanded it and his people deserved it. He explained how the company had suffered from his absence. Mark was reintroduced (he had met the TBG people when he conducted the QUOCA) and presented the results of the analyses, took questions, and emphasized the need for organizational changes if TBG and its people were to regain the success they had previously enjoyed.

3. Turner then described OCC's vision for the business—to be a top-quality, customer-responsive welding protective garment supplier with expanded civilian market penetration and access through

OCC to military markets and, eventually, other government markets. Specific Goals and Objectives and the Strategic Direction and Intent for TBG would be developed and articulated shortly after the close of the sale. Turner emphasized to the TBG employees that their employment was secure; TBG would operate as an autonomous unit of OCC and that, other than Sam, the management team would remain intact.

4. Turner stated that OCC considered the TBG acquisition to be an investment and that its strategy was to invest in TBG's people and their capabilities as well. He referred to the culture survey and explained that consultants would be brought in to improve Coordination and Integration. Technical development programs would be offered to all employees to facilitate Capability Development and personal growth.

5. Turner said that a marketing manager would be either promoted from within TBG or hired from outside to improve Customer Focus. In addition, a company newsletter and web site would be launched to share information with all employees concerning the company's performance, opportunities for improvement, and customer feedback.

6. Sam Blackett closed the meeting by thanking everyone for their contribution to the company's success and stating how pleased he was that OCC understood the business and its people. When he and Turner shook hands, the TBG people applauded.

7. On the day the deal closed, Turner toured the plant, met all of the people, and held a staff meeting with all managers and supervisors to develop and implement specific goals and processes for the integration plan he had outlined at the introduction meeting.

Meanwhile, in Charleston, David Claghorn was meeting with the OCC people to announce the TBG deal, to welcome Jim Alsup as the new president of OCC, and to congratulate Hal Turner on his promotion to head of TBG. David stated that as CEO of both operations, he wanted to take the opportunity provided by the organizational changes to implement some process improvements. David reintroduced Mark Iorio, who led a presentation and discussion of the OCC QUOCA. David then turned the meeting over to Jim Alsup, who presented the following information regarding OCC's developmental response to the QUOCA findings:

1. A company newsletter and web site will be launched to share information with all employees concerning the company's Goals and

Objectives, its Strategic Direction and Intent, and its Vision for the future.

2. Management development programs will be offered to all employees and complemented with a weekly staff meeting to improve Coordination and Integration of OCC activities.

3. Technical development programs would be offered to all employees to facilitate Capability Development and personal growth.

4. A development program for the marketing team, including professional training, participation in trade shows, and an expanded budget for customer visits, would be employed to improve Customer Focus. Further, the OCC marketing team would form an ad hoc group with their TBG counterparts to develop cross-selling capabilities.

David Claghorn closed the meeting by thanking everyone for his or her contribution to the success that had enabled OCC to expand by acquiring TBG. He promised that in his new role as CEO, he would enjoy the time, opportunity, and the assistance from Alsup and Turner to continue the future success of the business and all of its people. He, too, got a standing ovation.

# REFERENCES

## Introduction

1. Terrence E. Deal and Allan A. Kennedy, *Corporate Cultures: The Rites and Rituals of Corporate Life* (Reading, Mass.: Addison-Wesley, 1982).
2. Charles J. Fombrum, *Leading Corporate Change* (New York: McGraw-Hill, 1992).
3. *Webster's New Collegiate Dictionary* (Springfield, Mass.: Merriam-Webster, 1981).
4. "(The) Daily Deal.com". Corporate Control Alert. 24 May 2000. <http://www.thedailydeal.com/features/A22956-2000may24.html.

## Chapter 1

1. Mansel G. Blackford and K. Austin Kerr, *Business Enterprise in American History*, 2nd ed. (Boston: Houghton Mifflin, 1990).
2. Anya Schiffren, "Waiting for the Mergers...and Waiting," *The Standard*. 19 Feb. 2001. <http://www.thestandard.com/article/display/0,1151, 22227,00.html?Nl =met>.

## Chapter 2

1. Albert J. Viscio, John R. Harbison, Amy Asin, and Richard D. Vitaro, *Journal of Strategy and Business* (New York: Booz-Allen & Hamilton, Fourth Quarter, 1999).
2. Christopher Caggiano, "Merge Now, Pay Later," *Inc.*, April 2000: 86–96.
3. Andrew J. Sherman, *Mergers and Acquisitions from A to Z* (New York: AMACOM, 1998).
4. Stephen L. Keys, *The Ernst & Young Guide to Mergers and Acquisitions* (New York: Wiley, 1989).
5. Mitchell Lee Marks and Philip H. Mirvis, *Joining Forces: Making One Plus One Equal Three in Mergers, Acquisitions and Alliances* (San Francisco: Jossey-Bass, 1998).
6. Sharon L. Blanding, *Acquisitions: How to Expand, Extend and Defend Your Business* (Chicago: Probus, 1991).

7. Ibid.
8. Mitchell Lee Marks and Philip H. Mirvis, *Joining Forces: Making One Plus One Equal Three in Mergers, Acquisitions and Alliances* (San Francisco: Jossey-Bass, 1998).
9. Ibid.
10. Larry Senn as quoted from Stephen L. Keys, *The Ernst & Young Management Guide to Mergers and Acquisitions* (New York: Wiley, 1989).
11. Daniel R. Denison, *Corporate Culture and Organizational Effectiveness* (Ann Arbor, Mich.: self-published, 1997).
12. Jay W. Lorsch, "Note on Organization Design," note for classroom discussion, Harvard Business School, 1975.
13. Manfred F. R. Kets de Vries and Danny Miller, *The Neurotic Organization: Diagnosing and Revitalizing Unhealthy Companies* (New York: HarperCollins, 1984).
14. Denison.
15. Caroline J. Fisher, *Corporate Culture and Perceived Business Performance: A Study of the Relationship between the Culture of an Organization and the Perceptions of Its Financial and Qualitative Performance.* Doctoral dissertation, California School of Professional Psychology, 1997.

## Chapter 3

1. Edgar H. Schein, *Organizational Culture and Leadership* (San Francisco: Jossey-Bass, 1992).
2. Simon Creedy Smith and Iqbal Dharamsi, *International Mergers and Acquisition Review 2001/2002* (Deloitte and Touche, London).
3. Steven Gunders and Alan Alpert, *International Mergers and Acquisitions Review, 2001/2002* (Deloitte and Touche, London).
4. Peter Krass, *Why Do We Do It?* The Conference Board, October 14, 2002, www.conference-board.org/cgi-bin/MsmGo.exe?grab_id=46566936&EXTRA_ARC.
5. A. T. Kearney, October 14, 2002, www.atkearney.com/main.taf?a=5&b=4&c=1&d=29.
6. Mitchell Lee Marks and Philip H. Mirvis, *Joining Forces: Making One Plus One Equal Three in Mergers, Acquisitions and Alliances* (San Francisco: Jossey-Bass, 1998).
7. Cynthia Overman, "Learning Your M&ABC's," *HR Focus*, August 1999.
8. Art Geis, "HR M&A Solutions International," excerpt from company brochure, http://www.hrmandasolutionsintl.com/excerpt.html.
9. George Anders, "How Are We Going to Make This Merger Work?" *Fast Company*, February 2001: 184, 186.
10. Andrew J. Sherman, *Mergers and Acquisitions from A to Z* (New York: AMACOM, 1998).
11. Marks and Mirvis.
12. Robert Porter Lynch, *Business Alliance Guide: The Hidden Competitive Weapon* (New York: Wiley, 1993).
13. Stanley M. Davis, *Managing Corporate Culture* (New York: Harper & Row, 1984).
14. Marks and Mirvis.

15. Ruth N. Bramson, "HR's Role in Mergers and Acquisitions," *Training & Development*, October 2000: 59–66.
16. Schein.
17. Marks and Mirvis.
18. Ibid.
19. Mercer United Kingdom Resource Center.

## Chapter 4

1. Edgar H. Schein, *Organizational Culture and Leadership* (San Francisco: Jossey-Bass, 1992).
2. *American Heritage Dictionary* ( New York: Dell, Paperback Edition, 1973).
3. Schein.
4. Terrence E. Deal and Allan A. Kennedy, *Corporate Cultures: The Rites and Rituals of Corporate Life* (Reading, Mass.: Addison-Wesley, 1982).
5. John P. Kotter and James L. Heskett, *Corporate Culture and Performance* (New York: The Free Press, 1992).
6. Ichak Adizes, *Corporate Lifecycles: How and Why Corporations Grow and Die and What to Do About It* (Paramus, N.J.: Prentice-Hall, 1988).
7. Ibid.
8. Daniel R. Denison, *Corporate Culture and Organizational Effectiveness* (Ann Arbor, Mich.: self-published, 1997).
9. Ibid.
10. Caroline J. Fisher, *Corporate Culture and Perceived Business Performance: A Study of the Relationship between the Culture of an Organization and the Perceptions of Its Financial and Qualitative Performance*. Doctoral dissertation, California School of Professional Psychology, 1997.
11. Denison.
12. Fisher.
13. Denison.
14. Ibid.
15. Ibid.
16. Fisher.
17. Ibid.
18. Denison.
19. Ibid.

## Chapter 5

1. Edgar H. Schein, *Organizational Culture and Leadership* (San Francisco: Jossey-Bass, 1992).
2. Terrence E. Deal and Allan A. Kennedy, *Corporate Cultures: The Rites and Rituals of Corporate Life* (Reading, Mass.: Addison-Wesley, 1982).
3. Terrence R. Deal and Lee G. Bolman, *Reframing Organizations: Artistry, Choice, and Leadership* (San Francisco: Jossey-Bass, 1997).
4. Thomas J. Peters and Robert H. Waterman, *In Search of Excellence: Lessons from America's Best Run Companies* (New York: Warner, 1982).

5. Jim Collins, *Good to Great* (New York: HarperCollins Business, 2001).

6. Larry Senn as quoted from Stephen L. Keys, *The Ernst & Young Guide to Mergers and Acquisitions* (New York: Wiley, 1989).

7. Ibid.

8. George Labovitz and Victor Rosansky, *The Power of Alignment: How Great Companies Stay Centered and Accomplish Extraordinary Things* (New York: Wiley, 1997).

9. Ibid.

## Chapter 6

1. Scott Spann and Caroline Fisher, *Facilitating Merger Success: Integrating the Cultures and the Denison Culture Survey* (ARC International, Ann Arbor, 1997).

2. Daniel R. Denison, *Corporate Culture and Organizational Effectiveness* (Ann Arbor, Mich.: self-published, 1997).

3. Ibid.

4. Ibid.

5. Ibid.

6. Caroline J. Fisher, *Corporate Culture and Perceived Business Performance: A Study of the Relationship between the Culture of an Organization and the Perceptions of Its Financial and Qualitative Performance.* Doctoral dissertation, California School of Professional Psychology, 1997.

7. Ibid.

8. Ibid.

9. Ibid.

## Chapter 7

1. Caroline J. Fisher, *Corporate Culture and Perceived Business Performance: A Study of the Relationship between the Culture of an Organization and the Perceptions of Its Financial and Qualitative Performance.* Doctoral dissertation, California School of Professional Psychology, 1997.

2. Daniel R. Denison, *Corporate Culture and Organizational Effectiveness* (Ann Arbor, Mich.: self-published, 1997).

## Chapter 8

1. George Labovitz and Victor Rosansky, *The Power of Alignment: How Great Companies Stay Centered and Accomplish Extraordinary Things* (New York: Wiley, 1997).

2. Ken Blanchard, Terry Waghorn, and Jim Ballard, *Mission Possible: Becoming a World Class Business While There's Still Time* (New York: McGraw-Hill, 1997).

3. Richard L. Daft, *Organization Theory and Design* (Cincinnati: Southwestern, 1998).

4. Rossabeth Moss Kanter, *The Change Masters: Innovation for Productivity in the American Corporation* (New York: Simon & Schuster, 1983).

5. Miles H. Overholt, *Building Flexible Organizations: The People-Centered Approach* (Dubuque, Iowa: Kendall/Hunt, 1996).

6. Stephen R. Covey, *The 7 Habits of Highly Effective People: Powerful Lessons in Personal Change* (New York: Fireside, 1989).

7. Blanchard, Waghorn, and Ballard.

8. James Champy, *Reengineering Management: The Mandate for New Leadership* (New York: HarperBusiness, 1995).

9. George S. Odiorne, *The Human Side of Management* (Lexington, Mass.: Lexington, 1987).

10. *American Heritage Dictionary* (New York: Dell, Paperback Edition, 1973).

11. Odiorne.

## Chapter 9

1. James Champy, *Reengineering Management: The Mandate for New Leadership* (New York: HarperBusiness, 1995).

2. Craig R. Hickman and Michael A. Silva, *Creating Excellence: Managing Corporate Culture, Strategy, and Change in the New Age* (New York: New American, 1984).

3. Benjamin B. Tregoe, John W. Zimmerman, Ronald A. Smith, and Peter M. Tobia, *Vision in Action: How to Integrate Your Company's Strategic Goals Into Day-To-Day Management Decisions* (New York: Fireside, 1989).

4. Gillette Corp. web site, http://www.gillette.com/company/ourvision.asp.

5. Wells Fargo, Inc., web site, www.wellsfargo.com/invest_relations/vision_values2.jthml.

6. Thomas S. Bateman and Scott A. Snell, *Management: Building Competitive Advantage* (Boston: Irwin-McGraw Hill, 1999).

7. Miles H. Overholt, *Building Flexible Organizations: The People-Centered Approach* (Dubuque, Iowa: Kendall/Hunt, 1996).

8. Jim Collins, *Good to Great* (New York: HarperCollins Business, 2001).

9. Pitney Bowes web site, www.pb.com.

10. Nucor web site, www.nucor.com.

11. Kroger web site, www.kroger.com.

12. Gillette Corp. web site, http://www.gillette.com/company/ourvision.asp.

13. Abbott Laboratories web site, www.abbott.com.

14. Richard L. Daft, *Organization Theory and Design* (Cincinnati: Southwestern, 1998).

15. Bruce A. Pasternack and Albert J. Viscio, *The Centerless Corporation: A New Model for Transforming Your Organization for Growth and Prosperity* (New York: Fireside, 1998).

16. Richard C. Whiteley, *The Customer Driven Company: Moving from Talk to Action* (Cambridge, Mass.: Perseus, 2000).

17. Ibid.

18. Ibid.

19. Pasternak and Viscio.

## Chapter 10

1. Craig R. Hickman and Michael A. Silva, *Creating Excellence: Managing Corporate Culture, Strategy, and Change in the New Age* (New York: New American, 1984).

2. Ibid.

3. Francis J. Gouillart and James F. Kelly, *Transforming the Organization* (New York: McGraw-Hill, 1995).

4. Hickman and Silva.

5. Richard C. Whiteley, *The Customer Driven Company: Moving from Talk to Action* (Cambridge, Mass.: Perseus, 2000).

6. Thomas F. Wallace, *Customer Driven Strategy: Winning through Operational Excellence* (Essex Junction: Wright, 1992).

7. Richard L. Daft, *Organization Theory and Design* (Cincinnati: Southwestern, 1998).

8. Jim Collins, *Good to Great* (New York: HarperCollins Business, 2001).

9. Gillette Corp. web site, www.gillette.com.

10. Fannie Mae web site, www.fanniemae.com.

11. Kimberly-Clark Corp. web site, www.kimberly-clark.com.

12. Walgreens, Inc., web site, www.walgreens.com.

13. Wallace.

14. Ibid.

15. Thomas S. Bateman and Scott A. Snell, *Management: Building Competitive Advantage* (Boston: Irwin-McGraw-Hill, 1999).

16. Collins.

17. Gouillart and Kelly.

18. Bateman and Snell.

19. Ibid.

20. Peter F. Drucker, *The Effective Executive* (New York: HarperBusiness, 1966).

## Chapter 11

1. Thomas S. Bateman and Scott A. Snell, *Management: Building Competitive Advantage* (Boston: Irwin-McGraw-Hill, 1999).

2. William G. Ouchi, *Theory Z* (New York: Avon, 1981).

3. *Webster's New Collegiate Dictionary* (Springfield, Mass.: Merriam-Webster, 1981).

4. Ibid.

5. Ouchi.

6. Ken Blanchard, Terry Waghorn, and Jim Ballard, *Mission Possible: Becoming a World Class Business While There's Still Time* (New York: McGraw-Hill, 1997).

7. George Labovitz and Victor Rosansky, *The Power of Alignment: How Great Companies Stay Centered and Accomplish Extraordinary Things* (New York: Wiley, 1997).

8. Ibid.

9. Bateman and Snell.

10. James Champy, *Reengineering Management: The Mandate for New Leadership* (New York: HarperBusiness, 1995).

11. James C. Collins and Jerry I. Porras, *Built to Last: Successful Habits of Visionary Companies* (New York: HarperCollins, 1994).

12. Ibid.

13. Kenneth Hildebrand, American clergyman.

14. Bateman and Snell.

15. Lao-tzu, Chinese philosopher (604–531 B.C.).

16. Jim Collins, *Good to Great* (New York: HarperCollins Business, 2001).

17. Daft.
18. Bateman and Snell.
19. Daft.

## Chapter 12

1. Thomas S. Bateman and Scott A. Snell, *Management: Building Competitive Advantage* (Boston: Irwin-McGraw-Hill, 1999).
2. Ibid.
3. *Webster's New Collegiate Dictionary* (Springfield: Merriam-Webster, 1981).
4. Daniel R. Denison, *Corporate Culture and Organizational Effectiveness* (Ann Arbor, Mich.: self-published, 1997).
5. Bateman and Snell.
6. Richard L. Daft, *Organization Theory and Design* (Cincinnati: Southwestern, 1998).
7. Ibid.
8. Caroline J. Fisher, *Corporate Culture and Perceived Business Performance: A Study of the Relationship between the Culture of an Organization and the Perceptions of Its Financial and Qualitative Performance*. Doctoral dissertation, California School of Professional Psychology, 1997.

## Chapter 13

1. Daniel R. Denison, *Corporate Culture and Organizational Effectiveness* (Ann Arbor, Mich.: self-published, 1997).
2. Richard L. Daft, *Organization Theory and Design* (Cincinnati: Southwestern, 1998).
3. Thomas S. Bateman and Scott A. Snell, *Management: Building Competitive Advantage* (Boston: Irwin-McGraw-Hill, 1999).
4. Edgar H. Schein, *Organizational Culture and Leadership* (San Francisco: Jossey-Bass, 1992).
5. Ibid.
6. Bateman and Snell.
7. Ibid.
8. George S. Odiorne, *The Human Side of Management* (Lexington, Mass.: Lexington, 1987).
9. Bateman and Snell.
10. Daft.
11. Caroline J. Fisher, *Corporate Culture and Perceived Business Performance: A Study of the Relationship between the Culture of an Organization and the Perceptions of Its Financial and Qualitative Performance*. Doctoral dissertation, California School of Professional Psychology, 1997.
12. Ibid.

## Chapter 14

1. Peter M. Senge, *The Fifth Discipline: The Art and Practice of the Learning Organization* (New York: Currency Doubleday, 1990).
2. Thomas S. Bateman and Scott A. Snell, *Management: Building Competitive Advantage* (Boston: Irwin-McGraw-Hill, 1999).

3. Beverly A. Potter, *Changing Performance on the Job: Behavioral Techniques for Managers* (New York: AMACOM, 1980).

4. Alfred J. Marrow, *The Practical Theorist: The Life and Work of Kurt Lewin* (Annapolis, Md.: BDR, 1969).

5. Richard L. Daft, *Organization Theory and Design* (Cincinnati: Southwestern, 1998).

6. Ibid.

7. Ibid.

8. Manfred F. R. Kets de Vries and Danny Miller, *The Neurotic Organization: Diagnosing and Revitalizing Unhealthy Companies* (New York: HarperCollins, 1984).

9. George S. Odiorne, *The Human Side of Management* (Lexington, Mass.: Lexington, 1987).

10. Ibid.

11. William G. Ouchi, *Theory Z* (New York: Avon, 1981).

12. Senge.

13. John Naisbitt and John Patricia Aburdene, *Re-Inventing the Corporation: Transforming Your Job and Your Company for the New Information Society* (New York: Warner, 1985).

14. Malcolm Kushner, *The Light Touch: How to Use Humor for Business Success* (New York: Simon & Schuster, 1990).

15. Bateman and Snell.

16. Ibid.

17. Bruce A. Pasternack and Albert J. Viscio, *The Centerless Corporation: A New Model for Transforming Your Organization for Growth and Prosperity* (New York: Fireside, 1998).

18. Alfred J. Marrow, *The Practical Theorist: The Life and Work of Kurt Lewin* (Annapolis, Md.: BDR, 1969).

19. Potter.

20. Daniel Goleman, *Emotional Intelligence: Why It Can Matter More than IQ* (New York: Bantam, 1995).

21. Daft

22. Ibid.

23. Stephen R. Covey, *The 7 Habits of Highly Effective People: Powerful Lessons in Personal Change* (New York: Fireside, 1989).

## Chapter 15

1. Thomas S. Bateman and Scott A. Snell, *Management: Building Competitive Advantage* (Boston: Irwin-McGraw-Hill, 1999).

2. Ibid.

3. Wal-Mart, Inc., web site, www.walmart.com.

4. James C. Collins and Jerry I. Porras, *Built to Last: Successful Habits of Visionary Companies* (New York: HarperCollins, 1994).

5. George S. Odiorne, *The Human Side of Management* (Lexington, Mass.: Lexington, 1987).

6. Bateman and Snell

7. Ibid.

8. Kroger, Inc., web site, www.kroger.com.

9. Francis J. Gouillart and James F. Kelly, *Transforming the Organization* (New York: McGraw-Hill, 1995).

10. John P. Kotter and James L. Heskett, *Corporate Culture and Performance* (New York: The Free Press, 1992).

11. P. J. Bouchard and Lizz Pellet, *Getting Your Shift Together: Making Sense of Organizational Change* (Phoenix: CCI Press, 2000).

12. Gouillart and Kelly.

13. Ken Blanchard, Terry Waghorn, and Jim Ballard, *Mission Possible: Becoming a World Class Business While There's Still Time* (New York: McGraw-Hill, 1997).

14. Jim Collins, *Good to Great* (New York: HarperCollins Business, 2001).

15. Bateman and Snell.

16. Collins and Porras.

17. Richard L. Daft, *Organization Theory and Design* (Cincinnati: Southwestern, 1998).

18. Peter F. Drucker, *The Effective Executive* (New York: HarperBusiness, 1966).

19. Joni Mitchell, "Big Yellow Taxi."

20. Collins and Porras.

21. Gouillart and Kelly.

## Chapter 16

1. Thomas F. Wallace, *Customer Driven Strategy: Winning through Operational Excellence* (Essex Junction: Wright, 1992).

2. Daniel R. Denison, *Corporate Culture and Organizational Effectiveness* (Ann Arbor, Mich.: self-published, 1997).

3. Caroline J. Fisher, *Corporate Culture and Perceived Business Performance: A Study of the Relationship between the Culture of an Organization and the Perceptions of Its Financial and Qualitative Performance*. Doctoral dissertation, California School of Professional Psychology, 1997.

4. Edgar H. Schein, *Organizational Culture and Leadership* (San Francisco: Jossey-Bass, 1992).

5. Fisher.

## Chapter 17

1. Bruce A. Pasternack and Albert J. Viscio, *The Centerless Corporation: A New Model for Transforming Your Organization for Growth and Prosperity* (New York: Fireside, 1998).

2. Warren Bennis, *An Invented Life: Reflections on Leadership and Change* (Reading, Mass.: Addison-Wesley, 1993).

3. Thomas S. Bateman and Scott A. Snell, *Management: Building Competitive Advantage* (Boston: Irwin-McGraw-Hill, 1999).

4. Daniel R. Denison, *Corporate Culture and Organizational Effectiveness* (Ann Arbor, Mich.: self-published, 1997).

5. George S. Odiorne, *The Human Side of Management* (Lexington, Mass.: Lexington, 1987).

6. Richard L. Daft, *Organization Theory and Design* (Cincinnati: Southwestern, 1998).

7. John H. McConnell, Chairman & CEO Worthington Industries as quoted in James Champy, *Reengineering Management: The Mandate for New Leadership* (New York: HarperCollins, 1996).

8. Daft.

9. Peter M. Senge, *The Fifth Discipline: The Art and Practice of the Learning Organization* (New York: Currency Doubleday, 1990).

10. James A. Belasco and Ralph C. Stayer, *Flight of the Buffalo: Soaring to Excellence, Learning to Let Employees Lead* (New York: Warner Books, 1993).

11. Bateman and Snell.

12. Belasco and Stayer.

13. Daft.

14. Bennis.

15. George Labovitz and Victor Rosansky, *The Power of Alignment: How Great Companies Stay Centered and Accomplish Extraordinary Things* (New York: Wiley, 1997).

16. Belasco and Stayer.

17. Francis J. Gouillart and James F. Kelly, *Transforming the Organization* (New York: McGraw-Hill, 1995).

18. Odiorne.

19. Bateman and Snell.

20. Caroline J. Fisher, *Corporate Culture and Perceived Business Performance: A Study of the Relationship between the Culture of an Organization and the Perceptions of Its Financial and Qualitative Performance.* Doctoral dissertation, California School of Professional Psychology, 1997.

21. Daft.

## Chapter 18

1. Bruce A. Pasternack and Albert J. Viscio, *The Centerless Corporation: A New Model for Transforming Your Organization for Growth and Prosperity* (New York: Fireside, 1998).

2. Thomas S. Bateman and Scott A. Snell, *Management: Building Competitive Advantage* (Boston: Irwin-McGraw-Hill, 1999).

3. Ibid.

4. Peter M. Senge, *The Fifth Discipline: The Art and Practice of the Learning Organization* (New York: Currency Doubleday, 1990).

5. Bateman and Snell.

6. Francis J. Gouillart and James F. Kelly, *Transforming the Organization* (New York: McGraw-Hill, 1995).

7. Joiner Associates, *The Team Memory Jogger* (Madison, Wis.: Joiner, 1995).

8. Rossabeth Moss Kanter, *The Change Masters: Innovation for Productivity in the American Corporation* (New York: Simon & Schuster, 1983).

9. Joiner Associates.

## Chapter 19

1. Francis J. Gouillart and James F. Kelly, *Transforming the Organization* (New York: McGraw-Hill, 1995).

2. Thomas S. Bateman and Scott A. Snell, *Management: Building Competitive Advantage* (Boston: Irwin-McGraw-Hill, 1999).

3. Gouillart and Kelly.

4. Rossabeth Moss Kanter, *When Giants Learn to Dance* (New York: Touchstone, 1989).

5. George S. Odiorne, *The Human Side of Management* (Lexington, Mass.: Lexington, 1987).

6. Terrence E. Deal and Allan A. Kennedy, *Corporate Cultures: The Rites and Rituals of Corporate Life* (Reading, Mass.: Addison-Wesley, 1982).

7. Warren Bennis and Burt Nanus, *Leaders: The Strategies for Taking Charge* (New York: HarperPerennial, 1985).

8. Gouillart and Kelly.

9. James Champy, *Reengineering Management: The Mandate for New Leadership* (New York: HarperBusiness, 1995).

## Chapter 20

1. James C. Collins and Jerry I. Porras, *Built to Last: Successful Habits of Visionary Companies* (New York: HarperCollins, 1994).

2. Ibid.

3. Peter M. Senge, *The Fifth Discipline: The Art and Practice of the Learning Organization* (New York: Currency Doubleday, 1990).

4. Ibid.

5. Stephen R. Covey, *The 7 Habits of Highly Effective People. Powerful Lessons in Personal Change* (New York: Fireside, 1989).

6. James A. Belasco and Ralph C. Stayer, *Flight of the Buffalo: Soaring to Excellence, Learning to Let Employees Lead* (New York: Warner Books, 1993).

7. Thomas J. Peters, *Thriving on Chaos* (New York: HarperPerennial, 1987).

8. Senge.

9. Ibid.

10. Milind M. Lele and Jagdesh M. Sheth, *The Customer Is Key: Gaining an Unbeatable Advantage through Customer Satisfaction* (New York: Wiley, 1991).

11. Caroline J. Fisher, *Corporate Culture and Perceived Business Performance: A Study of the Relationship between the Culture of an Organization and the Perceptions of Its Financial and Qualitative Performance*. Doctoral dissertation, California School of Professional Psychology, 1997.

12. Harvey Mackay, *Swim with the Sharks without Being Eaten Alive* (New York: Ivy, 1988).

13. Fisher.

14. Ibid.

## Chapter 21

1. Thomas F. Wallace, *Customer Driven Strategy: Winning through Operational Excellence* (Essex Junction: Wright, 1992).

2. Milind M. Lele and Jagdesh M. Sheth, *The Customer Is Key: Gaining an Unbeatable Advantage through Customer Satisfaction* (New York: Wiley, 1991).

3. Richard C. Whiteley, *The Customer Driven Company: Moving from Talk to Action* (Cambridge, Mass.: Perseus, 2000).

4. Neil Rackham, *The SPIN Selling Fieldbook* (New York: McGraw-Hill, 1996).

5. Noel M. Tichy and Stratford Sherman, *Control Your Own Destiny or Someone Else Will* (New York: Doubleday, 1993).

6. Wallace.

7. Whiteley.

8. Ibid.

9. Ibid.

10. James A. Belasco and Ralph C. Stayer, *Flight of the Buffalo: Soaring to Excellence, Learning to Let Employees Lead* (New York: Warner Books, 1993).

11. William H. Davidow and Bro Uttal, *Total Customer Service: The Ultimate Weapon* (New York: HarperPerennial, 1989).

12. Belasco and Stayer.

13. Whiteley.

14. Ibid.

15. Wallace.

16. Lele and Sheth.

## Chapter 22

1. Leon Martel, *Mastering Change: The Key to Business Success* (New York: Simon & Schuster, 1986).

2. Friedrich Oetinger, eighteenth-century theologian.

3. Charles J. Fombrum, *Leading Corporate Change* (New York: McGraw-Hill, 1992).

4. Rossabeth Moss Kanter, *The Change Masters: Innovation for Productivity in the American Corporation* (New York: Simon & Schuster, 1983).

5. Martel.

6. John P. Kotter and James L. Heskett, *Corporate Culture and Performance* (New York: The Free Press, 1992).

7. William G. Ouchi, *Theory Z* (New York: Avon, 1981).

8. Peter M. Senge, *The Fifth Discipline: The Art and Practice of the Learning Organization* (New York: Currency Doubleday, 1990).

9. Kotter and Heskett.

10. Chinese proverb.

11. Andrea Anania, Senior Vice President and Chief Information Officer, Cigna Corp. *Fast Company*. Issue 56. March 2002.

12. Caroline J. Fisher, *Corporate Culture and Perceived Business Performance: A Study of the Relationship between the Culture of an Organization and the Perceptions of Its Financial and Qualitative Performance*. Doctoral dissertation, California School of Professional Psychology, 1997.

13. Martel.

## Chapter 23

1. James C. Collins and Jerry I. Porras, *Built to Last: Successful Habits of Visionary Companies* (New York: HarperCollins, 1994).

2. Peter M. Senge, *The Fifth Discipline: The Art and Practice of the Learning Organization* (New York: Currency Doubleday, 1990).

3. Warren Bennis and Burt Nanus, *Leaders: The Strategies for Taking Charge* (New York: HarperPerennial, 1985).

4. Thomas F. Wallace, *Customer Driven Strategy: Winning through Operational Excellence* (Essex Junction: Wright, 1992).

5. Thomas S. Bateman and Scott A. Snell, *Management: Building Competitive Advantage* (Boston: Irwin-McGraw-Hill, 1999).

6. Aldous Huxley, British author (1894–1963).

7. Jim Collins, *Good to Great* (New York: HarperCollins Business, 2001).

8. Miles H. Overholt, *Building Flexible Organizations: The People-Centered Approach* (Dubuque, Iowa: Kendall/Hunt, 1996).

9. Edgar H. Schein, *Organizational Culture and Leadership* (San Francisco: Jossey-Bass, 1992).

10. Senge.

11. George S. Odiorne, *The Human Side of Management* (Lexington, Mass.: Lexington, 1987).

12. Robert Wood Johnson, Jr., American business leader, humanist, and philanthropist (1893–1968).

13. Collins.

14. Schein.

15. Bateman and Snell.

16. Francis J. Gouillart and James F. Kelly, *Transforming the Organization* (New York: McGraw-Hill, 1995).

17. Collins and Porras.

18. Senge.

19. Schein.

# INDEX

# ABOUT THE AUTHOR

**Stuart Ferguson** is the founder of Organization Change Resources, a consultancy that focuses on issues from culture assessment and development to organizational change, strategic planning, leadership development, and team building for such firms as Marriott, Merrill Lynch, MetLife, and others. Formerly a vice president of strategic alliances at American Re-Insurance Company, Dr. Ferguson is a frequent speaker at conferences in the United States and around the world. Stuart received a bachelor of arts with high honors in business administration from Northwood University, a master of education in adult education program management from Georgia State University, and a doctorate from Kennedy-Western University. His dissertation entitled "People Business: Mergers, Acquisitions, and Organizational Cultures" provided the research for this book.